# COMMON PROPERTY RESOURCE MANAGEMENT

# COMMON PROPERTY RESOURCE MANAGEMENT
## Reflections on Theory and the Indian Experience

Gopal K. Kadekodi

**OXFORD**
UNIVERSITY PRESS

# OXFORD

UNIVERSITY PRESS

YMCA Library building, Jai Singh Road, New Delhi 110001

Oxford University Press is a department of the University of Oxford. It furthers the University's objective of excellence in research, scholarship, and education by publishing worldwide in

Oxford New York

Auckland Bangkok Buenos Aires Cape Town Chennai
Dar es Salaam Delhi Hong Kong Istanbul Karachi Kolkata
Kuala Lumpur Madrid Melbourne Mexico City Mumbai Nairobi
São Paulo Shanghai Taipei Tokyo Toronto

Oxford is a registered trade mark of Oxford University Press
in the UK and in certain other countries

Published in India
By Oxford University Press, New Delhi

ISBN 0 19 566616 X

Typeset in Goudy
by Laser Print Craft, Delhi 110051
Printed at Roopak Printers, Delhi 110032
Published by Manzar Khan, Oxford University Press
YMCA Library Building, Jai Singh Road, new Delhi 110001

# An Old Chinese Wisdom on Common Property Resource Management
## The Concept of Well Field System

'Each square *li* of land should be divided into nine plots, the whole containing nine hundred *mu*. The central plot will be the public field and the eight households, each owing a hundred-*mu* farm, will collaborate in cultivating the public field. Not until the public has been properly attended to, may each household attend to its private plot. This is how the country men should be required to learn'.
Mencius, extracted from Ch'u Chai and Winberg Chai (1965), p. 118

This book is dedicated to
Late P. R. Mishra who did not waste time in translating
Chakriya Vikas Pranali into English
but put it on the ground
as the only solution to the management of the commons.

# Contents

# Preface

Writing a book as an enabling tool in curriculum building at the undergraduate level on topics in Environmental Economics is not easy. However, the need is felt in India and in several other countries, partly because of this gap in applied economics textbooks, which do not cover sufficient ground on current topics such as environmental economics, environmental law, environmental movements, and awareness etc. This book addresses one such topic within environmental resource management, which is extremely relevant in the Indian context.

A natural resource abundant and dependent country such as India has a variety of natural resources such as land varieties (ranging from dry desert lands of Rajasthan to the snow bound Himalayas), water resources (surface, underground, marine, under various methods of collections and storage), mineral resources, biodiversity resources (including rich microorganisms, birds, insects, wild life, forest plantations, grasslands, and so on), fishery resources (including coral richness), and many more. These resources are managed by a variety of institutional mechanisms, though management practices have changed from time to time in the history of the country.

Among the many, common property resources as a group has received special attention throughout the history of India, even as long ago as the reign of the Chalukyas (about 300 BC). Today, it has become even more important to understand such resources as demographic pressure, changing technology on resource use and requirement, and the process of globalization give natural resources a totally new paraphrase.

Common property resources are those which have certain specifically defined property rights for their users or those who are dependent on them; they have special characteristics in terms of their link with life support to human and animal life, and they have distinct local versus global linkages, and market or non-market characteristics.

This book explores all such features of common property resources, both in theory and in practice specifically from the Indian context. Theoretical expositions and examples or case studies are developed keeping the requirements of students in mind. Therefore, it should become an important source textbook at the undergraduate levels.

The writing of this book has been possible because of a Capacity Building Programme in India, initiated by the Ministry of Environment and Forests, with financial support from the World Bank. I am very thankful to all the people connected with this programme. Particular mention must be made of U. Sankar, National Coordinator for this programme. I received very generous support, encouragement, and conceptual and technical inputs from a large number of academicians, officials, and non-government organizations. In particular, I wish to place on record my sincere thanks to P.R. Panchamukhi, Katar Singh, Nirmal Sengupta, Ramachandra Bhatta, Kanchan Chopra, M.N. Murty, Kirit Parikh, Jyoti Parikh; and Minoti Kaul Chakravarty, Partha Das Gupta, N.S. Jodha, and Charles Perrings.

A large number of scholars working with me helped to put voluminous materials together, provided library and bibliographical support, and educated me on the use of modern computer techniques in developing the manuscript into a book. I am extremely grateful to Arabinda Mishra, Seema Hegde, Rajeshwari Mathad and Gururaj Haribhat for all such support, which added much more detail and clarity to the book.

It is hoped that this book will meet the requirements of undergraduate students entering the new field of environmental economics, as well as all the practising government and non-government officials and technical personnel in fulfilling their commitments of adding an environmental dimension to their tasks of nation building.

GOPAL K. KADEKODI
Dharwad

# Abbreviations

| | | |
|---|---|---|
| AC | – | average cost |
| AUSAID | – | Australian Agency for International Development |
| B/C | – | Benefit and Cost |
| BSF | – | Border Security Force |
| CAG | – | Comptroller and Auditor General |
| CAPART | – | Council for People's Action and Rural Technology |
| CAZRI | – | Central Arid Zone Research Institute |
| CIDA | – | Canadian International Development Agency |
| CITES | – | Convention on International Trade in Endangered Species |
| CMFRI | – | Central Marine Fisheries Research Institute |
| CMIE | – | Centre for Monitoring Indian Economy |
| CPPR | – | common pooled private resource |
| CPR | – | common property resources |
| CPWRs | – | Common Property Water Resources |
| CRIDA | – | Central Research Institute of Dry land Agriculture |
| CRPF | – | Central Reserve Police Force |
| CRZ | – | Coastal Regulation Zone |
| CSO | – | Central Staistical Organization |
| CSWCRTI | – | Central Soil and Water Conservation Research and Training Institute |
| CVP | – | Chakriya Vikas Pranali |
| CVS | – | Charagah Vikas Samiti |
| CWL | – | cultivable waste lands |
| DADP | – | Desert Area Development Programme |
| DANIDA | – | Danish International Development Agency |
| DDAP | – | Desert Development Area Programme |
| DDP | – | Desertland Development Programme |

| DEFO | – Department of Environment and Forest |
| DFID | – Department for International Development |
| DFO | – Divisional Forest Officer |
| DPAP | – Drought Prone Area Programme |
| DRDA | – District Rural Development Agency |
| EAS | – Employment Assurance Scheme |
| ECLA | – European Commission for Latin America |
| EEC | – European Economic Commission |
| EEZ | – Exclusive Economic Zone |
| EFO | – Environment and Forest |
| FDCS | – Forest Development Co-operative Societies |
| FPCs | – Forest Protection Committees |
| FSI | – Forest Survey of India |
| GATT | – General Agreement on Tariffs and Trade |
| GEF | – Global Environmental Facility |
| GJC | – Gramya Jungle Committees |
| GTZ | – German Technical Cooperation |
| HFD | – Haryana Forest Department |
| HRMS | – Hill Resource Management Society |
| IADP | – Integrated Area Development Programme |
| ICRISAT | – International Council for Research in Semi-Arid Tropics |
| IFFCO | – Indian Farmers' Fertilizer Co-operative |
| IGIDR | – Indira Gandhi Institute of Development Research |
| IPR | – Intellectual Property Rights |
| IRDP | – Integrated Rural Development Programme |
| IRR | – internal rate of return |
| IWDP | – Integrated Watershed Development Programme |
| JFM | – Joint Forest Management |
| JMA | – Joint Management Association |
| JRY | – Jawahar Rozgar Yojana |
| KAWAD | – Karnataka Watershed Development |
| KFW | – Kreditanstal fur Wiederanfban |
| LPG | – liquified petroleum gas |
| MA | – Management Association |
| MC | – marginal cost |
| MERC | – management of environmental resource through communities |

| MEY | – maximum economic yield |
| MOAY | – maximum open access yield |
| MoU | – Memorandum of Understanding |
| MoEF | – Ministry of Environment and Forests |
| MP | – management practice |
| MR | – marginal revenue |
| MRAE | – Ministry of Rural Areas and Employment |
| MSY | – maximum sustainable yield |
| MYRADA | – Mysore Resettlement and Development Agency |
| NABARD | – National Bank for Agriculture and Rural Development |
| NAEB | – National Afforestation and Eco-development Board |
| NBSAP | – National Biodiversity Strategy and Action Plan |
| NDDB | – National Dairy Development Board |
| NGO | – non-governmental organization |
| NPSB | – net present social benefit |
| NPVB | – net present value benefit |
| NREP | – National Rural Employment Programme |
| NRSA | – National Remote Sensing Agency |
| NSS | – National Sample Survey |
| NTFP | – non-timber forest product |
| NTGCF | – National Tree Growers Co-operative Federation |
| NWDB | – National Wastelands Development Board |
| NWDPRA | – National Watershed Development Projects for Rainfed Areas |
| OBC | – Other Backward Classes |
| OECF | – Overseas Economic Cooperation Fund |
| OTHFL | – fallow other than current |
| PCCF | – Principal Chief Conservator of Forests |
| $_pH$ | – hydrogen ion concentration |
| PI | – panchayat institutions |
| PIDOW | – Participatory and Integrated Development of Watersheds |
| PLCPR | – private land with CPR access |
| PPG | – permanent pasture and grazing lands |
| PPR | – private property resources |
| PRADHAN | – Professional Assistance for Development Action |
| PROT+UNCL | – protected and unclassed forest lands |

| | | |
|---|---|---|
| PWD | – | Public Works Department |
| RLEGP | – | Rural Landless Employment Guarantee Programme |
| SC/ST | – | Scheduled Caste/Scheduled Tribe |
| SF | – | social forestry |
| SHRMS | – | Society for Hill Resources Management School |
| SIDA | – | Swedish International Development Agency |
| SPWD | – | Society for Promotion of Wastelands Development |
| SWG | – | social welfare group |
| TBS | – | Tarun Bharat Sangh |
| TC | – | total cost |
| TERI | – | Tata Energy Research Institute |
| TGCF | – | Tree Growers' Co-operative Federation |
| TGCS | – | Tree Growers' Co-operative Society |
| TOTNFCPR | – | total non-forest common property land resources |
| TR | – | total revenue |
| TRAFFIC | – | Trade Record Analysis of Flora and Fauna in Commerce |
| TRIPS | – | Trade Related Intellectual Property Rights |
| TWDP | – | Tribal Welfare Development Programme |
| UNDP | – | United Nations' Development Programme |
| UK | – | United Kingdom |
| UTs | – | Union Territories |
| VFCs | – | village forest committees |
| VP | – | van panchayat |
| VPC | – | Village Protection Committee |
| WDP | – | Watershed Development Programme |
| WTO | – | World Trade Organization |
| WWF | – | World Wildlife Fund |

# Boxes

# Figures

# Tables

# Appendices

# 1

# Common Property Regime:
# An Introduction

## WHAT IS 'COMMONS'?

Before getting into a detailed discussion about common property resources (CPRs') as the term is understood today, it would be useful to ask the meaning of 'commons'. The context here is primarily natural resources, but it can also include man-made resources. Commons represent all natural resources used for human welfare, which are not necessarily owned by any individual or group of individuals. However, some exclusive group has common rights to utilize them. The set of individuals, households, and groups of individuals falling in this category (exclusive group) is also specific. Rights to grazing lands and pastures, rights to collect fuelwood, non-timber produce, and fodder from forest patches, rights to fish from fish ponds or rivers, rights to irrigation and drinking water are some examples of commons regimes.[1] One can even cite examples of rights to gather soap stones, coal, sand, and other minerals as also the remote cases of commons.[2] As much as such

[1]Very loosely, some people also talk about wastelands as commons, but this need not be so (as will be made clear later on).

[2]One can also make a distinction between renewable and non-renewable commons. Fishery is an example of a renewable common, whereas collection of minerals that of a non-renewable one.

resources are site specific, the individuals and households attached to them also have to be site specific. For instance, only the residents of a village have exclusive rights on fishing from their common village pond, unless such rights are leased out or rented to outsiders.

Of all these, the most commonly talked about commons is that of grazing lands, perhaps next only to collection of fuelwood and other non-timber products from forests. This sequence of importance is purely historical. Both in Asia (even today) and medieval Europe, fuelwood collected from common forest patches was used to meet a substantial part of the basic energy requirements. However, for want of own farmyard grass, fodder, or hay, livestock rearing in certain seasons was always seen to be dependent upon the extent of common grazing lands (Parker and Jones, 1975; Mearns, 1996; Chakravarty–Kaul, 1996; Jodha, 1996; Ciriacy-Wantrup and Bishop, 1975; Hardin, 1968). In ancient India as well as in medieval Europe and elsewhere, the communities evolved ways and means to use the existing grazing lands and pastures to get sufficient feed for their cattle, without exerting themselves too much.[3] For instance, the villagers in the Himalayan region evolved methods of protecting forests for their own common good under an institution known as *van panchayat* (Somanathan, 1991).

Likewise, societies have historically evolved methods to regulate ocean fishing by communities (Gordon, 1954; Dasgupta, 1982). Example from Kerala include division of fishermen into categories as Monday fishermen, Tuesday fishermen and so on, that is, the rights of fishing communities to fish are restricted to different days of the week. Stevenson (1991) cites the case of Swiss grazing alpine lands managed by communities by dividing them into different levels (by slopes) and regulating them in terms of number of cattle units per farmer. Chakravarty–Kaul (1996) documents a large number of cases from former British Punjab, where ancient systems of managing the commons as *shamlat* and *mauzas* land protected the wastelands.[4] Kadekodi *et al.*

[3]In the language of modern environmental economics, this is termed as maintaining the carrying capacity of land.

[4]For sake of clarity it may be useful to quote Chakravarty–Kaul (1996: p. 67): '… a sense of ownership over the waste existed among the cultivating communities within the mauzas. Further, that the waste at large, were not as they appeared, "howling wildernesses", even in the central and lower Himalayas of Kumaon and Kangra. Similarly, official reports in 1849–52 described vast areas on either side of

(2000) give an account of Kumaonis managing water distribution and exercising their rights over water.

One can also find historical examples of collapse of commons. Hoskin and Stamp (1967) give an account of decline of commons due to population pressure and open access to grazing lands in medieval England. Jodha (1985) also describes the declining state of commons in Rajasthan due to population pressure and commercialization. Decline in community based tank irrigation (as seen in India) has taken place due to the change of property rights regime, from commons to the state.

It is obvious that the most important characteristic that defines 'commons' is 'limitation to entry and a well-defined group to manage rights'. In the pre-industrial period, having realized the importance of such resources, over time, societies evolved rules and regulations to restrict entry of 'others', assigned responsibilities to communities, and instituted punishments for defaulters. These characteristics make commons a specific resource to be studied for the most efficient way of management and for achieving human welfare. That is the subject matter of this book.

A Brief Tour of Commons: Historical and Contemporary

As far as the commons in India go, one has to look back at least two thousand years, to the time when Kautilya (advisor to King Chandragupta Maurya of the Magadh dynasty) made several observations on property rights and the management of common land, water, minerals, and forests. He advocated three types of arable lands: crown land, private land, and pastures. The pastures were the common lands. Kautilya said that the king should never privatize pasture lands by giving them to noblemen. He believed that by privatization, it would not only become difficult to retrieve it back (a matter of better administration), but also that it made the noblemen too powerful (a matter of better governance). The more important advice was that for healthy animal growth pastures be maintained as commons, otherwise, the noblemen would convert them to other crop lands for their

the Sutlaj as "overgrown with grass and bushes, scantily threaded with sheep walks and the footprints of cattle", over which the "chief tenants are nomad pastoral tribes who knowing neither law nor property collect herds of cattle stolen from the agricultural districts".'

private gains.[5] The pasture lands were either administered by someone appointed by the king (Kautilya called them chief superintendent of pastures), or by the village headmen, who saw to it that such lands were kept productive (example, by undertaking land clearing, supply of water, etc.). They also raised revenue earnings from the common grazers. Common lands, as much as private lands, were used for both revenue purposes and for maintaining the productivity of land high enough for human and animal welfare.

Such profound wisdom was also found in ancient China. There was a system of distinctly identifying common grazing lands in every hamlet in ancient China. The quote on the cover of this book explains the story better. It was obligatory for every private land owner to first maintain the common, without which he was not allowed to reap the crop from his own private lands.

For the contemporary period, some examples from India of crop lands, forest lands, and water resources, and from England and Switzerland of grazing lands are summarily presented here, the interested readers can refer to the original sources of information and literature for details.

### The Commons of Punjab[6]

Prior to the British rule, Punjab had a mix of arable farming and pastoral activities plus municipal and collective activities based on common lands. The common lands (*banjar kadim*) were held collectively by the village custodian body (*malikan-deb*). There were also sub-sections of the village called *pattis*, which were held in common. Thus, with the village common (*shamlat-deh*), there were wastelands called shamlat-patti. The so called shamlat (and its variations such as *deh-shamlat*—wastelands jointly owned and shared) and *abadi-deh* or residential area, catchment areas (*johads*), or area around the village (*gora deh*) and village wood lots were all different types of commons. Shamlat lands, though recorded in the name of the village head, were treated as a common land for raising fodder crops (*barseen*) only. The

---

[5]The main message is that there should not be any scope for either negative externality or for a tragedy of the commons! *Source*: Arthashastra, Book 8, Chapter 4, Verses 37–40.

[6]From Chakravarty–Kaul (1996), with additional inputs through personal communication with her.

village head had no rights to sell or transfer the right to anyone else, except for passing it on to the next generation. Because of the great emphasis on settled agriculture during the British regime, there were always pressures to convert the commons. According to Darling (1984), population pressure, rising land values, rise of irrigation, and alienation of land all led to the collapse of the communal land management in Punjab. Chakravarty–Kaul (1996) provides a detailed account of changes in all such commons, for example, due to legislation, canal irrigation systems, population growth, and market factors. Historically, these changes occurred over time. Reduction of commons, shifting from long fallows to short fallows, conversion to private lands and other such factors have reduced the commons in Punjab to some extent. Some of the changes may be attributed to the revenue objectives of the British government. Chakravarty–Kaul (1996: p. 65) traces the events of shifting land use and policy towards the waste in Cis–Sutlej area, and the marking of revenue boundaries and separating land users from one another. When the village custodian body (*malikan deb*) had to comply with land taxes, they also had to pay for *shamlat lands*. Thus, the land use pattern and property rights changed significantly.

Unlike the open field system in England, several parts of former Punjab had a different pattern of sharing of common fallow lands. In England, the common was a compact field for grazing. In Punjab, different methods of scattering the commons among the villagers were practised. In one method (*khet bat*) such lands were classified by their soil type, moisture condition, and vegetation into *hars*. This was the first step in the division of village fields—these were then rotated between cultivation and grazing and then distributed among village shareholders by some method of lottery (*kura* or *dheri*). Alternatively, such fallow or wastelands were treated as a compact field and distributed among the members (*chak bat* system). This method ensured equity among the members to begin with, but the scattered holdings and the increasing number of family members led to inequity. However, the principle of sharing the common continued. Every member, even if he had no scattered holdings, still had rights to the commons of which the main right was that of decision making. Thus, ultimately, if a villager was a *malikan-deh* and a *skin-deh* he never lost his right to the decision making process.

Chakravarty–Kaul's analysis of the land tenurial systems in Punjab suggests that the type of partition of the commons as used by the British, partly for the revenue objective and partly to develop records of individual rights led to private motives among the villagers; and land resources began to be treated as 'marketable'. This process ultimately led to the transfer of land to outsiders and moneylenders who had no incentive to maintain the integrity of the villagers. Yet the commons of Punjab survived till 1947, but disappeared with the land reforms, which created open access to the commons; or rather brought about the tragedy of commons in Punjab.

## Tank Irrigation System in India

Prior to canal and other surface irrigation systems, tank irrigation was the predominant method of irrigation in ancient India.[7] Tanks were by and large, constructed and maintained as commons by the villagers and communities. The history of community based tanks dates back to the Chola period (eleventh century). Sengupta (1991) argues that tanks are even today the predominant means for utilizing surface water for irrigation, though much of the characteristics as 'common' might not be seen today. In the mid 18th century about three or four million hectares of command area was under tank irrigation in India. There were about 32,000 tanks irrigating about 785,000 hectares in Madras Presidency alone (Agarwal and Narain, 1997: p. 255). Even today, according to Agarwal and Narain (1997: p. 246) about one-third of irrigated area in Tamil Nadu is under tank irrigation.[8] The common tanks were maintained by assigning duties to certain sections of the communities known as *manyams* in Tamil Nadu and *numberdars* in north India. All activities of desilting, removing weeds, ward and watch, constructing bunds, repairing tanks, distributing water, collecting revenue were their responsibility, with community approvals under a system known as *kudimaramath* (basically voluntary village labour).

---

[7]Sengupta (1991) clarifies that village lakes and ponds are not to be mistaken as tanks. Tank irrigation is essentially a water harvesting system in a sloped terrain from the catchment or run-off, with three sided embankments, the fourth side being an opening as a channel.

[8]At the all-India level, about 6 per cent of net area irrigated is from tanks, which used to be about 17 per cent at the time of independence.

The British, because of land revenue motivation, took away all such community rights and responsibilities and created state institutions such as the public works department (PWD). At the same time, they realized that the tanks could not be maintained (for higher revenues) without the involvement of communities. They even tried to coerce voluntary village labour through legislation (for example, Madras Compulsory Labour Act of 1858). The typical negative externalities associated with state control led to the decline and end of the community managed tank systems in India. However, even today in some pockets, there remains a mix of state financed tank maintenance under some department or other, and community managed water distribution system, but quite often very informally.[9] In the 19th century at least in the former Madras state there were attempts to revive the *kudimaramath* system, but with no success.

Clearly, shifting of management of commons from the community to the state led to the collapse of this institution.

## Van Panchayats of Uttaranchal Pradesh

Prior to the entry of the East India Company in India, forests were managed by the people and kings and their noblemen, that is, by and large, they were community managed (Guha, 1989; Gadgil and Guha, 1992). With the institution of the Indian Forest Act, 1865 by the British colonial government, much of these community rights and management of forests vanished from India. As a result co-operation from the people also disappeared.[10]

Around 1921, the people of Garhwal and Kumaon hill regions of India were involved in mass violence against this state management of forests. This ultimately led to the recognition and formation of Van Panchayats in 1931 (with a regulation under the District Scheduled Act of 1874).

In the hilly regions of former Uttar Pradesh, till about 1832, all lands in the village boundary, except for some reserved forests, were classified

---

[9]Good examples of this are Sukhomajri village in Haryana, Relegan Siddhi village in Maharashtra, Chapri and Tanda villages of Jharkhand, and thousands others. See Chopra *et al.* (1990); Antia and Kadekodi (2002), Chopra and Kadekodi (1991).

[10]Prior to this, the villagers protected forests from fires, encroachments, trespassing, illegal felling, hunting, free grazing, and so on.

as measured that is, private land holdings (*nap*), and non-measured or common (*benap*) lands. In 1883, all *benap* lands were converted into state property (as district protected forest) under British rules. The government began to use them for revenue purposes. This continued until some major forest fires in the 1920s, at the same time when communities were asking for their rights to forest resources. Following the recommendations of the Kumaon Grievance Committee in 1921, the first move towards bringing the commons back was to classify forest lands as Class I (non-commercial, reserved) and Class II (commercial, reserved) forests, and permitting people to use Class I forests for their own bona fide use. They in turn voluntarily formed what are called *latha* panchayats for managing these forests. What began as protection committees for the commons, were converted formally into van panchayats in 1931.

Under the regulation, the people of Garhwal and Kumaon regions were permitted to form village protection committees to manage forest compartments outside the reserved and protected forests. The forest departments monitored the activities of these committees. Today, there are over 5000 such protection committees in Uttaranchal, spread over 4800 villages and covering about 13 per cent of forest area of the state. The van panchayats treat the allotted forest lands as the commons. By and large, these are revenue forest lands (*soyam*). The members check indiscriminate felling of trees, social fencing of forests, ensure equitable distribution of forest products, prevent encroachments, plant saplings and so on (Singh, 1994a). For instance, they have created rules against free grazing, trespassing, etc. Thus, van panchayat is a case of maintained commons seen even today. In 1995, the Van Panchayat Act of Uttar Pradesh was further amended to relax the hold of the forest department and also to encourage the participation of women.

As of now, even though van panchayats are functioning in the state, they are failing in their duty as protectors of the commons. There are many reasons for this; the major ones are: lack of role participation of women, re-emergence of illegal felling, not–recycling of income from forest protection, continued control of the forest department, and insufficient monetary incentives out of their contributions to forest protection (just about 40 per cent).

## Swiss Alpine Grazing Common Property[11]

Alpine grazing lands in the foothills of the Alps in Switzerland serve the purpose of summer grazing of cattle exclusively, and owing to their vast land area, also make a separate self-contained operation as a 'common' possible (a case of economies of scale). Additionally, land that can be used out of the home farm on a daily basis or at similar short intervals for grazing is considered as pasture. This system of identifying pasture and grazing lands has some economic rationale. During summer, while the cattle graze in the alpine lands, the farmers harvest the hay from their own fields and pastures for the next winter. In this manner they are able to support about 30 per cent more animals than otherwise (an example of some kind of positive externality).

This system of alpine grazing lands is a classic example of efficient management of the commons. It may be attributed mainly to a system of 'limited entry' and assignment of alpine landscape by different levels of land quality and height. The villagers at the different alpine levels and meadows are grouped as the main beneficiaries of the grazing lands. While the farmers are to use their 'village level fields' for grazing the cattle after the harvests, they are subsequently permitted to take the cattle to the second level 'may fields' (in upper reaches) for grazing. Finally, after the winter, they can take them still higher up in the alpine grazing fields. The farmers find this an economic solution for the use of commons. The salient features of this management system are summarized here.

1. Rights system: Three primary rights that limit entry are clearly defined. They are share rights alps, the community alps, and corporation alps. Under the share rights, a farmer can graze one cattle unit (equivalent to one cow). This system limits access to any party who may want to enter from outside the group and defines grazing pressure rights among the user groups. Under community rights, residency status is a must. Second, the farmer should have used his own hay during the winter. Under corporation alps, common ownership and rights are permitted to all members of certain family lineage only.

2. Investment on the commons: There are written regulations on work duty, fees, and maintenance.

[11]Extracted mainly from Stevenson (1991).

3. Enforcement: There is an overseer whose responsibility is to check the rights and use patterns.

4. Restrictions on types of animals: The alpine regions are classified as cow alps (for cows only), sheep and goat alps, bull alps and so on.

5. Protection of alps: The farmers use a variety of methods to improve the productivity of the alps, such as fertilization, grazing rotation etc.

One of the most striking features of the Swiss Alps grazing system is the strong link between the commons and private resources, in this case the cattle. Second, strict adherence to 'limiting entry' has removed any free rider problems and other externalities.

## English Open Field System

Common pasture rights in England appear to go back to a period before the Anglo-Saxon invasions, when the inhabitants claimed rights over vast expanses of moors and forests—the size of the present English counties. The Anglo-Saxons introduced settled agriculture in the 5th–6th centuries. The English open field system was characterized as open arable fields for community control of cropping and common pasturing of stubble. They consisted of fallows, meadows, and wastelands.

The village common was predominantly used for cropping and marginally for grazing with communal ownership. The open fields were rotated between arable and pasture. Dahlman (1980) argues that the English open field system was an efficient adaptation to a particular economic situation in which it was necessary to maintain livestock rearing and crop agriculture as two different activities around the commons. Each village had three or four large fields divided into narrow long strips, held by peasants in feudal tenancy. The feudal tenants left their strips unfenced, hence the name 'open field'. They plowed the strips using co-operatively formed teams of oxen with crop rotation. Geographically, common grazing rights varied across England.

Considering the problem as one of optimizing land use pattern, each farmer tilled strips of ownership lands scattered across the open fields, while cattle were grazed on the 'common' open fields. These differing approaches to the organization of arable and pasturage reflect the fact that although cultivation could be carried out on small plots, cattle needed to graze over large areas (a case of economies of scale). On the other hand, if the grazing land had been divided into many units of ownership, each owner would have to secure the agreement of several others to allow his cattle to graze on their lands (otherwise a case of negative externality or conflicts may arise). Further, movement of cattle in fields would have to be policed to prevent overgrazing of other people's land. The open field system was an exercise of economies of scale in grazing activities, with reduced overhead costs. Chakravarty–Kaul (1996: p. 9) argues that 'scattering of arable holdings made it impossible for any individual farmer to refuse grazing on the stubble after the harvest or to withdraw from the system, because he would then lose the benefits of grazing on large-scale compact grounds'. The communities had imposed strict rules that 'no farmer was allowed to withdraw any part of the common land from common use'. If he were allowed to do so, then, with economies of scale in grazing, it would mean imposing a negative externality on his neighbours. Thus, the combination of privately held strips scattered all over the open field, but used in common after the harvest, together with the system of communally held pastoral land in coherent blocks, made it possible to combine joint and individual wealth maximization. Certainly this was a superior solution to the alternative of private ownership of the commons and decision making from the stand point of both joint and individual wealth maximization.

## THE PROBLEMS OF COMMONS

The situation of commons in India gives the impression that wherever strong community hold persisted, the commons continued to serve the purpose of meeting everybody's requirements. Second, the decline of the commons in India in the past was not necessarily due to population pressure, industrialization (leading to negative externalities), or over-exploitation of the resource. It took place mainly because of the withdrawal of customary rights and rules, imposition of revenue motivation and even privatization in the management of such resources and the emergence of state control.

From the glimpse of commons in European history, it can be said that in medieval Europe, wherever the commons survived, the reasons were (a) low population pressure, (b) not subjecting them to over-exploitation, and (c) not having any alternative use for the commons, for example, conversion to crop agriculture. The success of managing commons was due to economies of scale.

The degradation of forest lands, drying up of tanks in India or degradation of open access grazing lands in England are all instances of some people being affected in their livelihood for no fault on their part. Why should they be left uncared for? Who should pay for these costs?

In economic terms, over exploitation may take place because there is no accountability or eligibility on the resource share for the communities, or because they do not have to pay for it. This is referred to as a case of 'free rider' problem—defined as getting something free, by not paying for it. Here, it is a case of positive externality. Whenever the commons were treated without limitations of entry, there was a 'free rider' problem. Hardin (1968) talked about this, although a bit incorrectly, in the context of free grazing lands, as a problem of population explosion and its effect on the commons. In fact, he was referring to the free entry of (additional) sheep and goats (due to individual rationality instead of community rationality), thereby bringing upon greater pressure on land. He termed this as the 'tragedy of the commons', and attributed it to the non-existence of any institution to limit the expansion of use, over exploitation, and limiting the capacity of use (for example, herd grazing), and there not being any identifiable group responsible for the tragedy.[12] This is a case of open access use of a resource. The Swiss Alps grazing, on the other hand, is a case of community management with rights and duties, with a limited entry and use pattern. On the other hand, the introduction of mechanized fishing in a lake or river that drives the livelihood of all the traditional fishermen is called a situation of negative externalities. Why should anyone get a free ride or be compelled to bear the cost of negative externality?[13]

In many cases, the commons are treated as a public good, for which no single or multiple group or community is responsible. Examples are enjoying public parks or beaches or river boating. A common problem observed with such a situation is the negative externalities associated

---

[12]Dasgupta (1982) refers to this situation as a case of not accounting for the private costs of raising goats and sheep. Hence he refers to this as a mistaken tragedy or ruin. If only the private costs of raising goats and sheep are kept in mind, the farmers in Hardin's example would not necessarily raise the herd size beyond that where it does not pay to keep extra livestock.

[13]Epicures, the famous Greek mathematician and philosopher had declared that 'there is nothing like free lunch'!

with them. Overcrowding, pollution, overuse, and exploitation can result. All such situations lead to a reduction of gains to someone, or someone else needs to pay extra to solve the problem. Who is responsible for such losses or costs?

Quite often commons are treated as state property. The takeover of forest resources from communities in 1865, or irrigation tanks by the British in India are some examples. However, the failure of the state to maintain them and make use of them even for meeting revenue objectives raises several questions about the options for the future. What must the government do beyond 'policing' the state properties?

All these questions arise out of historical lessons about commons. It is necessary to understand the commons, both in theory and in practice for better management and greater human welfare.

## THE CONTEXT OF PROPERTY RIGHTS

Resources are generally classified by their physical characteristics, ownership patterns, and use patterns. Going by physical characteristics, they represent natural occurrence or man-made creations. Examples are water, minerals, forests, crop land, man-made capital, human capital, and so on. In economic terms, all resources are viewed in two distinct forms, either as stocks or as flows from them, and sometimes both. If they are referred to as stock, it means that they are to be identified at a particular time, for example on every 31 March of a year. Then, the stock of the resource refers to its totality as of that date. Examples are that of crown forest land in area terms, panchayat lands measured in area or number, or a total count of wildlife animals or total stock of fish (in million tonnes) in a particular lake. Flow of a resource, is either an extraction or removal of some of it, or the resources generated by it as output or production or even natural and man-made degeneration. For instance, from a stock of forest resources measured in hectares of forest lands, are flows of other resources such as timber in tonnes or cubic metres, non-timber forest products (NTFPs), flowers, fruits, grass, and so on. These flows are examples of produce or output from the stock of the resource, namely the forests. Likewise, from a lake full of fish, the catch of fish (in kg) may be viewed as a flow. From a grassland resource (as a stock) there can be cutting of fodder grass in kg or head loads. From a tank (as a stock) there can be water extraction in cubic metres as a flow. Obviously, the use pattern from the resources can also be viewed as from the stock or out of the flows. Tourism in a wildlife sanctuary and deriving leisure is a case of use benefit directly from the stock while the consumption of fish out of the catch from a lake is a case of flow consumption benefit.

This distinction of any resource as a stock or flow or both will be useful for purpose of sorting out ownership and rights.

A variety of ownership patterns or property rights of such resources are also distinguishable. Examples are private ownership, state ownership, common or community ownership, open access, and several other variants. Property is the result of a 'secure claim to a resource or the services that the resources provide'. The ownership rights and regimes define or delineate the management systems. Among all these types of property ownership regimes, the one on 'common property' (and also 'open access regime' to some extent) has attracted maximum attention from researchers, scholars, scientists, political *pundits* and policy makers (J.S. Mill, 1985; Alfred Marshall, 1949; Schlager and Ostrom, 1992; Bromley and Cernea, 1989; Bromley, 1992b; Ciriacy-Wantrup and Bishop, 1975; Hardin, 1968; Olson, 1965; Runge, 1986; Singh, 1994b).[14] It is the common property regime and its management, mainly from the Indian perspective, which is the focus of this book.

[14]Quotes from J.S. Mills and Alfred Marshall show clearly that even the protagonists of private property resources, namely the classical and neo-classical economists, had recognized the need for and role of CPRs '...It is possible also to conceive that in this original appointment, compensation might be made for the injuries of nature and the balance redressed by assigning to the less robust members of the community, advantages in the distribution, sufficient to put them on at par with the rest... If individual property, on the contrary, were excluded, the plan which must be adopted would be to hold the land and all instruments of production as the joint property of the community, and to carry on the operations of industry on a common account... The division of the produce would in like manner be a public act... Whatever may be the merits or defects of these various schemes, they cannot be truly said to be impracticable. No reasonable person can doubt that a village community, composed of a few thousand inhabitants cultivating in joining ownership the same extent of land which at present feeds that number of people, and producing by combined labour and the most improved processes the manufactured articles which they required, could raise an amount of production sufficient to maintain them in comfort; and would find the means of obtaining, and if need be, exacting, the quantity of labour necessary for this purpose, from every member of the association who was capable of work.'

J.S. Mill in *Principles of Political Economy* (1985), p. 352–4.

What is the meaning of property rights? Economic theory normally refers to two broad sets of agents (under a *laissez faire* economic system) that manage the economy—'consumers' and 'producers'. The producers or the resource owners are further distinguished as private, state, community, and several other variants. The ownership rights set out different types of rules on the resources. These are: user rights, rights to prevent or admit others from using the resource, and rights to sell or not to sell. Along similar lines, consumers are further distinguished as individuals, state, community, and so on. The types of ownership rights and the interplay of the two agents establish the economic behaviour in respect of production, exchange, pricing, and consumption of goods and services. In this context, following North (1990: p. 33), property rights can be defined as an institutional framework in which individuals can appropriate or exercise their rights over their own labour, goods and services they possess. The sense or degree of appropriation depends upon legal rules, organizational forms, enforcement procedures, and norms of behaviour applicable to the individuals. The basic fact in this process of economic management is the description of resources (including their endowments) and their ownership patterns, and clearly linking beneficiaries to the ownership rights. This thinking provides a better definition of property rights, particularly in the context of natural resources.

A property right is a claim to a benefit stream that is recognized and respected by people conventionally, legally, or otherwise. It is an institutional system in which the ownership and management of various resources are identified and specified (modified from Singh, 1994b: p. 133).

Alternative forms of property rights are private, public, state, common property, and open access. Accordingly, the associated resources, goods, and services are designated as private resources (and

'... The rights of property, as such, have not been venerated by those master minds who have built up economic science... It may be well, therefore, to note that the tendency of careful economic study is to base the rights of private property not on any abstract principle, but on the observation that in the past they have been inseparable from solid progress; and that, therefore, it is the part of responsible men to proceed cautiously and tentatively in abrogating or modifying even such rights as may seem to be inappropriate to the ideal conditions of social life.'
Alfred Marshall, *Principles of Economics*, Macmillan and Co., eighth edition, 1949, p. 40.

goods), public goods, state owned goods, CPRs, and open access resources.

A distinction must be made at this stage between property rights and tenure. Using the given definition, property rights bring in some kind of management status to the ownership of property. Tenure, on the other hand, refers to an act of pure ownership with no reference to management (Singh, 1994b). For instance, in India there are several land tenurial systems in all the states. They are not associated with any specific or precise management system, except that the society is free to enjoy the resources under such rights.

Much before the classical economists from the West (Mill, 1985 edition), Indian wisdom from Kautilya (300 BC) and several others and Chinese thinking (quoted on the cover page) in the pre-Christian era had realized the property rights as a management approach, as a good tool for governance, and for better welfare.[15]

What are the alternative property rights regimes? When it comes to the management of resources, they can either be owned by someone or maintained under certain custodianship. Second, there can be situations in which there are rights that exclude others from using the resources or no such rights. Accordingly, different regimes of managing the resources emerge conceptually. Among these, the most commonly and operationally relevant ones are: private property regime, public good regime, common property regime, state property regime, and open access regime.

The most commonly known property rights regime is private property holding. Under this regime, individuals, households, or even groups (corporate bodies, and firms etc.) can own resources with exclusive rights to use them, rights to exclude others from using them, and rights to sell some or all of them, or buy more of them (Bromley, 1991).[16] Examples are private land and livestock ownership, privately owned machines, buildings, hotels, etc. Only the owner can draw

[15]Kautilya, for instance, refers to three types of land property as crown land, private land, and pasture land.

[16]Another characterization often added is about the possibility of subtractiveness of the resource use. For instance, a privately owned car occupied by some members of a family, makes less room for other members of the family. But not all private resource uses have this characteristic. A privately owned garden can be used by many members at the same time without reducing its use by others.

benefits or welfare from the use of these resources (or if he wishes he can distribute them). The benefits or flows such as crop income, income from the sale of milk or from sale of products produced by machines etc., also enjoy the same rights, hence they are also included under the same private property regime. Such entitlements make it possible for the owners to use the resource in whatever best way they think, or sell it, or exchange it for something else, or even lease it out.

There can be a situation in which a produce or income derived from a resource becomes private resource, but not the source itself. For example, a village pond may be maintained by all the villagers; but the catch of fish by any individual becomes his private resource. In India, it is quite common for landowners to lease out lands to other farmers or landless people, from whom they receive some rental incomes.[17] The lessee does not own the land, but owns the produce from that land.

Neo-classical economic thinking proposes that resources under private property regimes are efficiently manageable under a competitive market condition (Varian, 1984). In reality, such market situations do not exist for a large number of resources such as land, forests, water, or fishing. Apart from a lack of proper markets, often these resources such as water bodies, fishing sights, forests, meadows are not easy to fraction or divide and sell. Hence, in many instances, private property regimes are not practical. As argued by Singh (1994a), sometimes private property owners such as poor landowners may misuse them (because of a shortsighted view, or with very high discount rates), leading to socially inefficient uses. Examples are poor farmers selling fertile agricultural lands for building motels, etc. The social losses may overshadow the private benefits in such cases. Because of individual property rights, it is often extremely difficult for the government or the 'state' to regulate their use or abuse in the best interest of the people at large.

Next is the situation of public good regime. Public goods are resources which are not owned by any single individual, household, or firm; the use of these by one individual or firm (with or without payment) does not exclude others from using or enjoying them (or the users or consumers do not have any rivalry among them); they allow collective use and consumption, and often are indivisible (because of

---

[17]Often such resources are maintained for sake of prestige, and not necessarily for income or profits.

which, no single individual can appropriate them).[18] Sometimes it is also said that public goods are characterized by non-subtractiveness (Buchanan, 1968). Use of the resource by a member does not reduce the value or utility for others by using it at the same time, with a public park as a textbook example. Public goods may be owned by the government or the state, or certain public bodies. Alternatively, the government or the state may just be the custodian of the resource. Examples of public, natural, and environmental resources are public parks or wildlife sanctuary, oceans, waterways (for example, Ganga Water Authority, with or without toll fee), express roads with toll fee, marine fishery in exclusive economic zones (EEZs), and so on. Examples of ownership are the government owning the minerals, municipal corporations owning lakes and ponds, National Highway Authority owning public roads, etc.

In the management of such public goods, apart from application of the modified Pareto optimality condition that the 'sum of all the individual marginal rates of substitution be equal to the marginal rate of transformation', policy tools of taxes and subsidies, and several rules can be suitably designed to regulate their use. Also, several other allocative rules and policy imperatives drawn from the economics of public goods can be followed (Buchanan, 1968). For instance, in the case of public parks, there can be entry fees, time restrictions, security restrictions, and so on.[19] One comes across a large number of natural resources in India and elsewhere which are maintained under this public good domain.

A variant of public good regime is the state property regime. In this situation, the government or the state is the exclusive owner of the resource or property. The resource itself can either be a public good or

[18]A more rigorous definition of a public good requires an added condition that it is available at zero marginal cost to the user. It may also be owned by one single individual, firm or the state, but the owner cannot exclude anyone from using such a resource. For instance, a patent holder owns a technology, receives royalty from its users, but cannot restrict entry of others from using it on agreed royalty or payment. Once a royalty is paid, repeated use by the individual does not attract additional royalty. Similarly, once an entrance fee is paid, enjoying a public park over hours and hours does not require any additional fee.

[19]Interested readers are recommended reading of Atkinson and Stiglitz (1980) and Buchanan (1968).

anything else. For instance, national parks, wildlife sanctuaries and national highways are state properties which are public goods in character. The state can also own railways, airlines, hotels, etc. which are more like private goods. Because of their large size (and quite often indivisibility and advantages of economies of scale, the state emerges as the owner of such resources. By a similar argument, the reserved and protected forests or minerals owned by the government are often referred to as nationalized resources.[20]

The government or the state can treat such resources for revenue motive (that is, more as a private property resource (PPR)) and hence charge rents, fees, etc. on their use. Examples are earning rent from hotel rooms, royalty and income from the extraction of minerals, service charges from railways, airlines, etc. Alternatively, the state can act only as a custodian, and only be involved in 'policing'. An example is that of owning and maintaining panchayat lands, reserve and protected forests, Central Reserve Police Force (CRPF) or Border Security Force (BSF). There is also a third option of treating the resource as benevolent to the public and providing services from the resource at just the marginal cost or at no cost. Examples of such benevolence are releasing panchayat and degraded forest lands to the communities for joint forest management.

On practical grounds, state property management has been found to not be acceptable to large sections of people for the reason that the management tends to become very bureaucratic, and the rent seeking behaviour of the state and the bureaucracy makes the net benefits or gains to the public very dismal. Quite often, there are conflicts between the government and the communities (as was the case with the forests in Kumaon hills in the 1920s).

DEFINITION OF COMMON PROPERTY RESOURCES

Next to the case of public good or state property regime is the situation of CPR, which is the subject matter of this book. A definition of CPR, which is quite acceptable to most students of economics is: 'A property on which well defined collective claims by an exclusive group are established, the use of the resource is subtractive, having the characteristic of a public good such as indivisibility shall be termed as

. [20]For more details on nationalization of minerals see Kadekodi (1990).

common property resource.'

This definition has two distinct features. First, it refers to the nature of the resource itself. It is of the nature of a public good. This is the physical and intrinsic character of the resource. Second, more than this, it should have an association with a community or user group in a specific way, namely with collective claims (and hence governance). Without the second, such resources can be managed as state or public goods. As an example, when the British took away the community rights of village tanks in India by creating PWDs to look after them, there is a vivid example of a CPR having been converted into a state property.

All CPRs, in principle, have three basic characteristics: First, a well-defined group or community has to have exclusive rights on the use of the resource. Second, there is the non-excludability condition that no member of that community can be excluded from the use of the resource. However, no single individual in the group has any exclusive property rights on those resources either. Nor does any outside member have any rights. Third, the use of the resource is subtractive in the sense that use of it by any user would reduce accese and the welfare of other members in the group.

At this stage, it may be necessary to distinguish between CPRs and common pool resources (the two terms are often used interchangeably). The distinction is based on the existence of collective claim and user rights. In a CPR situation as defined, the resources are collectively claimed and used. Invariably, the sharing and access rules are well defined once and for all time to come. There are strict rights and duties defined for sharing of resources by the exclusive group. This definition is quite close to the legal and regulatory framework. In the common pool situation, the group may or many not have a collective claim, ownership, or custodianship but may have access or user rights to the resource. Moreover, the access may differ from situation to situation (example, in times of drought, flood and so on), from year to year, and so on. For instance, pastoral rights are accorded to nomadic tribes to graze their sheep and goats in private lands (after harvesting)—this is a case of common pool resource use. Another example of common pool resource is that of water distribution from a village common tank, wherein landowners in the *ayacut* having first rights to irrigation from the tank and then come those having land outside.

Two of the most important examples of CPRs in India are a variety of common lands such as panchayat lands (or other similar common lands, as reviewed in the case of Punjab in the section 'A Brief Tour of Commons...') and water (say from tanks) or canal irrigation water. Examples of CPR as stocks are land categories such as grazing lands, panchayat lands, or community lands. Examples of common property flows are grass and fodder from grazing lands; forests providing timber, NTFPs, beauty of wildlife; village panchayat lands, buffer areas or certain types of forests assigned to the communities (such as protected, unclassed). Examples of CPR flows from water resources are boating or navigation in oceans, lakes providing fish and tourism, or public tanks, wells, and water bodies providing drinking water and so on.[21] Can biodiversity and local indigeneous knowledge also be added to the category of CPRs? Yes, provided the rules of the game are well defined. For instance, in India, there are rich biodiversity reserves under a traditional system known as sacred groves. There is no perfect inventory of the sacred groves. Indications are that there are about 240 in the western ghats and Kerala state alone. There are as many as 11,193 well identified wetlands in India, six major ones under the Ramsar Convention (Kadekodi, 2002).

Common property resources as stocks can provide either CPR flows or other types of resources mentioned in the section entitled 'The Context of Property Rights', such as private resources. Examples are timber from a protected forest (a CPR) can be either a CPR (for the community as a whole) or the government may treat it as a state property or a private good (and hence auction them). Fodder grass from a community managed joint forest can be a CPR itself. Examples of private flows are fish catch (by individuals) from a village pond (which is a CPR) or NTFPs collected by individuals from a protected forest and so on. Often such resource flows are called fugitive goods. By fugitive resource it is meant that the ownership of the resource is determined by the capture or access to the resource. For example, each fisherman claims ownership to all the fish he captures (irrespective of what is left in the lake).

---

[21]There are a number of studies on each of these CPR resource situations in India. It is beyond the scope of this book to cite studies on all these CPR categories. However, two specific ones are mentioned here: studies by Jodha on the grasslands of Rajasthan (1994, 1986) and Sengupta's studies on water (1991).

In traditional societies, CPRs are either collectively owned or the community has exclusive user rights. Many of the rights are traditionally defined, rather than imposed by the state through law. Examples of traditionally given rights on CPRs are the 'timber rights' to villagers in Himachal Pradesh,[22] forest user rights through Van Panchayats in Uttar Pradesh (Somanathan, 1991), or *shamlat-deh* lands held jointly by the village community in Delhi and surrounding areas since the Mughal period (Chakravarty–Kaul, 1996), or NTFP rights from a joint forest management of protected forest (Singh and Ballab, 1989).

What is the relationship between CPRs, PPRs, and public goods? Often, CPRs are viewed as a type of impure public goods. They can also be viewed as something between a private property and public good in character. Examples of pure public goods are atmosphere, oceans, etc., they have no exclusive user group identified, their use is not subtractive and is non-excludable. They are also indivisible. Under private property rights, use of a resource is exclusive and subtractive. Moreover, such rights allow the owner of the resource the right to buy and sell the property.

In practical terms, however, there are a few additional characteristics of common property resources. First, almost like a public good, there can be some degree of indivisibility of the resource. A forest compartment or a village pond or tank are typical examples. Second, a particular group or community can have exclusive rights on the use of and access to the resource without ownership rights. 'Shamlat' lands in Haryana and Punjab villages are examples. Third, exclusion of users (or control of access) to those resources from outside of the group is often problematic, for example, the rights of nomadic sheep rearers from Rajasthan. Fourth, there ought to be a set of rules regarding the use of the resource and sharing of its benefits such as having well defined rules on sharing fuelwood, water, or fodder grass. Finally, there ought to be an institution within the group to impose rules and regulations, outside of legal institutions such as courts. Examples are village protection committees (under joint forest management (JFM)), 'Pani' panchayats in Maharashtra, or hill resource management societies (HRMS) in Haryana.

[22]On an average, in recent times, villagers in Himachal Pradesh extract about 1.06 lakh cubic metres of timber as a matter of this right, without paying anything to the Forest Department.

DEFINITION OF OPEN ACCESS RESOURCE

There is a further variant of CPR, observed in many parts of the world, called an 'open access resource'. Is it the same as a CPR? The answer is 'no'. Whenever an exclusive group is not identified to manage a CPR, a state of conflict, rivalry and over exploitation of the resource can occur. This is a case of open access resource. Basically, it is a situation where there are no enforceable property rights over the use of the resource. A well-known biologist, Garrett Hardin (1968), termed it as a situation of tragedy of the commons.[23] In general, whenever one or the other characteristic or rules related to CPR are violated, individual choice may prevail over social choice. In such a situation, it is rational for an individual to over-extract or over-use the CPR, and yet not be individually responsible for the damage, here the CPR assumes the nature of open access resource. However, to the extent that the use or exploitation rates are below the carrying capacity of the resources, the situation may go unnoticed. In reality, one does not get many examples of CPRs but many more of open access resource. Examples of open access resources are fishing in the open sea, river, or ponds, ill-managed village common grazing lands, buffer areas of forests, groundwater, wildlife hunting without any restrictions, customs, rules, or regulations.

A rigorous definition of open access resource may be useful at this stage: An open access resource is a depletable fugitive resource characterized by rivalry in extraction; it is subject to use by any person who has the capability and desire to enter into harvest or extraction of it; and its extraction results in symmetric or asymmetric negative externalities (Stevenson, *Common Property Economics*, 1991: p. 8).

Theoretically speaking, an open access situation is treated as a case of negative externality (resulting from non-existence of property rights). A further distinction can be made between symmetric and asymmetric negative exernalities. The symmetric externality refers to the case of any user imparting negative externality on all the others and *vice versa.*

---

[23]Hardin, of course, stressed this as a problem of population growth and the need for a moral approach to bring the population within the 'carrying capacity' of the limited earth. He also advocated mutually agred coercion method as an alternative.

Gordon (1954: pp. 135) describes this situation as, 'everybody's property is nobody's property'.

An example of symmetric externality is over-fishing in a lake. Asymmetric open access use is a situation in which one user creates an externality on other agents but others are not able to do the same to him/her. An example is a tannery polluting a river and destroying the fish culture, but the fishermen being unable to do anything to the tannery.

## OTHER TYPES OF COMMONLY POOLED RESOURCES

With the experience of managing privately owned resources by communities in several parts of India, for example Chakriya Vikas Pranali (CVP) in Jharkhand, one can add another category of resource, commonly pooled private resource (CPPR). This is a situation where people while retaining their individual or private property rights, pool their resources such as water or private lands to collectivize and manage. Once again, as in the case of CPRs, management of such resources ought to have the conditions of excludability, subtractiveness, as well as rules of sharing. The only added characterization is that, because of their individual property rights, individuals also retain the right of withdrawing from the pool at any time, unless the poolers frame rules of penalty and restrictions on withdrawal (Kadekodi, 1992, 1998). This kind of pooling and creating a common asset and management regime is not easy. It requires several new catalytic inputs and a well-structured institutional framework of village society. First, there is the question of leadership. Motivating PPR owners to pool their resources requires strong leadership which gets heard. Second, well-designed and transparent sharing rules are necessary. Third, stronger rules and penalties on withdrawals from the pool and restrictions on membership (for example, on absentee land poolers) are needed.[24]

## WHY A 'COMMON PROPERTY REGIME' IS RELEVANT

In the context of natural resource management with CPRs, two questions emerge. First, when is a common property regime relevant? Second, how does it emerge? These questions can be answered if one looks at CPRs from the point of view of both efficiency and sustainable

[24]In Chapter 10 a case study on such a land, water, and forest resource management institution from Jharkhand is presented.

institutions to manage them. The first question is dealt with briefly here and the second will be taken up in Chapters 5 and 6.

Should one view a CPR regime as a case of scale economies? The answer is both 'yes' and 'no'. From the point of management efficiency, there are scale advantages in evolving CPR regimes. Pooling of human power and indigenous and modern technical knowledge that go with the CPR management leads to economies of scale in its productive use. However, equally relevant is the case of higher carrying capacity of CPR. Consider, for the moment, three alternative management regimes: private, CPR, and open access (leaving out for the moment the 'state' as another alternative). As illustrated in Figure 1.1, considering land productivity as an indicator of efficiency, up to level $P_1$, private ownership is preferable. Beyond $P_1$, in terms its carrying capacity, CPR management has an edge over private management. Open access is, in any case, a fallout of the failure of CPR resource or even private resource management, and is least efficient. The carrying capacity of private management defined as the maximum productivity is also much lower than that under CPR regime.

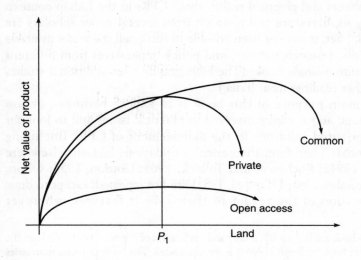

**Figure 1.1:** Efficiency of Land Use and Property Rights Regimes

Evolution of CPR institutions takes place, either (i) when private resource management fails (in terms of cost efficiency) or, (ii) because of scale advantages of the resource or, (iii) when the state fails to manage the resource as a public good. In the first instance, owners of private resources may even hand over or sell their small and marginal resources to create CPRs. In the second instance (of large scale), they may ask the state to intervene to takeover the resource for better management. In the third instance, the state itself may invite the community to come forward and join it in managing resources. An example of the first is pooling of small and fragmented private lands with low productivity to create a CPR institution. A good example of this is the CPV institution operating in Jharkhand in which poor tribals and small farmers of Chhotanagpur region have pooled their private lands to create a CPPR. An example of the second is the state (government) managing large irrigation systems, forest resources, and community grazing lands. An example of the third situation is the emergence of JFM.

ABOUT THE BOOK

This book is designed to provide both the relevant recent theoretical developments and practical reality about CPRs in the Indian context. In doing so, literature and research from several major scholars are included.[25] Yet, it has not been possible to survey all the major available documents, research outputs, and policy imperatives from different sources into a single book. (The bibliography cites additional studies and further readings from India.)

The main purpose of this book is to expose planners, action researchers, and students involved in practical issues and to look for policy-oriented solutions in the management of CPRs (including wastelands). Therefore, theoretical foundations laid out elsewhere (Singh, 1994a; Buchanan and Tullock, 1965; Gordon, 1954; Olson, 1971; Bromley, 1991; Dasgupta, 1982) are not repeated, except to draw the attention of the reader to their salient features, wherever

[25]For a basic reading on the theory and application of common pool resources, the most recent book by Singh (1994a) is recommended. The book provides summaries of most theoretical foundations, institutional mechanisms on management, political economy, as well as case studies.

necessary. Rather, the focus is on the most recent theoretical frameworks that address CPR management in India. The analysis uses Indian data. Second, there is a felt need to understand and appreciate the dimensions of Indian CPRs and the changes in them. This is necessary for designing strategies for the management of CPRs. Third, some selected case studies are reproduced or summarized from the available studies, highlighting the issues, the methods of dealing with them, and policy imperatives. It is hoped that they will provide some clues for policy research and guidelines.

The book is divided into three parts. The first part deals with the definitions, database, and some conceptualization of CPRs. In doing so, comparison is made between several types of resources and property right regimes. Along with CPRs, PPRs and wastelands are also analysed, compared, and contrasted.

In the second part, theories of CPR management, evolution of CPR institutions, and an inventory of existing institutions in India are presented, elaborated, and commented on. Relevant theories are highlighted.

The third part of the book presents four selected case studies on CPR management in India. They cover four different site-specific situations; three different types of CPR resources, namely grassland, forests, and water; and four different institutional frameworks of CPR management and to some extent refer to different methods of evaluating them.

# 2

# Dimensions of Common Property Land Resources in India

## INTRODUCTION

Having viewed CPRs in a conceptual framework in the first chapter, we now take a look at their magnitude and relevance in India. The first question is about the types of CPRs in India. Going by the definition from Chapter 1 or by customary management practices, one can list a large number of CPRs. They include lands under different community uses (such as thrashing grounds, grazing pastures), wastelands (barren lands, shrub lands, etc.), forest lands, water resources (both ground and surface), and water bodies (tanks, ponds), fishery resources, biodiversity resources (such as sacred groves) common dumping grounds, and many more.[1] Unfortunately, there are no official estimates on the magnitudes, types and variation in CPRs in India. If any, they are shown in revenue, irrigation, or forest records under different types of holdings (pasture lands, barren lands, reserved, and protected forests) and managements (shamlat, van panchayat, sacred grove), canals, tanks, and wells. It is necessary to look at the details and identify them as a CPR, state property, public good and so on.

[1]One can also add a list of global commons such as climate, ozone layer etc., but these are not dealt with in this book.

There is a great diversity of CPRs, relevant in the Indian context. Their importance has to be gauged using a particular criterion. Generally, their magnitude, their relevance to the communities at large, significance in terms of sustainability are used to assign importance to them. Second, regeneration of wastelands, reversing biodiversity losses, promoting institutions to act on a carrying capacity basis on fishery, NTFP extraction and management of CPRs have become part of the ongoing policy and action plans for agricultural and rural development in India (Government of India, 1989). There is an underlying policy current to say that the poor are dependent upon the commons and something needs to be done for them.[2] Over the last three decades, a number of land development and regeneration programmes have been initiated in selected pockets in India, some on an experimental basis by non-governmental organizations (NGOs), some by donor agencies and communities, many others at the initiative of development administrators. The concerned ministries, Ministry of Environment and Forests (MoEF), Agriculture, National Wastelands Development Board (NWDB), Ministry of Rural Areas, have so far undertaken a number of programmes such as Social Forestry (SF), Joint Forest Management (JFM), Watershed Development Programme (WDP), Desert Area Development Programme (DADP), Drought Prone Area Programme (DPAP), National Biodiversity Strategy and Action Plan (NBSAP) and so on. In 2002, the Government of India came out with the National Water Policy with some reference to the issues related to the commons in water. Many of these programmes and experiments have been evaluated, from which several models of rural development and transformation have been developed (Chopra et al., 1990; Chopra and Kadekodi, 1991; Kadekodi, 1997a; Ravindranath et al., 2000; Antia and Kadekodi, 2002). In many programmes, the question of property rights, both conventional and traditional, versus externally created ones (tree *patta* rights or scheme, joint forest scheme) are to be considered for instituting local level institutions to manage them. That is the stronger reason for having the necessary database on CPRs and proper analysis of the data to meet policy interests.

In this chapter, an attempt is made to review the most important land resources for their dimensionality, broadly classified as land and

[2]This dependency will be discussed in detail in Chapter 4.

forest, and wastelands. Chapter 3 carries the same issue of dimensionality in respect of water, fisheries, and biodiversity resources in India.[3] All these are viewed, wherever relevant, first as stocks of resources and subsequently their flows. The issues of identifying them as CPRs and their statistical magnitudes are discussed. Wherever possible, the existing and prevailing links between the communities and the commons are identified. The purpose is to provide some picture of the relevance of CPRs to the communities and people at large in India.

## LAND RESOURCES

Communities all over India had access to several types of commons, by tradition and in some cases by convention. With the breaking up of such traditional rights, and the coming of land reforms all over the country, the nature of holdings has changed.

Common property land resource refers to lands identified with a specific type of property rights. On the other hand, wastelands are a class of lands reflecting specific ecological characteristics (without regard to property rights). As mentioned in the previous section, it is important to recognize that at the time of implementing a land regeneration programme, the issue of property rights cannot be ignored. This is all the more relevant in creating a common pool of lands for regeneration and for designing proper benefit sharing rules and self-governing design principles (a phrase borrowed from Elinor Ostrom 1990, and also suggested by Katar Singh, 1994b). Given the strength of the commonness, the types of sharing rules may have to be worked out at the time of implementation.[4]

In a study by Chopra et al. (1990), an attempt was made to quantify the magnitudes of common property land resources in the 1970s at the all-India level.[5] This was followed by a study by Bagchi and Phillip

[3]This grouping is only for convenience, and its details are guided by the extent of reliable data and information available. However, many other types of CPRs will be referred to and described, without much data, for example, indigenous knowledge.

[4]See Chapter 10, for an example of creating a common pool of wastelands out of PPRs. Even to promote government programmes such as JFM, declaring certain forest areas such as buffer areas as common lands may become controversial due to traditional rights given to certain exclusive groups.

[5]On the other hand, a large number of micro-level studies are now available, as

(1993) sponsored by the NWDB. A third set of estimates was made in a United Nations Development Programme (UNDP) sponsored study (Kadekodi, 1997b). With the availability of satellite data from the National Remote Sensing Agency (NRSA), further refinements in the estimates of CPRs are now possible. Most recently, another set of data on common property land resources was generated by the National Sample Survey (NSS), 54th Round, for 1998. Based on all this information, several alternative estimates of common property land and forest resources for recent periods in India are presented and analysed.[6]

Rights to CPRs may either be ownership, user rights, or both. However, the methodologies based on secondary data cannot capture all the ramifications of access and different sources of rights, or access to resources. Broad orders of magnitude of common property land resources can only be based on some assumptions with respect to ownership, tenurial status, and user rights. The basic source for such data in India is the Land Use Statistics compiled by the Ministry of Agriculture. Under certain assumptions, the corresponding estimates of common property land resources can be culled out at the state and district levels. Table 2.1 presents the land categories, assumptions, and concepts used here in identifying common property land resources in India.

The methodology of arriving at the estimates of common property land resources from the Land Use Statistics is described briefly. The estimates are derived at the state level. Some states are left out either for want of land record data or lack of reliability of data. Net sown area, including area under miscellaneous tree crops, and current fallow constitutes a PPR to which non-owners do not have access. However, it is often found that partial common access does exist even on ownership lands, which are uncultivated due to some contingency. This could be the absence of capital investment or the sheer fact that the owner does not consider it worthwhile to invest on marginal or sub-marginal land. Estimation of such 'open to common access' but 'private' land is made by comparing data on owned land obtained from the Agricultural

---

case studies and by regions, giving estimates of common land categories. See Iyengar (1988), Singh (1994a, b), Pasha (1992), Jodha (1985), Bon (2000); for a glimpse of selected state-level estimates of CPR dry lands, see Jodha (1997).

[6]It should also be useful to analyse the trends in such resources over decades, but lack of consistent time series data makes this task untenable.

Table 2.1
Identification of CPRs

| Classification of land | Current property rights | Can it be accounted as a CPR? | Included in source of sanction for access (as assumed in the estimation) |
|---|---|---|---|
| Net sown area | Private | No | On uncultivated owned land: limited user rights |
| Current fallow | Private | No | On uncultivated owned land: limited user rights |
| Fallow other than current fallow | Private | Yes | User rights by convention |
| Cultivable waste | Revenue Dept | Yes | Partial user rights by convention |
| Pastures and other grazing land | Panchayat | Yes | User rights by law |
| Barren and Uncultivable land | Revenue Dept | May be | No access |
| Area put to non-agricultural use | Public | May be | No access |
| Forest area | Forest Dept | | |
| 1. Reserved | | No | No access |
| 2. Protected | | Partial | Partial user rights |
| 3. Unclassed | | Yes | User rights by law |

Census with that on net area sown and current fallow obtained from official statistics. Since, at the state level, 'total land leased in' is approximately equal to 'land leased out', it is assumed that area owned and area operated are equal for each state. Wherever area owned obtained from the Agricultural Census exceeds the sum of net area sown and current fallow as obtained from the Land Use Statistics, it is assumed that rights of common access exist on this surplus land which will be called private land with CPR access (PLCPR).

The next component of lands is fallow other than current (OTHFL). These have common user rights by convention. While partial use rights exist on cultivable wastelands (CWL), permanent pasture and grazing lands (PPG) have user rights by law. Table 2.2 shows these at the state level, by the category of land use.

Table 2.2
Common Property Land Resources of India, 1990–1

*(in thousand hectares)*

| State | PLCPR | PPG | CWL | OTHFL | TOTNFCPR (2+3+4+5) | Forest CPR** PROT+UNCL | Total CPR (6+7) |
|---|---|---|---|---|---|---|---|
| | | | Non-forest areas | | | | |
| 1 | 2 | 3 | 4 | 5 | 6 | 7 | 8 |
| Andhra Pradesh | 1953 | 843 | 780 | 1377 | 4953 | 1333 | 6286 |
| Assam | 366 | 184 | 104 | 84 | 738 | 1246 | 1984 |
| Bihar*** | 1433 | 126 | 372 | 999 | 2930 | 2418 | 5348 |
| Gujarat | 0 | 849 | 1920 | 60 | 2829 | 557 | 3386 |
| Haryana | 0 | 23 | 21 | 0 | 44 | 143 | 187 |
| Himachal Pradesh | 392 | 1136 | 125 | 15 | 1668 | 3351 | 5019 |
| Jammu & Kashmir | 182 | 127 | 138 | 6 | 453 | 72 | 525 |
| Karnataka | 649 | 1098 | 446 | 457 | 2650 | 1011 | 3661 |
| Kerala | 0 | 2 | 95 | 27 | 124 | 189 | 313 |
| Madhya Pradesh*** | 1790 | 2734 | 1579 | 826 | 6929 | 7180 | 14,109 |
| Maharashtra | 2120 | 1519 | 1028 | 983 | 5650 | 1546 | 7196 |
| Meghalaya | 39 | 17* | 493 | 167 | 716 | 851 | 1567 |
| Nagaland | 662 | 0* | 99 | 110 | 871 | 854 | 1725 |
| Orissa | 0 | 726 | 597 | 214 | 1537 | 3010 | 4547 |
| Punjab | 0 | 10 | 35 | 28 | 73 | 286 | 359 |
| Rajasthan | 2779 | 1912 | 5567 | 1927 | 12,185 | 2011 | 14,196 |
| Tamil Nadu | 627 | 124 | 290 | 1044 | 2085 | 314 | 2399 |

(Contd.)

33

(in thousand hectares)

| State | Non-forest areas | | | | | | Forest CPR** | Total CPR (6+7) |
| | PLCPR | PPG | CWL | OTHFL | TOTNFCPR (2+3+4+5) | | PROT+UNCL | |
| 1 | 2 | 3 | 4 | 5 | 6 | | 7 | 8 |
| Tripura | 39 | 0* | 1 | 1 | 41 | | 270 | 311 |
| Uttar Pradesh*** | 0 | 303 | 1034 | 884 | 2221 | | 1524 | 3745 |
| West Bengal | 0 | 7 | 106 | 51 | 164 | | 482 | 646 |
| Total | 13,031 | 11,740 | 14,830 | 9,260 | 48,861 | | 34,869 | 83,730 |

Definitions:

PLCPR = Private lands to which common access may exist;

CWL = Culturable wastelands;

PPG = Permanent pastures and grazing lands;

OTHFL = Other than current fallow;

PROT+UNCL = Protected and unclassed forest lands;

TOTNFCPR = PLCPR+CWL+PPG+OTHFL

TOTNFCPR : (Total non forest common property land resources)

TOTNFCPR = PLCPR+CWL+PPG+OTHFL

TOTCPR = TOTNFCPR+(PROT+UNCL)

TOTCPR: (Total common property resources (forest and non-forest together))

*Notes:* * NWDB data; ** Statistics on forest areas are for 1997. The Land Use Statistics of non-forest areas are for 1990-1; *** These are the states prior to the formation of Uttaranchal, Chattisgarh, and Jharkhand states; data from not all the states are shown.
*Source:* CMIE and Land Utilization Statistics of Ministry of Agriculture

34

FOREST RESOURCES

Another category of land for which common property rights may exist is land under forests. To begin with, there is considerable controversy even around estimates of the total forest cover in the country, mainly between NRSA data and data from Forest Working Plans and records. According to recorded forest statistics, based on land use and legal status data, 75.30 million hectares, comprising 22.73 per cent of the total geographical area of India can be classified as forest area. However, NRSA and FSI (Forest Survey of India) assessment show only 65.7 million hectares under actual forest cover (Forest Survey of India, 1999). This discrepancy is basically due to differences in methods of data collection and definitions of status. In the late 1980s, an exercise was carried out by FSI to reconcile the two data sources by undertaking a critical comparison of their respective methodologies. By now, it is clear from the reports of FSI that the gap in the two assessments is due to discrepancy between legal records and ground truthing.

The break-up of total forest area on the basis of legal status and ownership can be still more controversial. According to the forest statistics of India, legal ownership of 95.8 per cent of the forest area is vested in the states. Only 2.5 per cent of the forest area is with corporate bodies defined as municipal and other corporate bodies, and village panchayats, etc. Local communities, however, have rights of access to parts of the state owned forest. Though reserve forests have always been treated as inaccessible, protected and unclassed forests are partly accessible. In 1907, the Imperial Gazetteer recorded that the unclassed or public forest lands are those given over with even fewer restrictions for the use of the public. It further maintained that protected forests may be either in a state of transition to reserves or intended to remain permanently in that class. In the latter case, more beneficial exercise of rights by local communities was allowed. It can, therefore, be concluded that access of local communities to protected forests would be inversely related to the magnitude of their conversion to reserve forests. The Government of India Gazetteer of 1975 held that the local people have virtually unrestricted rights of felling trees and grazing livestock in protected forests. On the basis of this indirect evidence, it can be concluded that whereas no access to reserve forests has been granted either by law or by use, local communities have had access to protected forests, both by law, and more significantly by convention.

Unclassed forests, with very low productivity, are always open to use by local communities. Accordingly, both protected and unclassed forests are treated as forming a part of common property forest resources, keeping in mind that this may yield an overestimate of land to which common access may exist. It is, therefore, the subset of total forest area minus reserve forests to which common property rights are assumed to exist. (Data for these are taken from various reports of FSI.)

Table 2.2 shows estimates of common property lands and forest areas for the year 1990–91, based on the methods and assumptions described.

States such as Rajasthan and Madhya Pradesh have very large chunks of common lands. According to Jodha (1986) there is a heavy concentration of CPRs in the dry land regions of India. The states having the least common lands are Haryana, Punjab, Tripura, Kerala, and West Bengal. Table 2.2 shows that there is a considerable degree of variation in the extent of CPR land and forests in different states (and also over time). In order to analyse such variations, four different indicators can be developed at this macro-level analysis. They are: (i) ratio of CPR land and forest to geographical area; (ii) per capita CPR land and forest area; (iii) ratio of CPR land and forest to wastelands; (iv) comparing the Ratio of CPR in the 1990s to, say, 1980s.[7]

Jodha (1994) suggests several other micro-level indicators which can be broadly grouped into physical degradation indicators and CPR management indicators. The physical degradation indicators are: number of CPR products collected by the communities; trees and shrubs per hectare; number of ponds; number of CPR plots where biodiversity has declined; and CPR area where grazing capacity has declined. Common property resource management indicators include protection of CPR area; regulation of CPR usage; and investment in development of CPRs. Using these indicators, some major inferences are drawn in Box 2.1.

---

[7]Though data similar to those in Table 2.2 are not shown here for 1980, they are available in Chopra *et al.* (1990).

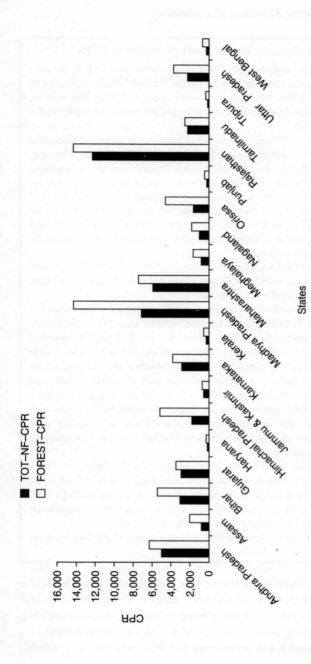

**Figure 2.1:** Common Property Land Resources of India (in thousand hectares)

37

---

**Box 2.1: Categorization of States According to CPRs**

1. CPR as a percentage of geographical area ranges between 4 and 30 per cent in different states, barring states such as Himachal Pradesh, which are known to have protected forest CPRs. In the north eastern states and other hilly regions, the non-forest CPRs are relatively less. Three broad groups can be made on the basis of CPR intensities.

a. States where the CPR area is low, being less than or around 10 per cent of geographical area in both the years. In this category are Punjab, Haryana, Uttar Pradesh, West Bengal, and Kerala. Andhra Pradesh can also be included in this category in the sense that CPRs as a percentage of geographical area are less than 10 per cent in 1990-1. Punjab and Haryana have a high level of agricultural development and there is a larger percentage of the land under private ownership and a low level of forest area per capita. Uttar Pradesh and Andhra Pradesh, by virtue of being states with diverse agro-climatic zones, exhibit the marginal characteristics.

b. States where the CPR area falls in the range of around 10 to 30 per cent. A number of states such as Bihar, Gujarat, Karnataka, Maharashtra, Orissa, Tamil Nadu, and Tripura fall in this group.

c. The outliers with more than 30 per cent area under CPRs. Rajasthan has a CPR area of around 42 per cent, not because of forest areas but by the nature of land use pattern mainly as pastures. Himachal Pradesh and Jammu and Kashmir, being hilly states, show varying characteristics. This is because of large areas of protected forests in Himachal Pradesh, which make the area under CPRs unduly high; similarly, large areas in the category of reserve forests exist in Jammu and Kashmir, which decrease the CPR area to an unusually low level.

2. In a majority of the states, there has been a decrease in the lands with CPR rights. Per capita CPR land has also gone down. These decreases are more pronounced in the arid and semi-arid states of Madhya Pradesh, Maharashtra, Gujarat, Karnataka, and Rajasthan.

3. A very important indicator for policy purposes is the ratio of CPR to wastelands. Restricting to non-forest categories only, except for Nagaland, in all the states the CPR area is much less than the wastelands. At the all-India level this ratio is 50.2 per cent. In other words, much of the scope for wastelands development programmes will have to be outside of CPR areas.

4. Finally, there is an indication that in some states there has been an increase in CPR areas in the 1980s.

---

It is found that, in spite of the severe data limitations, both the levels of common property land resource areas in different states and the changes taking place over time have exhibited some interesting patterns. River basins, where crop production on private land is a profitable activity, have a low percentage of CPRs, whereas high rainfall mountains and sub-mountainous regions have a high percentage. Arid and semi-arid states, where livestock rearing is an important activity, also have large amounts of land as common pastures which add to common property land resource area. The dry lands of India invariably have very high CPRs enabling the poor with some subsistence livelihood (Jodha, 1994).

WASTELAND RESOURCES

From the point of view of ecological development, it is important to understand the extent and magnitude of wastelands. While CPRs are defined and identified within the property rights regimes, wastelands are to be understood within the framework of ecological configurations and characteristics, beyond the property rights regimes. Therefore, a wasteland situation is quite distinct from a common property situation. As part of policies on the revival of land from degradation in India, a large number of programmes have been developed by the concerned departments such as agriculture, rural development, wastelands development, soil conservation, eco-regeneration and so on. Therefore, the dimensions of wastelands in India, their ecological characteristics, gaps in the data and information about them, and the institutions to manage them, are some of the important issues to be addressed.

Why is there a need for a separate definition and estimates of wastelands? There are two basic reasons for this. First (as will be made clear later), wastelands and CPRs are two different things. Second, the criteria to be used for developing land regeneration and monitoring programmes are to be linked precisely to the criteria used in defining and estimating lands classified into different categories. Regeneration capability depends upon the quality of lands whereas monitoring and implementation depends upon property rights or ownership patterns. In the ultimate land regeneration programmes, both the quality and the ownership patterns (to be more precise, the property rights systems) need to be taken into account. At the outset, therefore, it is useful to draw the distinction between them, for purposes of identification, data collection, analysis, and policy use.

What is the definition of wasteland? Currently in India, there are at least three different official definitions of wastelands. Basically they differ, not so much in their magnitudes but, in the manner in which they are identified and estimated. The Ministry of Agriculture (1992) used land productivity as an economic criterion for defining wastelands. Bombla and Khare (1984) went by land productivity as well as quality or ecological characteristics. The NWDB used both ecological and economic criteria, namely, economic recoverability, regeneration, and productivity. Accordingly, three different definitions and sets of estimates have emerged, with some degree of overlapping.

What causes wastelands?[8] Wastelands can result from inherent or imposed disabilities on land such as location, environment, chemical and physical properties of the soil, and financial management constraints. The Technical Task Force Group constituted by the NWDB in 1986 had classified wastelands into 13 categories (see Box 2.2).

---

**Box 2.2: Classification of Wastelands**

- Gullied and/or ravinous land
- Land with or without scrub
- Waterlogged and marshy land
- Land affected by salinity/alkalinity
- Shifting cultivation area
- Under-utilized/degraded notified forest land
- Degraded pastures/grazing land
- Degraded land under plantation crops
- Sands (coastal and desert)
- Mining/industrial wastelands
- Barren rocky/stony waste/sheet rock area
- Steep sloping area
- Snow covered and/or glacial area

---

The Ministry of Agriculture, in its earliest estimates (1982), assumed some degree of land productivity consistent with soil and water availability to arrive at the proportion of 'problem areas' within different land use categories. Bombla and Khare (1984), on the other hand, have used ecological quality such as salinity, alkalinity, water erosion, wind erosion, floods, and water logging as the basis for arriving at the estimates of wastelands. Discounting any economic criteria, they used

---

[8]Lands are classified by the use pattern. Generally, they are distinguished into eight categories as, area sown, area under pasture and grazing land, current fallow, fallow other than current, cultivable wastes, barren and uncultivable waste lands, area put to non-agricultural uses and forest area.

ecological instability, complete loss of topsoil, and toxicity in the root zones as the additional ecological criteria. They pointed out two demerits in the conventional productivity linked definition of the Ministry of Agriculture. First, productivity—either potential or actual—is dependent upon the state of availability or non-availability of technology and its utilization. Second, the definition is biased towards economics and ignores ecological considerations completely. Subsequently, they tried to establish relationships between ecological problems and land use categories, and derived consistent estimates of wastelands.

The NWDB's 'Technical Group Report', 1986 stated that standardizing the definition of wastelands is imperative as different organizations have categorized wastelands differently because of which there is non-uniformity of database and gross variations in the extent of estimated wastelands in the country. After much deliberation, the NWDB arrived at the following definition of wasteland and it's categorization. This definition is comprehensive enough to refer to the ecological factors behind the erosions, and the economic approach to deal with the problem. 'Wastelands mean degraded lands which can be brought under vegetative cover, with reasonable effort and which are currently lying underutilized, and land which is deteriorating for lack of appropriate water and soil management or on account of natural causes' (Technical Group Report of NWDB, 1986).

The productivity and ecology-linked definitions, however, have difficulties of measurement on a practical basis, particularly on a continuous basis over the years. Often sampling techniques are resorted to. Sampling techniques, however robust they are, may lead to erroneous conclusions due to non-availability of complete topo-sheets and the minimal topographic information. Second, over the sampled blocks or watersheds, the recorded data may be totally remote from the truth. Furthermore, 'ground truthing' on an all-India sampling basis is also extremely expensive.

What are the basic differences between wastelands and CPRs? Wastelands refer to the quality of land resources based on some definitions or concept of quality whereas, CPRs are based purely on ownership or property rights systems; hence the two differ in concept as well as magnitude.

The basic source of information for identifying wastelands is the

Land Use Statistics published by the Ministry of Agriculture. Taking into account the causes and the land use categories, wastelands can be broadly divided into 10 groups. While identifying the common property land and forest resources, the same land use statistics are used. A comparison of land use categories identified as wastelands along with those classified under CPRs is presented in Box 2.3. One notices that, based on measurements and empirical estimates, some categories of wastelands also fall under the category of CPRs and *vice-versa*.

---

**Box 2.3: Operational Measures of CPRs and Wastelands**

| CPRs | Wastelands |
|---|---|
| 1. That part of land, which, though officially classified as privately owned, allows partial common access if it is not sown. | 1. Permanent pastures and grazing lands. |
| 2. Cultivable wastes. | 2. Land under miscellaneous trees and groves. |
| 3. Fallow other than current fallow. | 3. Part of current fallow. |
| 4. Common pastures and grazing land. | 4. Culturable wastelands. |
| 5. Protected and unclassed forests. | 5. Fallow other than current fallow. |
| | 6. Barren and uncultivable lands. |
| | 7. Water logged areas. |
| | 8. *Usar* lands. |
| | 9. Lands under shifting cultivation. |
| | 10. Degraded forest lands and coastal sand dunes. |

---

These differences between CPRs and wastelands are mainly based on land use patterns.

Estimates of Wastelands

Chopra *et al.* (1990) analysed these issues on a systematic basis and came up with a set of land categories to be classified as wastelands. According to them, current management practices may provide some logical basis for clubbing land use categories as wastelands. The land use categories that can qualify as wastelands are shown in Box 2.3.[9]

---

[9]Bagchi and Phillip (1993), on the other hand, included current fallow lands under the wastelands. But they did not consider water-logged areas, '*usar*' lands,

Such a classification is simplistic yet operationally easy to derive estimates. It is a matter of empirical verification as to how many assumptions hold true against ground realities, based on either productivity or ecology-linked estimates.

What are the sources of data for estimating wastelands? There are four sources of data for estimating wastelands (or their components) in India: (i) the eight-fold classification of Land Use Statistics published by the Ministry of Agriculture, (ii) the State of Indian Forests that classifies forests by crown densities, published by the Ministry of Environment and Forests, (iii) the remote sensing data from NRSA. They are to be collated with additional information on the ecological quality characteristics of lands already listed and economic criteria such as land productivity and biomass regeneration etc., (iv) finally, a number of studies and experiments carried out by NGOs and researchers at the micro-level also provide some data on wastelands.

Of these, only two are presented here at the state level.[10] The first is from NWDB for 1986, the second from NRSA for 1999, based on remote sensing and ground truthing. Some comments offered, are, however, based on other available estimates.

Table 2.3 and 2.4 present the NWDB estimates of wastelands across different states of the country. On the basis of detailed satellite mapping of 146 districts of the country in 1986, the NWDB (1989) arrived at an estimate of wastelands at 129.57 million hectares, of which 93.69 million hectares are in non-forest areas. As compared to the total geographical area of India of 329 million hectares, the magnitude of this degradation is almost 45 per cent. The NWDB used Bombla and Khare's (1984) estimates of non-forest degraded lands and added estimates of wastelands in the forest areas.

The major causes of wastelands are water logging, salinity, marshiness, ravine land, sandy dunes, strip lands, mined areas, and coastal lands. They can be grouped into three categories: saline and alkali lands, wind-eroded areas, and water-eroded areas (see Table 2.4). (For some broad comments on NWDB data see Box 2.4).

---

ravinous lands, lands under shifting cultivation, degraded forestlands, and sand dune lands.

[10]For several other alternative estimates, see Kadekodi (1997b).

Table 2.3
Estimates of Wasteland in India

*(lakh ha)*

| State | Non-forest area | Non-forest degraded area | Reported forest area | Forest degraded area | Total degraded area | Total geographical area |
|---|---|---|---|---|---|---|
| Andhra Pradesh | 211.27 | 76.82 | 63.80 | 37.34 | 114.16 | 275.07 |
| Assam | 47.74 | 9.35 | 30.70 | 7.95 | 17.30 | 78.44 |
| Bihar* | 144.67 | 38.96 | 29.20 | 15.62 | 54.58 | 173.87 |
| Gujarat | 176.62 | 71.53 | 19.40 | 6.83 | 78.36 | 196.02 |
| Haryana | 42.54 | 24.04 | 1.67 | 0.74 | 24.78 | 44.21 |
| Himachal Pradesh | 20.34 | 14.24 | 35.33 | 5.34 | 19.58 | 55.67 |
| Jammu & Kashmir | 202.05 | 5.31 | 20.18 | 10.34 | 15.65 | 222.23 |
| Karnataka | 153.07 | 71.22 | 38.72 | 20.43 | 91.65 | 191.79 |
| Kerala | 27.64 | 10.53 | 11.22 | 2.26 | 12.79 | 38.86 |
| Madhya Pradesh* | 288.96 | 129.47 | 154.49 | 71.95 | 201.42 | 443.45 |
| Maharashtra | 243.68 | 115.60 | 64.01 | 28.41 | 144.01 | 307.69 |
| Manipur | 7.17 | 0.14 | 15.15 | 14.24 | 14.38 | 22.32 |
| Meghalaya | 12.94 | 8.15 | 9.49 | 11.03 | 19.18 | 22.43 |
| Nagaland | 7.96 | 5.08 | 8.62 | 8.78 | 13.86 | 16.58 |
| Orissa | 98.53 | 31.57 | 57.18 | 32.27 | 63.84 | 155.71 |
| Punjab | 47.46 | 11.51 | 2.90 | 0.79 | 12.30 | 50.36 |
| Rajasthan | 310.54 | 180.01 | 31.70 | 19.33 | 199.34 | 342.24 |
| Sikkim | 4.38 | 1.31 | 2.73 | 1.50 | 2.81 | 7.10 |
| Tamil Nadu | 107.54 | 33.92 | 22.52 | 10.09 | 44.01 | 130.06 |

(Contd.)

44

(lakh ha)

| State | Non-forest area | Non-forest degraded area | Reported forest area | Forest degraded area | Total degraded area | Total geographical area |
|---|---|---|---|---|---|---|
| Tripura | 4.20 | 1.08 | 6.29 | 8.65 | 9.73 | 10.49 |
| Uttar Pradesh* | 253.33 | 66.35 | 41.08 | 14.26 | 80.61 | 294.41 |
| West Bengal | 76.87 | 21.77 | 11.88 | 3.59 | 25.36 | 88.75 |
| Union Territories | NA | 8.89 | NA | 27.15 | 36.64 | 14.67 |
| Total | 2103.07 | 936.85 | 753 | 358.89 | 1295.74 | 2856.07 |

Notes:
1. For some of the north east states, the figures of recorded forest and non-forest are not consistent with the corresponding degraded areas, due to different data source.
2. NA is not available.
3. *These are the states that existed prior to the formation of Uttaranchal, Chattisgarh, and Jharkhand.
Source: NWDB (1989), Indian Council of Forestry Research and Education.

Table 2.4
Details of Non-forest Wastelands by Ecological Problems

*(lakh ha)*

| State | Saline/alkaline lands | Wind eroded area | Water eroded area | Total |
|---|---|---|---|---|
| Andhra Pradesh | 2.40 | – | 74.42 | 76.82 |
| Assam | – | – | 9.35 | 9.35 |
| Bihar* | 0.04 | – | 38.92 | 38.96 |
| Gujarat | 12.14 | 7.04 | 52.35 | 71.53 |
| Haryana | 5.26 | 15.99 | 2.76 | 24.04 |
| Himachal Pradesh | – | – | 14.24 | 14.24 |
| Jammu & Kashmir | – | – | 5.31 | 5.31 |
| Karnataka | 4.04 | – | 67.18 | 71.22 |
| Kerala | 0.16 | – | 10.37 | 10.53 |
| Madhya Pradesh* | 2.42 | – | 127.05 | 129.47 |
| Maharashtra | 5.34 | – | 110.26 | 115.60 |
| Manipur | – | – | 0.14 | 0.14 |
| Meghalaya | – | – | 8.15 | 8.15 |
| Nagaland | – | – | 5.08 | 5.08 |
| Orissa | 4.04 | – | 27.53 | 31.57 |
| Punjab | 6.88 | – | 4.63 | 11.51 |
| Rajasthan | 7.28 | 106.23 | 66.59 | 180.01 |
| Sikkim | – | – | 1.31 | 1.31 |
| Tamil Nadu | 0.04 | – | 33.88 | 33.92 |
| Tripura | – | – | 1.08 | 1.08 |
| Uttar Pradesh* | 12.95 | – | 53.40 | 66.35 |
| West Bengal | 8.50 | – | 13.27 | 21.77 |
| Union Territories | 0.16 | – | 8.73 | 8.89 |
| Total | 71.65 | 736 | 129.26 | 936.91 |

*Notes:* '-' means either negligible or not present; *these are the states prior to the formation of the new states of Uttaranchal, Chattisgarh, and Jharkhand.
*Source:* NWDB (1989)

---

**Box 2.4: Characterization of Wastelands as per NWDB**

1. The overall picture about wastelands is very pessimistic. About 45 per cent of the total geographical area has degraded due to one factor or another. Their share within forest and non-forest areas is fairly the same (44.54 per cent within non-forest and 47.66 per cent within forest areas).

2. Within the category of non-forest areas, states such as Haryana, Karnataka, Madhya Pradesh, Meghalaya, and Rajasthan have registered higher than the all-India proportions of wastelands (in percentage terms). Likewise, within

the category of forest areas, Andhra Pradesh, Bihar, Jammu and Kashmir, Karnataka, Manipur, Meghalaya, Nagaland, Orissa, Rajasthan, and Sikkim have more than the all-India proportions.

3. Among the non-forested areas, 'degradation due to water erosion' dominates with 78.55 per cent area, followed by saline and alkaline areas. Further, water-related degradation is observed in almost every state. It is, however, found to be quite high in Maharashtra, Madhya Pradesh, Gujarat, Karnataka, Rajasthan, Uttar Pradesh, and Andhra Pradesh, cutting across almost all agro-climatic zones in India.

The NRSA estimates for 1999 are presented in Table 2.5. Grouping of these data by ecological characteristics makes some comparison possible with NWDB data (presented in Tables 2.3 and 2.4). There are many surprises in the data, apart from major changes from NWDB data for the early 1980s. These are briefly enumerated.

1. According to NRSA, the total all-India wastelands in 1999 stand at 64 million hectares, as against 44 million hectares in 1988–9. This amounts to a sharp rise in wastelands by almost 44 per cent over ten years.

2. The NWDB estimate of wastelands in India in 1986 was 130 million hectares, suggesting gross overestimation. This is because the NWDB estimates are based on 146 sample districts only. Hence they may not reflect the complete and true picture at the all-India level.

3. It is extremely alarming that about 20 per cent of the geographical area of the country is categorized as wastelands or degraded lands.

4. The states with substantial increase in wastelands are Bihar, Goa, Jammu and Kashmir, Kerala, Orissa, Sikkim, Tamil Nadu, West Bengal, and all union territories.

5. On the basis of ecological categorization, further comments can be made by taking into account the Bobla and Khare. (1984: Table 3.3) estimates.

(a) As far as saline and alkaline areas are concerned, as against 71 lakh hectares (Bombla and Khare ), the NRSA data put the figure at 20 lakh hectares. The major states with substantial saline affected areas are Uttar Pradesh, Tamil Nadu, Rajasthan, and Gujarat.

(b) The magnitude of water-eroded areas also seems to have come down from 129 lakh hectares to 16 lakh hectares. The major affected states are West Bengal, Uttar Pradesh, Gujarat, Bihar, Assam, and Andhra Pradesh.

Table 2.5

Wastelands Data from National Remote Sensing Agency, 1999

(sq. km)

| State | 1 | 2 | 3 | 4 | 5 | 6 | 7 | 8 | 9 | 10 | 11 | 12 | 13 | 14 | 15 | 16 |
|---|---|---|---|---|---|---|---|---|---|---|---|---|---|---|---|---|
| Andhra Pradesh | 629.68 | 20,256.64 | 1035.02 | 603.26 | 13.80 | 22,237.78 | 709.29 | 52.91 | 464.70 | 98.88 | 5196.27 | 388.96 | 0.00 | 51,750.19 | 275,068.00 | 18.81 |
| Arunachal Pradesh | 0.00 | 3326.78 | 41.47 | 0.00 | 3088.08 | 1416.67 | 2134.99 | 6.07 | 309.43 | 0.30 | 1262.36 | 7.93 | 6732.17 | 18,326.25 | 83,743.00 | 21.88 |
| Assam | 0.00 | 843.72 | 1633.56 | 0.00 | 8391.48 | 3112.71 | 2217.85 | 0.00 | 3764.54 | 0.43 | 54.88 | 0.00 | 0.00 | 20,019.17 | 78,438.00 | 25.52 |
| Bihar* | 559.17 | 4689.93 | 1198.87 | 0.51 | 45.45 | 13,066.53 | 164.97 | 79.80 | 222.08 | 184.23 | 688.91 | 97.10 | 0.00 | 20,997.55 | 173,877.00 | 12.08 |
| Goa | 0.00 | 292.83 | 41.02 | 0.00 | 0.00 | 71.99 | 2.47 | 32.19 | 0.00 | 110.83 | 58.55 | 3.49 | 0.00 | 613.27 | 3702.00 | 16.57 |
| Gujarat | 1013.39 | 21,786.72 | 2656.26 | 7637.34 | 0.00 | 5443.02 | 387.45 | 78.32 | 188.42 | 49.66 | 3293.39 | 487.31 | 0.00 | 43,021.28 | 196,024.00 | 21.95 |
| Haryana | 49.50 | 988.42 | 238.30 | 285.63 | 0.00 | 732.52 | 721.65 | 134.10 | 465.01 | 13.72 | 105.12 | 0.00 | 0.00 | 3733.98 | 44,212.00 | 8.45 |
| Himachal Pradesh | 121.89 | 2056.50 | 15.69 | 1.36 | 0.00 | 4589.98 | 4278.17 | 2457.50 | 105.04 | 85.66 | 3858.04 | 1529.67 | 12,559.42 | 31,659.00 | 55,673.00 | 56.87 |
| Jammu and Kashmir | 21.25 | 4495.30 | 246.50 | 0.00 | 0.00 | 2491.66 | 267.51 | 640.56 | 869.26 | 0.31 | 32,821.50 | 1685.42 | 21,904.97 | 65,444.24 | 101,387.00 | 64.55 |
| Karnataka | 301.52 | 9087.68 | 32.76 | 125.11 | 0.00 | 8299.41 | 97.46 | 104.74 | 43.96 | 77.78 | 2627.89 | 40.97 | 0.00 | 20,839.28 | 191,791.00 | 10.87 |
| Kerala | 0.00 | 357.93 | 136.00 | 0.00 | 0.00 | 609.30 | 3.99 | 25.65 | 27.87 | 0.49 | 146.46 | 140.49 | 0.00 | 1448.18 | 38,863.00 | 3.73 |
| Madhya Pradesh* | 7569.11 | 36,977.87 | 51.72 | 162.81 | 0.00 | 20,437.77 | 302.44 | 910.40 | 24.57 | 141.44 | 2950.97 | 184.65 | 0.00 | 69,713.75 | 443,446.00 | 15.72 |
| Maharashtra | 1700.37 | 31,386.91 | 527.57 | 251.66 | 0.00 | 13,430.67 | 1349.40 | 687.43 | 77.63 | 100.45 | 2587.42 | 1389.57 | 0.00 | 53,489.08 | 307,670.00 | 17.38 |
| Manipur | 0.00 | 1.32 | 324.60 | 0.00 | 12,014.06 | 608.64 | 0.00 | 0.00 | 0.00 | 0.00 | 0.00 | 0.00 | 0.00 | 12,948.62 | 22,327.00 | 58.00 |
| Meghalaya | 0.00 | 4190.63 | 14.87 | 0.00 | 2086.77 | 3612.11 | 0.00 | 0.00 | 0.00 | 0.00 | 0.00 | 0.00 | 0.00 | 9904.38 | 22,429.00 | 44.16 |
| Mizoram | 0.00 | 0.00 | 0.00 | 0.00 | 3761.23 | 310.45 | 0.00 | 0.00 | 0.00 | 0.00 | 0.00 | 0.00 | 0.00 | 4071.68 | 21,081.00 | 19.31 |
| Nagaland | 0.00 | 1596.46 | 0.00 | 0.00 | 5224.65 | 1582.99 | 0.00 | 0.00 | 0.00 | 0.00 | 0.00 | 0.00 | 0.00 | 8404.10 | 16,579.00 | 50.69 |
| Orissa | 185.82 | 8358.68 | 379.10 | 51.49 | 115.28 | 10,014.07 | 13.43 | 193.95 | 212.49 | 35.45 | 1574.09 | 207.88 | 0.00 | 21,341.71 | 155,707.00 | 13.17 |
| Punjab | 168.52 | 339.44 | 352.10 | 173.29 | 0.00 | 353.29 | 113.71 | 81.50 | 619.67 | 26.89 | 0.00 | 0.00 | 0.00 | 2228.40 | 50,362.00 | 4.42 |
| Rajasthan | 4952.77 | 27,152.76 | 289.66 | 2722.99 | 0.00 | 12,541.89 | 12,208.44 | 21.10 | 40,639.51 | 128.65 | 4799.02 | 182.28 | 0.00 | 105,639.11 | 342,239.00 | 30.87 |

(Contd.)

48

| State | 1 | 2 | 3 | 4 | 5 | 6 | 7 | 8 | 9 | 10 | 11 | 12 | 13 | 14 | 15 | 16 |
|---|---|---|---|---|---|---|---|---|---|---|---|---|---|---|---|---|
| Sikkim | 0.00 | 1073.11 | 0.00 | 0.00 | 0.00 | 1060.57 | 0.00 | 0.00 | 0.00 | 0.00 | 10.34 | 0.00 | 1425.56 | 3569.58 | 7096.00 | 50.30 |
| Tripura | 0.00 | 286.87 | 0.11 | 0.00 | 400.88 | 588.18 | 0.00 | 0.00 | 0.00 | 0.00 | 0.00 | 0.00 | 0.00 | 1276.03 | 10,486.00 | 12.17 |
| Tamil Nadu | 226.12 | 7697.91 | 415.80 | 2479.73 | 0.53 | 9634.25 | 168.94 | 221.96 | 590.80 | 120.46 | 1155.92 | 301.50 | 0.00 | 23,013.90 | 130,058.00 | 17.70 |
| Uttar Pradesh* | 2806.52 | 5498.99 | 4981.43 | 5811.94 | 0.00 | 3338.32 | 446.36 | 50.44 | 470.21 | 29.26 | 1180.13 | 992.83 | 13,166.37 | 38,772.80 | 294,411.00 | 13.17 |
| West Bengal | 171.90 | 1245.16 | 1931.54 | 131.25 | 0.00 | 777.58 | 384.97 | 2.93 | 879.13 | 47.34 | 130.46 | 16.24 | 0.00 | 5718.48 | 88,752.00 | 6.44 |
| Union Territories | 12.83 | 25.74 | 24.60 | 39.01 | 0.00 | 289.97 | 5.43 | 46.34 | 47.33 | 0.00 | 83.05 | 0.00 | 0.00 | 574.30 | 10,973.00 | 5.23 |
| Total | 20,553.35 | 194,014.29 | 16,568.45 | 20,477.38 | 35,142.20 | 140,652.31 | 25,978.91 | 5828.09 | 500,21.65 | 1252.13 | 64,584.77 | 7656.29 | 55,788.49 | 638,518.31 | 3,166,414.00 | 20.17 |

*Notes:* *These are the states prior to the formation of Uttaranchal, Chattisgarh, and Jharkhand.

1. Gullied/ravinous land
2. Land with or without scrub
3. Waterlogged/marshy land
4. Saline/alkaline area
5. Shifting cultivation area
6. Degraded notified area
7. Degraded pastures/grazing lands
8. Deg. land under plantation crops
9. Sands—islands/coastal
10. Mining/industrial wastelands
11. Barren rocky area
12. Steel sloping area
13. Snow/glacier area
14. Total wastelands
15. Total geographical area
16. Percentage of wastelands to total geographical area

*Source:* Wastelands Atlas of India, 2000.

49

The major discrepancy seems to be in the interpretation of satellite data to translate into levels of degradation according to ecological categories. While the recorded data may overestimate the degradation rates, the satellite data present quite the opposite picture. The method of ground truthing may be a viable approach, though its precise statistical procedure has not yet been formulated.

Appendix 2.1

Table A2.1: Non-forest Wastelands in India, 1990-1

(in thousand hectares)

| State | | | Non-forest areas | | | | | Bagchi-Phillip |
| | BUL | PPG | MISCTR | CWL | CURFL | OTHFL | TOTNFWL | ESTIMATES[2] |
| --- | --- | --- | --- | --- | --- | --- | --- | --- |
| Andhra Pradesh | 4403 | 843 | 262 | 780 | 2485 | 1377 | 10,150 | 8019 |
| Assam | 2455 | 184 | 247 | 104 | 88 | 84 | 3162 | 2391 |
| Bihar* | 3126 | 126 | 291 | 372 | 1765 | 999 | 6679 | 4322 |
| Gujarat | 3772 | 849 | 4 | 1920 | 1039 | 60 | 7644 | 6272 |
| Haryana | 417 | 23 | 3 | 21 | 169 | 0 | 633 | 354 |
| Himachal Pradesh | 377 | 1136 | 48 | 125 | 45 | 15 | 1746 | 1418 |
| Jammu and Kashmir | 586 | 127 | 73 | 138 | 97 | 6 | 1027 | 699 |
| Karnataka | 2287 | 1098 | 17 | 446 | 1290 | 457 | 5595 | 4535 |
| Kerala | 355 | 2 | 34 | 95 | 44 | 27 | 557 | 319 |
| Madhya Pradesh* | 4458 | 2734 | 100 | 1579 | 762 | 826 | 10,459 | 8990 |
| Maharashtra | 2828 | 1519 | 180 | 1028 | 869 | 983 | 7407 | 6100 |
| Meghalaya | 226 | 17 | 153 | 493 | 59 | 167 | 1098 | 1160 |
| Nagaland | 28 | 0 | 125 | 99 | 118 | 110 | 480 | 555 |
| Orissa | 1245 | 726 | 859 | 597 | 119 | 214 | 3760 | 1899 |
| Punjab | 425 | 10 | 12 | 35 | 82 | 28 | 592 | 210 |
| Rajasthan | 4280 | 1912 | 22 | 5567 | 1814 | 1927 | 15,522 | 13,410 |
| Tamilnadu | 2329 | 124 | 234 | 290 | 1264 | 1044 | 5285 | 3841 |
| Tripura | 131 | 39 | – | 1 | 1 | 1 | 173 | 7 |
| Uttar Pradesh* | 3482 | 303 | 545 | 1034 | 1084 | 884 | 7332 | 5241 |

(Contd.)

(Appendix 2.1 Contd.)

(in thousand hectares)

| State | Non-forest areas | | | | | | | Bagchi-Phillip ESTIMATES[2] |
| --- | --- | --- | --- | --- | --- | --- | --- | --- |
| | BUL | PPG | MISCTR | CWL | CURFL | OTHFL | TOTNFWL | |
| West Bengal | 1816 | 7 | 46 | 106 | 395 | 51 | 2421 | 714 |
| Union Territories and others | 4884 | 42 | 448 | 184 | 218 | 330 | 5606 | 11712 |
| All India[1] | 43,910 | 11,804 | 3703 | 15,014 | 13,807 | 9590 | 97,328 | 82,168 |

Notes: *These are the states prior to the formation of Uttaranchal, Chattisgarh and Jharkhand states.

The estimates shown here are based on the method developed and shown in Box 2.3. The various components of wastelands considered here are: barren and uncultivable lands, permanent pastures and grasslands, land under miscellaneous tree crops, culturable wastelands, parts of current fallow, and other fallow. The table shows these estimates along with the estimates made by Bagchi and Phillip (1993). The estimated non-forest wastelands in 1990–1 were of the order of 97.33 million hectares, showing an increase of more than 3.6 million hectares over a 10-year period. The same cannot be said easily about degradation in forested areas. These estimates are quite high (almost 30 per cent) as compared to those obtained from National Remote Sensing Agency (Table 2.5).

Abbrevations:

BUL = Barren and uncultivable lands
PPG = Permanent pastures and grasslands
MISCTR = Land under miscellaneous tree crops
CWL = Culturable wastelands
CURFL = Current fallow
OTHFL = Other fallow
TOTNFWL = Total non-forest wastelands.

[1]. All-India totals are inclusive of all the remaining states and union territories.

[2]. Bagchi–Phillip data are for different years, ranging from 1978 to 1987.

Source: CMIE, Ministry of Agriculture, Land Utilization Statistics.

# 3

# Dimensions of Access to Common Property Resources

## INTRODUCTION

When one talks about access to CPRs, the reference is basically to the extractions, flows, and use patterns of the resources. Foremost among these are the flows from land and related resources, discussed in Chapter 2. Other than land and related resources, the most talked about CPRs are water, fishery, and biodiversity in general. Water can be viewed both as a stock (measured at any point of time) as well as flows used for various development activities as well as human and animal welfare. Fishery can also be viewed as a reservoir (a stock) or flows as the catch or extraction from the reservoir. Biodiversity consists of a variety of commons such as wildlife, diversity of religious, cultural, and socially relevant plants, and herbal and medicinal plants (of both economic and social relevance). The flows from such resources are tourism benefits, social, religious, and cultural security (a term borrowed from Ignachy Sachs who talked about cultural and social sustainability), and economic and livelihood supports. This chapter explores the dimensions of all such resources and flows.

Talking about access, there are three basic issues in the Indian context. First, there is some degree of dependency of certain section of people (including livestock and other animals) upon CPRs for their livelihood and security. The question, therefore, is about this dependency syndrome as part of a sustainable development strategy. Is this rate of dependency driven by poverty? Or is it driven by certain habits and culture? Second, what is their link with other property resources? The third question is about the sustainable and economically feasible flows of these resources under alternative property management regimes. Prior to all such questions is the issue of the dimensions of these resources, which is the focus of this chapter.

WATER RESOURCES

Water is considered to be the first right of all living beings. The National Water Policy Document of 2002 as well the earlier 1987 document stressed the point that water is a prime natural resource, a basic human need, and a precious national asset. The majority of natural water resources are glacier mountains, flows of rivers, tanks and natural lakes, groundwater, wetland and mangrove areas, and such other water bodies. Man-made water resources such as dams and canals, tube wells (for extraction of groundwater), other wells (for example, dug wells) and supply of all types of potable water (taps, tanker supplies, etc.) also fall in the category of CPRs depending upon property rights (public or private).

Getting an inventory of water resources distinctly as CPRs is difficult at the national level.[1] The major source of information are the Ministries of Water Resources and Agriculture. On the basis of available data, it is assumed that all the irrigation water resources coming from government sources, village tanks, public tube-wells and several other sources are considered as CPRs. Likewise, private canals and private wells are treated as PPR sources of water. Table 3.1 shows the changing pattern of the CPR and PPR water sources at the all-India level over the last thirty years. As can be seen (also observed in Chapter 1), community tank irrigation has come down significantly. The increase in CPR water sources is mainly due to the expansion of

[1]Watershed level case studies can, however, provide some information on them at the micro-regional levels. Attention can be drawn to selected watershed studies such as Katar Singh (1991, 1995), Chopra et al. (1990), Sengupta (1991), Parikh and Reddy (1997), Farington et al. (1999), Agarwal and Narain (1997), and Chopra and Rao (1996).

tube-well irrigation, as surface irrigation seems to have reached its peak potential. There is also a significant increase in private water harvesting.[2]

Table 3.1
Changing Pattern of CPR and PPR Sources of Water for Irrigation

('000 ha)

| Sources of Water | | 1970–1 | 1980–1 | 1990–1 | 1997–8 |
|---|---|---|---|---|---|
| Common | Government Canals | 11,972 | 14,450 | 16,973 | 16,617 |
| Property | Tanks | 4112 | 3182 | 2944 | 3100 |
| Sources | Tube Wells | 4461 | 9531 | 14,257 | 18,432 |
| | Other Sources | 2266 | 2551 | 2932 | 3491 |
| | Total CPR Sources | 22,811 | 29,714 | 37,106 | 41,640 |
| Private | Private Canals | 866 | 842 | 480 | 475 |
| Sources | Other Wells | 7426 | 8164 | 10,437 | 12,448 |
| | Total Private Sources | 8292 | 9006 | 10,917 | 12,923 |

Source: CMIE, Economic Intelligence Services, November 2001.

In order to understand the dependency syndrome of the people, the access to different sized land holders is presented in Table 3.2. The analysis of data reveals the following:

1. Access to irrigation from government canals increases with the size of holdings. For instance, marginal farmers are able to access just about 0.05 hectares of their operational area for irrigation from the government canal system, whereas the large farmers on an average get about 1.06 hectares of irrigation. This is also true with respect to access to tanks, tube-wells, and other water resources.

2. Second, wherever the property rights are very strictly defined, as is the case with government canal irrigation, per hectare access to water among marginal farmers, all other categories, and large farmers is generally in favour of the marginal farmers, or nearly equal among them. For instance, marginal farmers have about 0.13 hectares of their operational holdings under government canal irrigation, whereas the figure is about 0.06 hectares for large, 0.08 for medium, 0.09 for semi-medium, and 0.11 for small farmers.

[2]Whether this is due to the developmental process (including privatization, globalization, and liberalization) or due to shrinking of CPR water sources, or due to failure of CPR management institutions is a matter for detailed micro-level study.

Table 3.2
Access to Irrigation Water by Operational Land Holdings, 1990–1

| Holdings Sizes | Units | CPR Sources | | | | |
| --- | --- | --- | --- | --- | --- | --- |
| | | Govt Canals | Tanks | Tube Wells | Other Sources | Total |
| Marginal | Irr. area ('000ha) | 3348 | 940 | 3319 | 1850 | 9457 |
| (<1 ha) | Irr. area per ha of holding | 0.13 | 0.04 | 0.13 | 0.08 | 0.38 |
| | Irr. area (ha) per holding | 0.05 | 0.02 | 0.05 | 0.03 | 0.15 |
| Small | Irr. area ('000ha) | 3061 | 682 | 3013 | 2329 | 9085 |
| (<1–1.99 ha) | Irr. area per ha of holding | 0.11 | 0.02 | 0.10 | 0.09 | 0.32 |
| | Irr. area (ha) per holding | 0.15 | 0.03 | 0.15 | 0.12 | 0.45 |
| Semi-medium | Irr. area ('000ha) | 3645 | 654 | 3555 | 3117 | 10,971 |
| (<2–3.99 ha) | Irr. area per ha of holding | 0.09 | 0.02 | 0.09 | 0.09 | 0.29 |
| | Irr. area (ha) per holding | 0.26 | 0.05 | 0.25 | 0.22 | 0.79 |
| Medium | Irr. area ('000ha) | 3851 | 503 | 3442 | 3490 | 11,286 |
| (<4–9.99 ha) | Irr. area per ha of holding | 0.08 | 0.01 | 0.08 | 0.08 | 0.25 |
| | Irr. area (ha) per holding | 0.50 | 0.06 | 0.45 | 0.45 | 1.48 |
| Large | Irr. area ('000ha) | 1762 | 178 | 1364 | 1601 | 4905 |
| (>10 ha) | Irr. area per ha of holding | 0.06 | 0.00 | 0.05 | 0.96 | 0.17 |
| | Irr. area (ha) per holding | 1.06 | 0.11 | 0.82 | 0.96 | 2.94 |
| Total | Irr. area ('000ha) | 15,667 | 2957 | 14,694 | 12,386 | 45,704 |
| | Irr. area per ha of holding | 0.09 | 0.02 | 0.09 | 0.07 | 0.28 |
| | Irr. area (ha) per holding | 0.15 | 0.03 | 0.14 | 0.12 | 0.43 |

Source: Agriculture Census Division, Ministry of Agriculture.

3. Third, considerable breakdown of CPR institutions is visible in the distribution of water from other sources. For instance, large farmers get about 2.94 hectares per holding under irrigation from these sources, whereas marginal farmers get just about 0.15 hectares. This is perhaps

due to the 'open access nature' of the resources, and hence, the presence of unequal rights.

FISHERY RESOURCES

The major sources for fishery are inland and marine water resources. The extent of their availability and suitability determine the prospects for fishery outputs. Broadly speaking, fresh water and brackish water fish are extremely dependent upon water quality measured in terms of the hydrogen ion concentration (pH) values. For instance, for cultivation of prawns and crabs in brackish water, salinity levels at around 16 ppt are most ideal.

The changes in water resources over time have induced pressures and brought changes in access to and rate of extraction of fishery resources (such as pelagic, demersal, molluscus, crustaceans, and several miscellaneous species). Table 3.3 shows the changes in inland water sources in India for 1993 and 1995.[3] The CPR related inland water resources for fishery have increased at the aggregate level in the recent period. In particular, both tanks and brackish water sources have increased by about one-third. However, traditional sources such as beels, oxbow, and derelict water have come down by almost one-third. Marine sources such as the continental shelf and the length of the coastline are important indicators of prospects for marine fishery. India has about 506,000 sq. km of continental shelf of marine area and the coastline is about 8041 km.[4]

Table 3.3
Changes in Inland Water Resources

*(lakh sq. km)*

| Year | Rivers and Canals (length in km) | Reservoirs | Tanks, lakes, and ponds | Beels, oxbow, lakes and derelict water | Brackish water | Total water bodies |
|------|------|------|------|------|------|------|
| 1993 | 170,282 | 20.90 | 22.54 | 13.00 | 12.35 | 68.79 |
| 1995 | 171,334 | 20.50 | 31.30 | 8.28 | 16.32 | 76.40 |

*Source*: Handbook of Fisheries Statistics, Department of Agriculture and Co-peration.

[3]For state level details see Table A3.1.
[4]See Table A3.2 for state level information.

How much is the CPR fishery production in India? The answer to this is not an easy one, for want of precise estimates of CPR versus commercial fishery. However, certain safe assumptions may be made to get broad dimensions CPR fishery output in India: treat all the inland and marine 'capture' as coming from CPR sources; and treat all 'farmed fish production' such as aquaculture as commercial and hence not from CPR sources. Strictly speaking, most of the marine fishery production in India falls under the category of open access fishery, rather than CPR fishery.[5] Under these assumptions, the dimensions of CPR and non-CPR fishery outputs can be identified (see Table 3.4). Though the CPR fishery outputs from the marine sources have been increasing, the same from inland CPR sources have been fast declining. Considering the fact that the stock of common property water bodies with potential for fishery have been increasing, the declining trend in CPR inland fishery output suggests either serious over exploitation beyond the carrying capacity in some earlier period leading to the declining rates of current extraction,[6] or a breakdown of CPR community based institutions to regulate the yields. A third possibility of migration of a large number of fishermen to non-fishery based activities and hence declining dependency on fishery activities is also not ruled out.[7] The growth of non-CPR based aquaculture (about 2.3 million tonnes of annual prawn

Table 3.4

Identification of CPR and Non-CPR based Fishery Production ('000 tonnes)

| Type of fishery | | 1984–5 | 1989–90 | 1994–5 | 2000–01 |
|---|---|---|---|---|---|
| Capture = CPR | Marine | 1614.92 | 2208.60 | 2358.23 | 2668.48* |
| | Inland | 591.74 | 396.50 | 334.03 | 400.41 |
| Aquaculture = Non-CPR | | 511.50 | 1005.50 | 1762.70 | 2389.84 |
| Total Fishery Output | | 2718.16 | 3610.60 | 4454.96 | 5458.73 |

Note: *this figure is for the year 1998
Source: Marine Fisheries Information Service T and E Ser. No. 41, 52, 67, 136; Annual Reports of Central marine Fisheries Research Institute; Department of Agriculture and Co-operation.

[5]For want of sample survey data, or any village-wise census data, it is difficult to disaggregate the open access and CPR productions.

[6]A theoretical model on this will be presented in Chapter 4.

[7]Some micro-studies show the decline of active fishermen (Kadekodi and Gulati, 1999).

landings from prawn ponds) is mainly due to commercialization and breakdown of CPR based fishery institutions (Kadekodi and Gulati, 1999).

## BIOMES AND BIODIVERSITY RESOURCES

At the outset, a distinction needs to be made between biomes and biodiversity, the former refers to area dimensions and the latter is in terms of species, flows, etc. Biomes are distinguished broadly as marine, wetland (including mangrove), and terrestrial biodiversity (ecosystems including flora and fauna as well).[8] These resources are either in the form of open access or common property regimes. Whatever may be the property rights regime, they provide cultural, social, and economic support to human and animal life.

Marine biodiversity and biomes are the source of the rich cultural, religious, and economic life for over 20 million fishermen in India. They consist of a coastline of about 8041 km, with about 2333 landing centres, covering about 3726 villages and fishing grounds, coral reefs, seabeds, and a variety of endemic and endangered species. The total coral reef area is estimated at 1270 sq. km, spread in the Gulf of Kutch (458 sq. km), Gulf of Mannar (88 sq. km), and Lakshadweep islands (705 sq. km). Apart from these, the estuarine ecosystems in India consist of mangroves of 0.41 million hectares and wetlands (mainly fresh water bodies) of 3.90 million hectares.[9] Some details of wetland and coastline ecosystem CPRs are shown in Table 3.5. Among them, mangroves, beaches, salt pans, various vegetation areas, and mudflats have direct links with the communities dependent upon them. They also include inter-tidal affected areas bringing salinity to soil and hence are a home for crabs and molluscus, on which a large number of fishing communities depend.

The terrestrial biodiversity area consists of reserved and protected forest areas, wildlife sanctuaries, and national parks. The forests in

[8]If stretched, one can add such other groups as micro-organisms, domesticated biodiversity, agri-biodiversity, and other forms of biodiversity as well (Kadekodi, 2002b).

[9]A total of 1193 wetlands have been identified. The two most talked about among these are Chilka lake (Kadekodi and Gulati, 1999) and Keoladeo National Park (QChopra, in Kadekodi, 2002a).

Table 3.5
CPR Land Area under Various Eusterine Ecosystems

| Land Categories | Area in sq. km |
| --- | --- |
| Mudflats | 22,961 |
| Beaches/Spits | 1465 |
| Shoals/bars | 93 |
| Coral reefs | 1270 |
| Mangroves | 4121 |
| Marsh vegetation | 370 |
| Mudflats with vegetation | 6125 |
| Beach Vegetation | 290 |
| Lagoons/backwaters | 2132 |
| Flood-prone areas | 3437 |
| Coastal dunes | 2509 |
| Reclaimed area | 1212 |
| Paleo-beach ridges | 434 |
| Paleo-mudflats | 6821 |
| Strand plains | 1379 |
| Salt-affected area | 697 |
| Salt pans | 1617 |
| Total area | 56,933 |

Source: Sahai, (1993).

India have been classified into 16 major forest types, and 221 minor types with different degrees of common property and open access resources.[10] The total area of the forests, the kinds of species, and the nature of threats to them are presented in Tables 3.6 to 3.9. India has seven major biospheres covering about 21,000 sq. km of area. As many as 75 national parks, 420 wildlife sanctuaries, and 120 botanical gardens have been identified. Indian plant biodiversity is rich with about 17,000 flowering plant species and another 28,000 non-flowering plant species. For various reasons, such as over exploitation, and the collapse of community based protection institutions, as many as 500 species are already included in the list of rare and threatened plant species.

[10]The details of these forest areas have already been discussed in Chapter 2.

Table 3.6
Dimensions of CPR Biodiversity Resources

| Category | Number | Total Geographical Area (sq. km) |
|---|---|---|
| A. Within Habitats (*in situ*) | | |
| Biosphere Reserves | 7 | 21,067 |
| National Parks | 80 | 34,830 |
| Sanctuaries | 445 | 115,920 |
| Reserve Forests | NA | 415,896 |
| Other Protected areas | 19 | 29,716 |
| B. Outside Habitats (*ex situ*) | | |
| Botanical Gardens | 120 | NA |
| Gene Banks | 183,447* | NA |

*Note*: NA = not available; *denotes number of accessions.
*Source*: Compendium of Environment Statistics, 1999, CSO, 22.

Table 3.7
Rare and Threatened Fauna Species

| Category | Approximate Number | | | | | |
|---|---|---|---|---|---|---|
| | Mammals | Birds | Reptiles | Amphibians | Invertebrates | Total |
| Rare | – | 2 | – | | 12 | 14 |
| Vulnerable | 28 | 22 | 4 | – | 3 | 57 |
| Endangered | 29 | 21 | 16 | 1 | 1 | 68 |
| Critical* | 3 | 8 | – | – | 2 | 13 |
| Extinct** | 1 | 2 | – | – | – | 3 |
| Insufficiently Known | 16 | – | – | – | 4 | 20 |
| Total | 77 | 55 | 20 | 1 | 20 | 173 |

*Note*: *Mammal—Brow-altered deer, yak, hispid hara.
Birds—Christmas island frigate bird, Mrs. Hume's bartailed pheasant, burmese peafowl, blacknecked crane, hooded crane, masked finfoot, jerson's courser, forest spotted owlet.
**Mammal—Cheetah.
Birds—Pinkheaded duck, mountain quail.
*Source*: Compendium of Environment Statistics, 1999, CSO, 46.

ACCESS, DEPENDENCY, AND RESOURCE FLOWS FROM CPRs

As explained in Chapter 1, understanding of CPRs in terms of access and utilization pattern, and the degree of dependency is as important

Table 3.8
Endemic and Threatened Fauna Species

| Faunal Groups | Total Number | Species Endemic | Species Percentage | Threatened |
|---|---|---|---|---|
| Mammals | 372 | 38 | 10.21 | 77* |
| Birds | 1228 | 69 | 5.61 | 55* |
| Reptiles | 446 | 214 | 47.98 | 22* |
| Amphibias | 204 | 110 | 53.92 | 1 |
| Insects | 53,430 | 16,214 | 30.34 | – |
| Molluscs | | | | |
| Land | 1511 | 878 | 58.1 | – |
| Freshwater | 212 | 89 | 41.98 | – |

*Source*: Compendium of Environment Statistics, 1999, CSO, 47.

as the stocks or endowments of those resources. This is the question of flows from CPR stocks. There are, once again, a number of micro-level studies on the issues mentioned above, more as case studies.[11]

The only major source of information at the all-India or macro-level that throws light on these issues is from the NSS, with its special survey conducted in 1998 (January to June). As many as 78,900 rural households from about 11,000 villages in India were covered, regarding their links with a variety of CPRs. The major CPRs covered are common lands, forest areas, grazing lands, water resources, fishery, and extraction from biodiversity sources. Analysis based on NSS data is presented in subsequent sections.

Access to Land Resources

The common lands covered in the NSS enquiry are panchayat lands, government revenue lands, village common lands, village thrashing grounds, unclassed forest lands, woodlots, barren lands and wastelands, river banks, and lands belonging to other households used as commons. An aggregate picture of such commons per household is shown in Table 3.10. There is some kind of link between the privately owned lands per household and the amount of CPR land available to them (Table 3.10 and Figure 3.1).[12] On a statistical basis, the elasticity of

[11]Interested readers can refer to the Bibliography, which gives a glimpse of such micro-level case studies on CPR flows.
[12]As compared to the neighbouring states like Meghalaya, Tripura, Assam, and

Table 3.9
National Parks and Wildlife Sanctuaries of India

| States | National Parks | | Wildlife Sanctuaries | |
|---|---|---|---|---|
| | Number | Area (sq km) | Number | Area (sq km) |
| Andhra Pradesh | 1 | 352.62 | 20 | 12,084.59 |
| Arunachal Pradesh | 2 | 2468.23 | 9 | 6777.75 |
| Assam | 2 | 930 | 9 | 1381.58 |
| Bihar | 2 | 567.32 | 19 | 4624.30 |
| Goa | 1 | 107 | 4 | 335.43 |
| Gujarat | 4 | 479.67 | 21 | 16,744.27 |
| Haryana | 1 | 1.43 | 9 | 233.18 |
| Himachal Pradesh | 2 | 1440 | 33 | 6315.92 |
| Jammu and Kashmir | 4 | 3810.07 | 16 | 10,163.67 |
| Karnataka | 5 | 2472.18 | 20 | 4229.21 |
| Kerala | 3 | 536.52 | 12 | 1814.36 |
| Madhya Pradesh | 11 | 6143.12 | 32 | 10,847.29 |
| Maharashtra | 5 | 956.45 | 24 | 14,309.51 |
| Manipur | 2 | 81.80 | 1 | 184.85 |
| Meghalaya | 2 | 386.70 | 3 | 34.21 |
| Mizoram | 2 | 250 | 3 | 720 |
| Nagaland | 1 | 202.02 | 3 | 34.35 |
| Orissa | 2 | 1212.70 | 17 | 6175.49 |
| Punjab | Nil | Nil | 6 | 294.82 |
| Rajasthan | 4 | 3856.53 | 22 | 5698.02 |
| Sikkim | 1 | 850 | 4 | 161.10 |
| Tamil Nadu | 5 | 307.86 | 13 | 2527.29 |
| Tripura | Nil | Nil | 4 | 603.62 |
| Uttar Pradesh | 7 | 5409.05 | 28 | 8082.52 |
| West Bengal | 5 | 1692.65 | 16 | 1064.29 |
| A and N Islands | 6 | 315.61 | 94 | 437.16 |
| Chandigarh | Nil | Nil | 1 | 25.42 |
| Dadra and Nagar Haveli | Nil | Nil | Nil | Nil |
| Daman and Diu | Nil | Nil | 1 | 2.18 |
| Delhi | Nil | Nil | 1 | 13.20 |
| Lakshadweep | Nil | Nil | Nil | Nil |
| Pondicherry | Nil | Nil | Nil | Nil |
| Total | 80 | 34,829.53 | 445 | 115,919.58 |

*Source*: Compendium of Environment Statistics, 1999, CSO, 48.

Manipur, an unusually high CPR land is reported in Mizoram.

Table 3.10
Availability of CPR Land in Different States 1998

| States | Area owned per household (ha) | CPR land per household (ha) |
|---|---|---|
| Andhra Pradesh | 0.67 | 0.17 |
| Arunachal Pradesh | 1.52 | 1.15 |
| Assam | 0.79 | 0.05 |
| Bihar* | 0.59 | 0.08 |
| Gujarat | 1.17 | 0.72 |
| Haryana | 1.00 | 0.05 |
| Himachal Pradesh | 0.73 | 0.33 |
| Jammu and Kashmir | 0.68 | 0.14 |
| Karnataka | 1.23 | 0.25 |
| Kerala | 0.28 | 0.12 |
| Madhya Pradesh* | 1.52 | 0.74 |
| Maharashtra | 1.08 | 0.30 |
| Manipur | 0.66 | 0.17 |
| Meghalaya | 1.02 | 0.72 |
| Mizoram | 0.36 | 4.37 |
| Nagaland | 2.68 | 1.49 |
| Orissa | 0.58 | 0.28 |
| Punjab | 0.94 | 0.02 |
| Rajasthan | 2.21 | 2.04 |
| Sikkim | 0.49 | 0.25 |
| Tamil Nadu | 0.35 | 0.16 |
| Tripura | 0.30 | 0.01 |
| Uttar Pradesh* | 0.74 | 0.14 |
| West Bengal | 0.33 | 0.03 |
| India | 0.84 | 0.31 |

Notes: *These are the states prior to the formation of Uttaranchal, Jharkhand, and Chattisgarh states; see Table A3.2 for details.
Source: Cultivation Practices in India, NSS 54th round; Sarvekshana Vol. XXIV, Issue 84, July-September 2 no. p. 60

CPR land (per household) vis-à-vis the area owned (per household) in India is 1.584.[13] This high degree of dependency was pointed out by a number of micro-level studies (example, Jodha (1986, 1994b), Singh

[13]A regression between the two, using state level data is: CPR land per household = − 0.306 + 0.763 *Area owned per household
        (− 2.966)   (8.164)
   R = 0.872, df = 21; figures in brackets are t-statistic values.

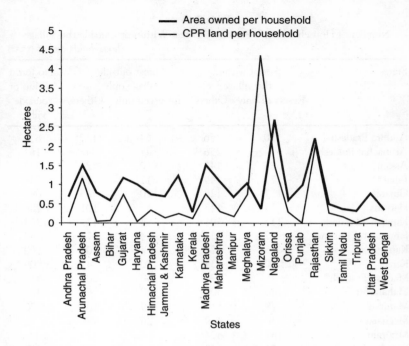

**Figure 3.1:** Availability of CPR and Ownership Land in Different States

(1994b), and Iyengar (1988). Other than the north eastern states, in states such as Rajasthan, Madhya Pradesh, and Gujarat this dependency on CPR lands is quite high. Table A3.2 shows the break-up of access to CPR lands by type of lands.

Access to Forest Resources

On similar line, NSS also provides some information regarding access of rural communities to forest lands. Table 3.11 shows that out of 1000 households at the all-India level, just about 68 have access to reserved forests within the village, and another 38 have access to reserve forests outside the village. As many as 62 per cent of households have no access to forest resources at all. This reflects either physical inaccessibility or non-existence of arrangements to access basic need requirements such as fuelwood and fodder. Invariably, states with high forested areas, show a larger percentage of households which are

Table 3.11

Number of Households with Access to Forest Within or Outside the Village

*(households out of ,000)*

| States | Forest within the village | | Forest outside village only | | No forest within or outside village |
|---|---|---|---|---|---|
| | Reserved only | Others | Reserved only | Others | |
| Andhra Pradesh | 120 | 56 | 64 | 137 | 624 |
| Arunachal Pradesh | – | 256 | 41 | 542 | 161 |
| Assam | 85 | 142 | 60 | 125 | 587 |
| Bihar* | 23 | 149 | 17 | 77 | 734 |
| Gujarat | 107 | 128 | 10 | 63 | 693 |
| Haryana | 51 | 143 | – | 101 | 706 |
| Himachal Pradesh | 112 | 501 | 54 | 129 | 203 |
| Jammu and Kashmir | 27 | 332 | 14 | 174 | 453 |
| Karnataka | 125 | 177 | 4 | 104 | 590 |
| Kerala | 40 | 34 | 70 | 47 | 809 |
| Madhya Pradesh* | 45 | 270 | 50 | 201 | 433 |
| Maharashtra | 140 | 300 | 30 | 69 | 461 |
| Manipur | 79 | 119 | 39 | 187 | 576 |
| Meghalaya | 30 | 429 | 26 | 438 | 78 |
| Mizoram | 167 | 804 | – | 29 | – |
| Nagaland | 54 | 155 | – | 443 | 347 |
| Orissa | 104 | 403 | 57 | 134 | 303 |
| Punjab | 5 | 21 | 6 | 25 | 944 |
| Rajasthan | 65 | 163 | 33 | 92 | 647 |
| Sikkim | 62 | 575 | 191 | 32 | 140 |
| Tamil Nadu | 85 | 130 | 101 | 111 | 573 |
| Tripura | 232 | 116 | 52 | 289 | 311 |
| Uttar Pradesh* | 37 | 143 | 22 | 78 | 719 |
| West Bengal | 18 | 71 | 31 | 103 | 777 |
| A and N Islands | 335 | 309 | 199 | 111 | 45 |
| India | 68 | 165 | 38 | 104 | 625 |

*Notes:* *These are the states prior to the formation of Jharkhand, Chattisgarh, and Uttaranchal.

*Source: Sarvekshana,* Vol. XXIV, Issue 84, July–September 2000, pp. S-252–3.

dependent upon the reserved forests as much as protected and other forests. Interestingly enough, in states such as Punjab, West Bengal, and Kerala where the area under forests is much less, people are dependent on them but outside own villages.

Access to CPR Flows from Land and Forests

What are the major CPR flows from the commons (of both land and forests)? Clearly, fuelwood and grass, fish from common ponds, lakes, and other water bodies, medicinal plants and herbs, leaf biomass, and fruits are some of the major products for which the communities depend upon the common land and forests. Tables 3.12 and 3.13 show state level details based on NSS data.

A majority of households depend on CPR land and forest resources for their requirements of fuelwood, fodder, bamboo, and fish, followed by medicinal plants and herbs, leaf biomass, and fruits roughly in that order. There are indications that these CPR flows have come down over time (Table 3.12). Between 1993 and 1998, the extent of consumption of fuelwood from CPR land and forests has come down significantly at the all-India level, from 87 per cent of households to 62 per cent. Only 45 per cent of rural households reported collecting fuelwood from the commons now. The quantity collected is just about half of the quantity of fuelwood actually consumed. Going by Table 3.13, which shows the dependency of households for different types of CPR collections or extractions, one gets the impression that at the all-India level, in terms of value of collections, about 40 per cent of it as fish comes from the CPRs, and 25 per cent from collection of leaf biomass, about 16 per cent from fodder and bamboo, and another 15 per cent out of collected fruits and roots, etc. The situation, however, differs from state to state. For instance, the maximum dependency for fishing is seen in West Bengal, followed by Maharashtra. As far as dependency for grass and bamboo is concerned, the north eastern states and Jammu and Kashmir are in the majority. Haryana, Himachal Pradesh, and Kerala show very high dependency for the collection of medicinal plants.

One striking information revealed by NSS data is the extent of dependency on the CPR based collections as part of the total consumption by rural households. Table 3.14 shows the same for various states. As seen from the table, compared to the annual per capita expenditures (including home grown imputed CPRs), the average value of collections from the CPR resources is about 15 per cent at the all-India level.[14] Forest and CPR rich states such as Madhya Pradesh,

[14]This comparison between annual per capita expenditure and value of total collection from the CPR is not strictly valid. It is assumed that for each type of CPR

Table 3.12
Estimates of Consumption and Collection of Fuelwood in Different States

| States | Percentage of households using fuelwood | | Percentage of households reporting collection in 1998 | Average Quantity (kg) | |
|---|---|---|---|---|---|
| | 1998 | 1993-94 | | Collected 1998 | Consumed 1993-94 |
| Andhra Pradesh | 81 | 94 | 59 | 545 | 950 |
| Arunachal Pradesh | 85 | 96 | 82 | 5448 | 3786 |
| Assam | 60 | 97 | 44 | 614 | 1411 |
| Bihar* | 58 | 70 | 41 | 446 | 623 |
| Gujarat | 73 | 83 | 55 | 483 | 877 |
| Haryana | 41 | 90 | 27 | 306 | 1013 |
| Himachal Pradesh | 59 | 91 | 56 | 1080 | 2346 |
| Jammu and Kashmir | 51 | 89 | 33 | 553 | 2234 |
| Karnataka | 79 | 96 | 53 | 484 | 1446 |
| Kerala | 53 | 95 | 13 | 204 | 1301 |
| Madhya Pradesh* | 76 | 96 | 56 | 621 | 1673 |
| Maharashtra | 67 | 82 | 59 | 522 | 776 |
| Manipur | 75 | 96 | 40 | 1157 | 1635 |
| Meghalaya | 93 | 94 | 86 | 2558 | 2282 |
| Mizoram | 98 | 99 | 97 | 6688 | 1532 |
| Nagaland | 98 | 99 | 67 | 2972 | 2816 |
| Orissa | 75 | 91 | 62 | 944 | 1290 |
| Punjab | 69 | 74 | 24 | 550 | 841 |
| Rajasthan | 34 | 94 | 21 | 267 | 1368 |
| Sikkim | 69 | 74 | 53 | 1805 | 1832 |
| Tamil Nadu | 70 | 93 | 61 | 497 | 816 |
| Tripura | 51 | 97 | 31 | 427 | 1417 |
| Uttar Pradesh* | 51 | 88 | 33 | 416 | 813 |
| West Bengal | 51 | 73 | 38 | 324 | 742 |
| India | 62 | 87 | 45 | 500 | 1015 |

Notes: *These are the states prior to the formation of Uttaranchal, Chattisgarh, and Jharkhand.
Source: Sarvekshana, Vol. XXIV, No. 1, Issue 84, July–September 2000, p. 74.

Assam, and Orissa have larger collection values than CPR poor states. Also in states with lower levels of per capita income or expenditure,

collection (for items shown in Tables 3.12 and 3.13) one member of the family is deputed or held responsible; hence the value of total collection also represents a per capita situation.

Table 3.13

Distribution of Households Collecting Selected Materials from CPR, 1998

*(Number of households per ,000)*

| State | Fruit, roots, tubers | Gums and resins | Honey | Medicinal herbs | Fish | Leaves | Weed, grass, bamboo | Value of collections (R. million) |
|---|---|---|---|---|---|---|---|---|
| Andhra Pradesh | 73 | 12 | 5 | 13 | 479 | 298 | 119 | 1044 |
| Arunachal Pradesh | 211 | 0 | 10 | 10 | 374 | 129 | 265 | 137 |
| Assam | 27 | – | 5 | 1 | 763 | 27 | 177 | 1540 |
| Bihar* | 208 | – | 6 | 2 | 256 | 321 | 207 | 1010 |
| Gujarat | 182 | 1 | 3 | 0 | 64 | 529 | 220 | 343 |
| Haryana | 314 | – | 9 | 655 | – | – | 22 | 17 |
| Himachal Pradesh | 61 | – | 41 | 745 | 89 | 53 | 10 | 32 |
| Jammu & Kashmir | – | – | – | – | 10 | 11 | 979 | 2 |
| Karnataka | 453 | – | 13 | – | 295 | 81 | 157 | 642 |
| Kerala | 6 | – | 9 | 167 | 477 | 4 | 337 | 505 |
| Madhya Pradesh* | 350 | 5 | 5 | 9 | 101 | 461 | 69 | 2849 |
| Maharashtra | 49 | 0 | 2 | 2 | 750 | 99 | 98 | 1707 |
| Manipur | 108 | – | 6 | 0 | 122 | 444 | 321 | 64 |
| Meghalaya | 140 | – | 11 | 2 | 184 | 210 | 452 | 320 |
| Mizoram | 175 | 0 | 18 | 0 | 307 | 296 | 204 | 112 |
| Nagaland | 234 | – | 69 | 22 | 201 | 170 | 303 | 25 |
| Orissa | 259 | 1 | 1 | 4 | 136 | 443 | 156 | 1923 |
| Punjab | – | – | – | – | – | – | – | – |
| Rajasthan | – | 194 | 183 | – | – | 614 | 9 | 29 |

(Contd.)

(Number of households per ,000)

| State | Fruit, roots, tubers | Gums and resins | Honey | Medicinal herbs | Fish | Leaves | Weed, grass, bamboo | Value of collections (R. million) |
|---|---|---|---|---|---|---|---|---|
| Sikkim | 2 | – | – | 1 | – | 203 | 794 | 60 |
| Tamil Nadu | 139 | 0 | 0 | 8 | 205 | 183 | 464 | 525 |
| Tripura | 69 | 2 | 3 | 4 | 427 | 0 | 675 | 134 |
| Uttar Pradesh* | 20 | – | 12 | 3 | 254 | 306 | 404 | 778 |
| West Bengal | 7 | 0 | 5 | – | 842 | 115 | 30 | 2331 |
| A and N Islands | 224 | 22 | 47 | 13 | 163 | 181 | 349 | 4 |
| India | 154 | 2 | 6 | 11 | 415 | 250 | 162 | 16,156 |

*Note:* *These are the states prior to the formation of Uttaranchal, Chattisgarh, and Jharkhand.

*Source: Sarvekshana*, Vol. XXIV, Issue 84, July–September 2000, p. S-426.

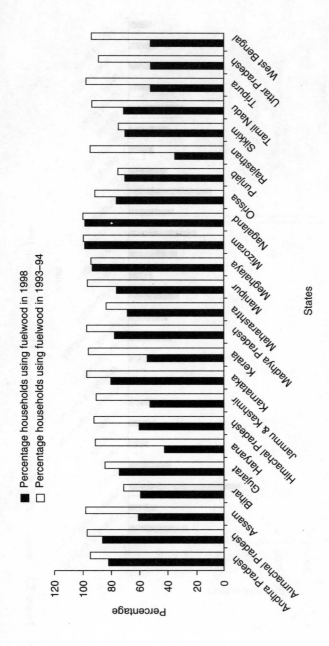

**Figure 3.2:** Percentage of Households Using Fuelwood in 1993–4 and 1998.

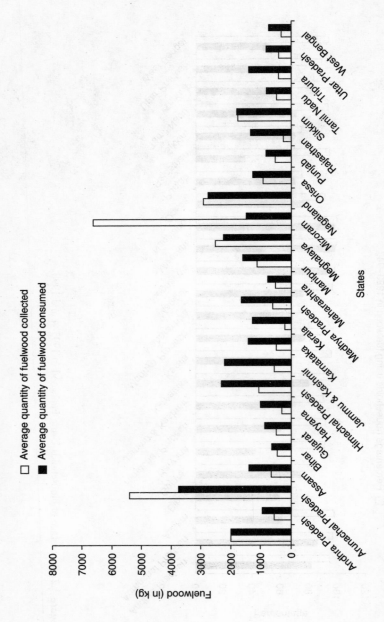

**Figure 3.3:** Pattern of CPR Collection and Consumption of Fuelwood (in kg) in 1998

the extent of dependency on such collections from the CPRs is higher.[15] Thus, accounting for CPR collections will show better income distribution at the per capita levels, a fact as highlighted by Jodha (1986).

Table 3.14
Average Value of Collections from CPRs and Average Consumption Expenditure

| State | Average value of collections from CPR (Rs) | Annual consumption expenditure (Rs) | Ratio of value of collection to consumption expenditure (%) |
|---|---|---|---|
| Andhra Pradesh | 554 | 4632 | 11.96 |
| Assam | 1071 | 4056 | 26.41 |
| Bihar* | 519 | 3468 | 14.97 |
| Gujarat | 663 | 4992 | 13.28 |
| Haryana | 1174 | 6552 | 17.92 |
| Karnataka | 635 | 4380 | 14.50 |
| Kerala | 390 | 7248 | 5.38 |
| Madhya Pradesh* | 984 | 3912 | 25.15 |
| Maharashtra | 799 | 4608 | 17.34 |
| Orissa | 929 | 3612 | 25.72 |
| Punjab | 1057 | 7368 | 14.35 |
| Rajasthan | 266 | 5424 | 4.90 |
| Tamil Nadu | 667 | 4572 | 14.59 |
| Uttar Pradesh* | 690 | 4476 | 15.42 |
| West Bengal | 450 | 4296 | 10.47 |
| India | 693 | 4584 | 15.12 |

Note: Annual consumption expenditure are derived from estimates taken from Sarvekshana Issue No. 81 (October–December 1999), Household Consumption Expenditure and Employment Situation in India, 54th Round, NSS. *These are the states prior to the formation of Uttaranchal, Chattisgarh, and Jharkhand states.
Source: Sarvekshana, Vol. XXIV, Issue 84, July–September 2000, p. 67.

This fact is much more vivid from Table 3.15 in which the quantity of fodder collected from CPR land and forest resources and that from own farms (cultivated) is shown. Out of 1000 households at the all-India level, as few as 20 get their fodder requirements from own farms

[15]The correlation between annual per capita expenditure and annual per capita collection from CPRs is –0.56, indicating such a negative link.

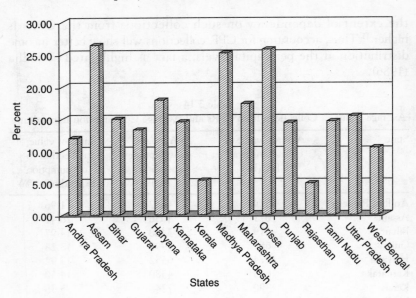

**Figure 3.4:** Ratio of Value of CPR Collection to Total Consumption Expenditure in Percentage

by cultivation, and about 127 of them depend on the commons. In states such as Sikkim, Uttar Pradesh (including Uttaranchal), north eastern states, and Karnataka this dependency on collection is much higher than the national average. The access to grazing lands from the commons also differs from state to state as shown in Appendix Table A3.1. At the all-India level, as few as 17 of 1000 households have access to village forests for grazing, 109 households report access to other types of CPRs, and 47 access to government forests. Most other households depend upon wastelands that come under revenue and other departments.

Access to Water Resources

There are a variety of resources of water which are in the public domain and a significant part of these are included in the category of the commons. The National Water Policy of 2002 categorically states that all the stakeholders have to have a say in planning, development, and management of water resources in India. Unfortunately, even after

Table 3.15
Number of Households Reporting Use of CPR
Collection and Cultivation of Fodder

*(Number of households per ,000)*

| State | Collection | Cultivation |
|---|---|---|
| Karnataka | 158 | 24 |
| Kerala | 46 | 9 |
| Madhya Pradesh | 87 | 12 |
| Maharashtra | 111 | 11 |
| Manipur | 63 | 39 |
| Meghalaya | 22 | 10 |
| Mizoram | 206 | 61 |
| Nagaland | 221 | 106 |
| Orissa | 73 | 5 |
| Punjab | 180 | 27 |
| Rajasthan | 29 | 52 |
| Sikkim | 325 | 72 |
| Tamil Nadu | 66 | 3 |
| Tripura | 14 | 1 |
| Uttar Pradesh | 232 | 22 |
| West Bengal | 93 | 2 |
| Andaman and Nicobar | 45 | – |
| India | 127 | 20 |

*Source: Sarvekshana*, Vol. XXIV, No. 1, Issue 84, July–September 2000, pp. S-348–9.

all the debates about property rights (such as traditional rights, community rights, and basic need human rights), water has not yet been declared a CPR in India, though references are made in the Water Policy document indirectly.

When it comes to estimates of the extent of water sources, once again, other than the estimates by Agarwal and Narain (1997), there is no consistent set of complete official information at the all-India level about water harvesting structures and their property rights regimes, etc. However, NSS data for 1998 based on a sampling method provide some clues.

How are the different water sources managed in India? By and large, water resources in India are in common property regimes only. Irrigation canals are managed jointly by the government (as a custodian) and communities. Traditionally, tanks, village ponds, and

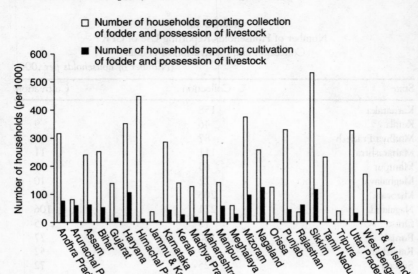

**Figure 3.5:** Pattern of CPR Collection and Cultivation of Fodder in 1998

lakes—all of which are treated as CPRs—are sources of water for drinking, livestock rearing, washing, fishing and bathing, and several sanitary-related activities.

There are two ways to look at water resources in the common property regime, one as access to or availability of water from different common based sources and two, the extent of their management by the communities. Talking of dimensions of common property water resources, this distinction is important. As far as access to potable water is concerned, some of the major findings from the NSS data are shown in Tables 3.16 and summarized here.

1. Access to potable water depends upon the proximity to such water sources. At the all-India level, about 758 out of 1000 households reported that they live near community tube wells, 665 near community wells, 266 near other water sources, and 952 households near one or more of these sources, on average. Interestingly, in states like West Bengal, Karnataka, and Andhra Pradesh this accessibility to community

Table 3.16
Number of Households Residing in Villages
with Common Potable Water Resources (CPWRs)

*(Number of households per ,000)*

| State/UT | Community tube wells | Community wells | Other than tube wells and wells | Any CPWR |
|---|---|---|---|---|
| Andhra Pradesh | 822 | 728 | 346 | 990 |
| Arunachal Pradesh | 217 | 167 | 269 | 449 |
| Assam | 782 | 512 | 241 | 926 |
| Bihar* | 849 | 789 | 164 | 987 |
| Gujarat | 785 | 675 | 234 | 982 |
| Haryana | 536 | 697 | 193 | 917 |
| Himachal Pradesh | 97 | 487 | 424 | 813 |
| Jammu & Kashmir | 130 | 310 | 255 | 501 |
| Karnataka | 967 | 697 | 155 | 991 |
| Kerala | 583 | 898 | 280 | 928 |
| Madhya Pradesh* | 714 | 797 | 369 | 985 |
| Maharashtra | 877 | 846 | 155 | 983 |
| Manipur | 319 | 176 | 451 | 591 |
| Meghalaya | 147 | 311 | 668 | 922 |
| Mizoram | 32 | – | 336 | 368 |
| Nagaland | 195 | 588 | 435 | 861 |
| Orissa | 958 | 803 | 219 | 1000 |
| Punjab | 254 | 208 | 282 | 575 |
| Rajasthan | 591 | 642 | 364 | 938 |
| Sikkim | – | – | 806 | 806 |
| Tamil Nadu | 887 | 753 | 465 | 978 |
| Tripura | 974 | 774 | 437 | 974 |
| Uttar Pradesh* | 609 | 566 | 303 | 911 |
| West Bengal | 956 | 309 | 108 | 997 |
| A and N Islands | 37 | 867 | 204 | 867 |
| India | 758 | 665 | 266 | 952 |

Note: *These are the states prior to the formation of Uttaranchal, Chattisgarh, and Jharkhand states.
Source: *Sarvekshana*, Vol. XXIV, No. 1, July–September 2000, pp. S-276–7.

sources is nearly 100 per cent.

2. As far as community tube-wells are concerned, the dependency of the households on them is the highest in Karnataka, Orissa, Tamil Nadu, and West Bengal.

3. Andhra Pradesh, Bihar, Karnataka, Madhya Pradesh, Maharashtra, Orissa, Rajasthan, and Tamil Nadu show very high dependency of the households on community wells.

The major uses of water other than drinking for rural households are irrigation, livestock rearing, fishing, and household enterprises, etc. Some major findings from NSS (see Table 3.17) are summarized here.

1. Out of 1000 households, about 228 of them use community or government water sources for irrigation, 298 households for live stock rearing, 28 for household enterprises and 25 for fishing, on average.

2. But interestingly, in states like Haryana, Himachal Pradesh, Jammu and Kashmir, Orissa, Madhya Pradesh, and Rajasthan the dependency of the households on the common water for livestock rearing is quite high (invariably, more than 450 out of 1000 households have reported dependency).

3. As far as community based or government irrigation is concerned, Bihar and Uttar Pradesh  top the list.

4. Fishing is the next  most important activity which is dependent upon the commons. In states such as West Bengal, and certain pockets of Arunachal Pradesh, Assam, Mizoram, and Nagaland, this dependency is quite high.

Do the communities manage the common water resources in India? The answer is yes and no, and varies from state to state (and also region to region). As far as management of common water resource is concerned, not all the resources are managed by the communities, as seen from NSS data in Table 3.18. Out of a total of 1000 households, only 41 households reported that common water resources in their villages are managed by the community only, 30  households reported management by the government only, 26 reported management by community and government. Interestingly enough, as many as 236 households reported no management by communities, 111 reported no management by government, 73 reported no management either by the community or government. On the other hand, a large number of households, 483 of reported that private water resources are made available to them. Clearly, there is evidence of a breakdown of some of the traditional systems of water management by the communities, and the government institutions are also unable to manage them.

Table 3.17<br>
Number of Households Reporting Use of Water Resources by Purpose<br>
(Number of households per ,000)

| State | Community or government water resources used for | | | |
| | Irrigation | Livestock rearing | Household enterprise | Fishing |
|---|---|---|---|---|
| Andhra Pradesh | 182 | 200 | 28 | 6 |
| Arunachal Pradesh | 194 | 155 | 19 | 310 |
| Assam | 76 | 223 | 60 | 306 |
| Bihar* | 300 | 226 | 46 | 20 |
| Gujarat | 205 | 358 | 14 | 1 |
| Haryana | 245 | 586 | 35 | – |
| Himachal Pradesh | 165 | 484 | 52 | 1 |
| Jammu & Kashmir | 619 | 671 | 55 | – |
| Karnataka | 161 | 386 | 33 | 5 |
| Kerala | 68 | 73 | 4 | 9 |
| Madhya Pradesh* | 161 | 471 | 24 | 6 |
| Maharashtra | 76 | 270 | 13 | 4 |
| Manipur | 280 | 65 | 48 | 108 |
| Meghalaya | 15 | 11 | 54 | 96 |
| Mizoram | 9 | 143 | 203 | 423 |
| Nagaland | 315 | 318 | 54 | 375 |
| Orissa | 152 | 468 | 108 | 100 |
| Punjab | 155 | 78 | 2 | 1 |
| Rajasthan | 171 | 471 | 22 | 0 |
| Sikkim | 338 | 389 | 270 | 2 |
| Tamil Nadu | 117 | 112 | 6 | 7 |
| Tripura | 73 | 39 | 2 | 5 |
| Uttar Pradesh* | 472 | 347 | 16 | 2 |
| West Bengal | 243 | 248 | 25 | 70 |
| Andaman and Nicobar Islands | 19 | 57 | 6 | 8 |
| India | 228 | 298 | 28 | 25 |

*Note:* *These are the states prior to the formation of Uttaranchal, Chattisgarh, and Jharkhand states.
*Source: Sarvekshana,* Vol. XXIV, Issue 84, July–September 2000, pp. S-428–9

## SOME LESSONS FROM THE DIMENSIONALITY OF CPRs

The analysis of the dimensions, extent of management institutions, and the rate of change in these, as revealed by macro-level data are quite striking. First, one notices from the macro-level as well as from

Table 3.18

Distribution of Households by Availability of Community and Government
Water Resources in Villages of their Residence and Presence of Local
Management of Common Water Sources for Irrigation

*(Households per ,000)*

| State | Households in Villages with local management and water resources belonging to | | | Households in Villages without local management and with water resources belonging to | | | HHs in other villages |
|---|---|---|---|---|---|---|---|
| | Community only | Govt only | Both | Community only | Govt only | Both | |
| Andhra Pradesh | 142 | 135 | 92 | 194 | 97 | 72 | 268 |
| Arunachal Pradesh | 10 | 27 | – | – | 247 | 57 | 659 |
| Assam | 16 | 5 | – | 262 | 90 | 42 | 585 |
| Bihar* | 20 | 29 | 12 | 177 | 160 | 74 | 527 |
| Gujarat | 32 | 27 | 22 | 263 | 86 | 99 | 471 |
| Haryana | 49 | – | – | 414 | 109 | 131 | 298 |
| Himachal Pradesh | 18 | 36 | 20 | 63 | 149 | 64 | 651 |
| Jammu and Kashmir | 23 | 31 | 6 | 121 | 135 | 32 | 652 |
| Karnataka | 10 | 5 | 3 | 292 | 148 | 72 | 470 |
| Kerala | 18 | 31 | 28 | 239 | 114 | 90 | 481 |
| Madhya Pradesh* | 39 | 21 | 23 | 303 | 78 | 76 | 461 |
| Maharashtra | 7 | 43 | 13 | 86 | 226 | 59 | 565 |
| Manipur | 71 | 26 | 34 | 193 | 65 | 13 | 598 |
| Meghalaya | – | 11 | – | 102 | 127 | - | 760 |
| Mizoram | – | – | – | 115 | 103 | 26 | 757 |
| Nagaland | 56 | 39 | – | 216 | 133 | 209 | 348 |
| Orissa | 23 | 5 | 21 | 569 | 55 | 149 | 177 |
| Punjab | – | 6 | – | 194 | 51 | 87 | 662 |
| Rajasthan | 42 | 20 | 11 | 216 | 119 | 53 | 539 |
| Sikkim | – | 17 | – | 29 | 192 | 17 | 745 |
| Tamil Nadu | 89 | 51 | 97 | 224 | 154 | 168 | 217 |
| Tripura | – | – | 31 | 310 | 65 | 131 | 464 |
| Uttar Pradesh* | 29 | 1 | 9 | 286 | 66 | 37 | 572 |
| West Bengal | 50 | 18 | 17 | 122 | 67 | 15 | 711 |
| A and N Islands | – | – | 46 | 167 | 116 | 34 | 637 |
| India | 41 | 30 | 26 | 236 | 111 | 73 | 483 |

Note: *These are the states prior to the formation of Uttaranchal, Chattisgarh, and
Jharkhand states;

Source: *Sarvekshana*, Vol. XXIV, Issue 84, July–September 2000, pp. S-285–6.

village level data that, in regions and states where CPRs are still maintained, the dependency on them continues. Wherever they are not maintained, the villagers depend on CPRs in the neighbouring villages. This is particularly true of forest land and related resources. As far as water resources are concerned, access by marginal and small farmers is limited. On the whole, there is evidence to show that the stock and flows of CPRs have been dwindling over time in India. Third, a broad picture of the breakdown or weakening of both traditional and governmental institutions for management of the commons in India emerges from NSS data. Finally, a number of biodiversity rich CPR resources have entered the list of rarity and endangerment.

## Appendix 3.1

### Table A3.1

Number of Households Reporting Grazing of Livestock on CPR Land and Forest and Reporting Possession of Livestock for each Climatic Zone

*(Number of households per ,000)*

| State | Type of CPR land | | | Forest | | | No. of hhs reporting grazing of livestock on CPR or forest est. (00) | sample |
|---|---|---|---|---|---|---|---|---|
| | Village forest | Others | Any | Govt forest | Others | Any | | |
| Andhra Pradesh | 4 | 63 | 66 | 16 | 91 | 136 | 16,220 | 774 |
| Arunachal Pradesh | 117 | 108 | 185 | 35 | 41 | 256 | 416 | 224 |
| Assam | 9 | 162 | 166 | 27 | 99 | 235 | 8237 | 723 |
| Bihar | 15 | 79 | 85 | 38 | 135 | 157 | 23,558 | 1203 |
| Gujarat | 15 | 227 | 228 | 28 | 120 | 250 | 13,611 | 761 |
| Haryana | 1 | 77 | 79 | – | 88 | 150 | 3814 | 179 |
| Himachal Pradesh | 20 | 26 | 35 | 221 | 227 | 345 | 3526 | 651 |
| Jammu & Kashmir | 9 | 90 | 97 | 130 | 79 | 248 | 1959 | 417 |
| Karnataka | 14 | 112 | 117 | 37 | 195 | 249 | 17,333 | 797 |
| Kerala | 2 | 1 | 3 | 4 | 25 | 32 | 1470 | 105 |
| Madhya Pradesh | 55 | 213 | 245 | 148 | 230 | 422 | 45,388 | 2308 |
| Maharashtra | 12 | 52 | 61 | 33 | 66 | 110 | 12,189 | 623 |
| Manipur | 27 | 97 | 100 | 14 | 16 | 109 | 273 | 85 |
| Meghalaya | 14 | 61 | 61 | – | – | 61 | 212 | 60 |
| Mizoram | 22 | 37 | 52 | – | 7 | 53 | 38 | 36 |

(Contd.)

82

*(Number of households per ,000)*

| State | Type of CPR land | | | Govt forest | Others | Any | No. of hhs reporting grazing of livestock on CPR or forest | |
|---|---|---|---|---|---|---|---|---|
| | Village forest | Others | Any | | | | est. (00) | sample |
| Nagaland | 68 | 156 | 157 | 12 | 21 | 157 | 137 | 146 |
| Orissa | 114 | 214 | 258 | 150 | 279 | 349 | 22,127 | 1146 |
| Punjab | – | 2 | 2 | – | 10 | 11 | 313 | 24 |
| Rajasthan | 8 | 227 | 230 | 16 | 83 | 282 | 17,586 | 1000 |
| Sikkim | – | 1 | 1 | 15 | 6 | 21 | 18 | 42 |
| Tamil Nadu | 3 | 62 | 63 | 3 | 58 | 86 | 8267 | 520 |
| Tripura | 1 | 1 | 1 | 6 | 33 | 36 | 204 | 39 |
| Uttar Pradesh | 10 | 141 | 146 | 68 | 114 | 219 | 50,293 | 1946 |
| West Bengal | 1 | 26 | 26 | 12 | 161 | 165 | 18,244 | 906 |
| Andaman and Nicobar Islands | 17 | 9 | 26 | 139 | 113 | 187 | 84 | 86 |
| India | 17 | 109 | 117 | 47 | 123 | 197 | 265,645 | 14,827 |

*Source: Sarvekshana*, Vol. XXIV, Issue no. 84, July–September 2000, pp. 5-364-71.

Table A3.2

CPR Land Per Household by Type of Land and Ratio of CPR Land to Total Geographical Area and to Total Non-residential Geographical Area

(land in ha.)

| State | Type of land | | | | ratio of CPR area to | | Estimated no hhs. (00) | Estd. area CPR (00 ha) |
|---|---|---|---|---|---|---|---|---|
| | Grazing | Village forest | Others | All | Total geo. area | Non-resi. geo. area | | |
| Andhra Pradesh | 0.02 | 0.01 | 0.13 | 0.17 | 0.09 | 0.11 | 119,332 | 20,546 |
| Arunachal Pradesh | 0.29 | 0.64 | 0.22 | 1.15 | – | – | 1625 | 1874 |
| Assam | 0.02 | 0.01 | 0.01 | 0.05 | 0.07 | 0.09 | 35,114 | 1613 |
| Bihar | 0.02 | 0.02 | 0.05 | 0.08 | 0.08 | 0.1 | 150,258 | 12,627 |
| Gujarat | 0.20 | 0.03 | 0.49 | 0.72 | 0.27 | 0.33 | 54,468 | 39,165 |
| Haryana | 0.01 | 0.01 | 0.02 | 0.05 | 0.03 | 0.04 | 25,388 | 1221 |
| Himachal Pradesh | 0.07 | 0.16 | 0.1 | 0.33 | 0.12 | 0.13 | 10,226 | 3404 |
| Jammu & Kashmir | 0.05 | 0.00 | 0.09 | 0.14 | – | – | 7907 | 1133 |
| Karnataka | 0.09 | 0.02 | 0.14 | 0.25 | 0.10 | 0.11 | 69,693 | 17,505 |
| Kerala | 0.05 | 0.02 | 0.05 | 0.12 | – | – | 45411 | 5392 |
| Madhya Pradesh | 0.22 | 0.15 | 0.36 | 0.74 | 0.22 | 0.26 | 107,483 | 79,715 |
| Maharashtra | 0.09 | 0.10 | 0.10 | 0.30 | 0.11 | 0.12 | 111,247 | 33,174 |
| Manipur | 0.05 | 0.08 | 0.04 | 0.17 | – | – | 2505 | 430 |
| Meghalaya | 0.16 | 0.28 | 0.28 | 0.72 | – | – | 3457 | 2487 |
| Mizoram | 0.06 | 3.43 | 0.87 | 4.37 | – | – | 718 | 3137 |
| Nagaland | 0.14 | 0.57 | 0.78 | 1.49 | 0.08 | 0.02 | 871 | 1301 |
| Orissa | 0.11 | 0.1 | 0.07 | 0.28 | 0.11 | 0.12 | 63,451 | 17,487 |

(Contd.)

(land in ha.)

| State | Type of land | | | Ratio of CPR area to | | Estimated no hhs. (00) | Estd. area CPR (00 ha) |
| | Grazing | Village forest | Others | All | Total geo. area | Non-resi. geo. area | | |
| --- | --- | --- | --- | --- | --- | --- | --- | --- |
| Punjab | 0.00 | 0.00 | 0.01 | 0.02 | 0.01 | 0.01 | 27,971 | 490 |
| Rajasthan | 0.24 | 0.08 | 1.72 | 2.04 | 0.32 | 0.27 | 62,377 | 127,094 |
| Sikkim | 0.05 | – | 0.20 | 0.25 | 0.14 | 0.19 | 849 | 213 |
| Tamil Nadu | 0.02 | 0.02 | 0.12 | 0.16 | 0.12 | 0.13 | 96,287 | 15,129 |
| Tripura | 0.01 | 0.01 | 0.00 | 0.01 | 0.01 | 0.01 | 5602 | 77 |
| Uttar Pradesh | 0.04 | 0.02 | 0.08 | 0.14 | 0.12 | 0.15 | 230,000 | 31,705 |
| West Bengal | 0.00 | 0.01 | 0.02 | 0.03 | 0.02 | 0.02 | 110,379 | 3186 |
| Andaman and Nicobar | 0.05 | 0.07 | 0.02 | 0.13 | 0.09 | 0.10 | 426 | 57 |
| India | 0.07 | 0.05 | 0.19 | 0.31 | 0.15 | 0.16 | 13,48,687 | 420,219 |

*Note:* Villages where non-residential geographical area are not available, the total geographical area has been deducted from the total geographical area of the respective regions.
*Source: Sarvekshana,* Vol. XXIV, Issue 84 July–September 2000, pp. s-243-44.

Table A3.3

Inland Fishery Water Resources of India, 1995

| State/UT | Length of rivers and canals (kms) | Area of reservoirs sq. km | Area under tanks and ponds sq. km | Beels, oxbow, and derelict water sq. km | Brackish water sq. km | Total water bodies other than rivers and canals |
|---|---|---|---|---|---|---|
| Andhra Pradesh | 11,514 | 2340 | 5170 | Nil | 640 | 8150 |
| Assam | 4820 | 20 | 230 | 1100 | Nil | 1350 |
| Bihar | 3200 | 600 | 950 | 50 | Nil | 1600 |
| Goa | 250 | 30 | 30 | Nil | Nil | 60 |
| Gujarat | 3865 | 2430 | 710 | 120 | 3760 | 7020 |
| Haryana | 5000 | Neg. | 100 | 100 | Nil | 200 |
| Himachal Pradesh | 3000 | 420 | 10 | Nil | Nil | 430 |
| Jammu and Kashmir | 27,781 | 70 | 170 | 60 | Nil | 300 |
| Karnataka | 9000 | 2200 | 4140 | Nil | Nil | 6420 |
| Kerala | 3029 | 300 | 300 | 2430 | 2430 | 5460 |
| Madhya Pradesh | 20,661 | 2940 | 1190 | Nil | Nil | 4130 |
| Maharashtra | 1600 | 2790 | 500 | Nil | 100 | 3390 |
| Manipur | 3360 | 10 | 50 | 400 | Nil | 460 |
| Meghalaya | 5600 | 80 | 20 | Neg | Nil | 100 |
| Nagaland | 1600 | 170 | 500 | Neg | Nil | 670 |
| Orissa | 4500 | 2560 | 1140 | 1800 | 4170 | 9670 |
| Punjab | 15,270 | Neg. | 70 | Nil | Nil | 70 |
| Rajasthan | NA | 1200 | 1800 | Nil | Nil | 3000 |
| Sikkim | 900 | Nil | Nil | 30 | Nil | 30 |

(Contd.)

| State/UT | Length of rivers and canals (kms) | Area of reservoirs sq. km | Area under tanks and ponds sq. km | Beels, oxbow, and derelict water sq. km | Brackish water sq. km | Total water bodies other than rivers and canals |
|---|---|---|---|---|---|---|
| Tamil Nadu | 7420 | 520 | 6910 | NA | 560 | 7990 |
| Tripura | 1200 | 50 | 120 | Nil | Nil | 170 |
| Uttar Pradesh | 31,200 | 1500 | 1620 | 1330 | Nil | 4450 |
| West Bengal | 2526 | 170 | 2760 | 420 | 2100 | 5450 |
| Arunanchal Pradesh | 2000 | Nil | 2760 | 420 | 2100 | 5280 |
| Mizoram | 1395 | Nil | 20 | Nil | Nil | 20 |
| Andaman and Nicobar | 115 | 10 | 30 | Nil | 370 | 410 |
| Chandigarh | 2 | Nil | Neg. | Neg. | Nil | 0 |
| Delhi | 150 | 40 | Nil | Nil | Nil | 40 |
| Lakshadweep | Nil | Nil | Nil | Nil | Nil | 0 |
| Pondicherry | 247 | Nil | Neg. | 10 | 10 | 20 |
| Dadra and Nagar Haveli | 54 | 50 | Nil | Nil | Nil | 50 |
| Daman and Diu | 12 | Nil | Nil | Nil | Nil | 0 |
| Total | 171,334 | 20,500 | 31,300 | 8270 | 16,320 | 76,390 |

*Source:* Handbook on Fisheries Statistics, 1996, Department of Agriculture and Co-operative.

Table A3.4
Marine Fishery Resources of India

| State/UTs | Continental shelf (thousand sq. km) | Number of landing centres | Number of villages | Approx. Length of coastline (km) |
|---|---|---|---|---|
| Andhra Pradesh | 31 | 379 | 409 | 974 |
| Goa | 10 | 87 | 91 | 104 |
| Gujarat | 164 | 854 | 851 | 1600 |
| Karnataka | 27 | 28 | 204 | 300 |
| Kerala | 40 | 226 | 222 | 590 |
| Maharashtra | 112 | 184 | 395 | 720 |
| Orissa | 24 | 63 | 329 | 480 |
| Tamilnadu | 41 | 362 | 442 | 1000 |
| West Bengal | 17 | 47 | 652 | 157 |
| Andaman and Nicobar | 35 | 57 | 45 | 1912 |
| Pondicherry | 1 | 28 | 45 | 45 |
| Lakshadweep | 4 | 11 | 10 | 132 |
| Daman and Diu | 0 | 7 | 31 | 27 |
| Total | 506 | 2333 | 3726 | 8041 |

*Source*: Handbook on Fisheries Statistics, 1996, Department of Agriculture and Co-operative.

# 4

# Common Property Resources, Private Property Resources, and Livelihood

## INTRODUCTION: THE SETTING

In this chapter we return to the issue of the relevance of CPRs, more specifically in the Indian context. Being part of the natural resource system, invariably the context is the sustainable development of CPRs. Talking of relevance in the Indian context, four questions can be posed.

1. First, what are the relative merits and demerits of managing a particular natural resource under different property rights regimes such as common property, private property, and open access resource?

2. In reality, a variety of resources co-exist under different property rights regimes. The question is about the link between different common and private property resources, and also between other property rights regimes. Do PPRs and CPRs have any production relationship? Do they act as substitutes or complements?

3. Third, what is the extent of dependency of local communities upon CPRs for their livelihood? Under what kinds of social and economic conditions together with property rights regimes do the communities depend upon CPRs strongly or weakly? In both cases, it is important to analyse the links between CPR and PPR.

4. Is it feasible to define a sustainable rate of extraction and use of CPRs?

From among the Indian studies, Jodha (1986, 1994), Katar Singh (1994a), Iyengar (1988), Kadekodi (1997a), Murty (1994), Chopra *et al.* (1990), Jyoti Parikh and S. Reddy (1997), Chopra and Gulati (2001), Chopra and Rao (1996), Sengupta (1995), Bhatta and Bhat (2001) and others have looked into some of these questions. Each of these questions raises several alternative ways of formulating theoretical models to examine the issues and to empirically test the hypotheses.

The first issue is with respect to efficiency and feasibility of resource management under alternative property rights regimes. This will be examined in a theoretical framework in the second section. Referring to the second hypothesis, the mutual dependency between CPRs and PPRs as two productive resources is quite well known among the users of the two (Hardin, 1968; Dasgupta, 1982). Historically, as examined in Chapter 1, there is evidence of strong links between crop agriculture and livestock rearing in medieval England as well as Switzerland. In the Indian context, even in the contemporary period, strong links between CPRs, PPRs, and livelihood are observed among the tribals (nomads), forest dwellers (van panchayats in Uttaranchal).

An alternative approach is to treat common and private property resources as substitutes. Known examples are substitution of good topsoil and nutrient contents (a CPR) by chemical fertilizer (a PPR), fuelwood by liquified petroleum gas (LPG) or electricity, and so on (Ciriacy-Wantrup and Bishop, 1975; Jodha, 1990; Chopra and Kadekodi, 1991). In many neo-classical economic models, even land itself (be it a CPR or PPR) is treated as substitutable by man-made capital. An example is an air conditioner replacing an open green landscape. On the contrary, in the context of sustainable development, more so in the Indian context, it is the complementarity between common and private resources that needs to be understood in theory and strengthened in practice. Economic theory has dealt with complementarity problems very marginally, with the exception of Hicks (1939), who devoted one entire chapter to it. An associated question is about the recognition of labour working on CPR management. This labour also acts as a complement to the deployment of private labour. All these aspects of complementarity will be explored further in the third and fourth sections with a case study in the fifth section.

As far as the third hypothesis is concerned, the question of CPR and livelihood linkage is essentially an issue of welfare, quality of life, or consumption pattern. The degree of dependency of the communities can be linked to the availability of alternative resources, non-purchasing power (or degree of poverty), culture and habits, and subsistence level of living. Some of these may or may not actually hold. This issue is dealt in the sections on CPR-livelihood linkages followed by a case study. On the matters of sustainability, two standard statements are generally made: First, CPRs are generally over exploited, which may not necessarily be true (Conrad, 1999). Second, there are both positive and negative externalities associated with CPRs (Dasgupta, 1982). The second last section addresses the question of a sustainable rate of use of CPRs and the problems of positive and negative externality associated with them, followed by the last section with a case study of fishery in Karnataka.

## A SIMPLE THEORY OF PROPERTY RIGHTS REGIMES

The choice between a common property regime and a private property regime has been the debate in theoretical literature, for over fifty years now (Gordon, 1954; Anderson, 1977; Howe, 1979; Stevenson, 1991; Singh, 1994a; Sengupta, 1995). Much of this theoretical development is centred around the relative merits of the three property rights regimes, namely private, common, and open access. It may be useful to take a look at this debate, for its relevance to India.

In Chapter 1, Figure 1.1 showed the possible relative productivities under the three regimes, with the necessary arguments. For the sake of simplicity, an assumption is added here without any loss of generality, that productivity under the open access regime is also the same as that under CPR management. Otherwise, as shown in Figure 1.1, the productivity under open access regime would be much lower (as in Hardin's grazing land example or in a typical open access fishery situation). Let the resource under question be designated as a grazing land (more relevant for the Indian situation), which yields an output such as fodder.[1] Let the price of fodder be given externally (may be by a market situation). To begin with, consider private versus common

---

[1]Following Gordon (1954), Anderson (1997), and others, one can also consider efforts to reap the benefits of the resource, instead of the resource such as grazing land, as the relevant input for CPR output.

property regimes as the two alternative management options. In Figure 4.1, curve OXc stands for the value of the marginal fodder product under CPR management at different levels of use of the grassland resource. Likewise, OXp stands for the same under a PPR management.[2] As argued in Chapter 1 and depicted in Figure 4.1, the level of grassland use up to Rx, yields higher marginal returns from private management. Beyond that level, due to crowding of resource users, too much of competition and uncertainty, and also due to indivisibility of the resource, the net marginal private productivity of the resource declines very fast. Beyond Rx, the resource management under a CPR regime is relatively better, yielding higher marginal productivity as shown by the curve OXc . For the sake of simplicity, let the cost of using incremental grassland resource be an increasing one, with the corresponding marginal resource cost curves under the two regimes as straight lines.

Line OYc stands for the marginal resource cost under the CPR regime and OYp under PPR. There is an implicit assumption here that the cost of rearing the benefits under the CPR regime are generally lower.[3] Under the usual net benefit maximizing rules, the efficient level of grazing land to be used will be Rc for the CPR management regime, and Rp for PPR regime, at which the corresponding marginal productivity and resource costs are equal.[4] As generally argued, under the CPR management, the exploitation of the resource is higher (as also the output of fodder)[5] so also the net benefits.

---

[2]Both these stand for the total productivities of all the individuals, households, or firms taken together, more like an industry level productivity.

[3]This is not too difficult to see in reality, as long as transaction costs and other risk costs are lower under CPR management. For example, much less policing is required under CPR management than under a PPR regime. Some amount of risk pooling also takes place under CPR regime.

[4]This result follows from the familiar optimization rule that under the objective of net benefit maximization, the value of marginal productivity of the resource (that is, of the grazing land) be equal to the cost of hiring or using that marginal resource. Since the only resource input is the amount of grazing land, the marginal cost and marginal resource cost are the same.

[5]This result is generally misunderstood by saying that a CPR regime is bad as it uses more resources and hence can lead to higher rates of degradation (for example, an argument used by Hardin, in his analysis of free grazing situation). If only better collective and community management rules are introduced, the difference between

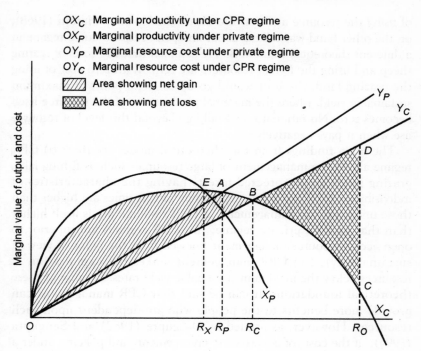

OX_C  Marginal productivity under CPR regime
OX_P  Marginal productivity under private regime
OY_P  Marginal resource cost under private regime
OY_C  Marginal resource cost under CPR regime
▨ Area showing net gain
▩ Area showing net loss

**Figure 4.1:** Grazing Land Resource

In the event that the resource is to be treated as an open access resource, the option open for the resource users is to go up to the level of resource use where total resource cost is just equal to the total benefit. Or total net benefit is equal to zero. In Figure 4.1, this situation is shown at Ro when all the net positive benefits upto Rc (area between the marginal productivity and marginal resource cost under a CPR regime, shown by the light shaded area) are neutralized by the negative net benefits from using the resources between Rc and Ro (area between marginal resource cost and marginal productivity curves, shown by the dark shaded area). Gordon (1954) identifies this situation

the private marginal cost and CPR marginal cost can be collected or saved by the community as rental or for future benefit and/or resource development. Furthermore, contrary to the argument in the literature, the social discount rate under a CPR regime need not be too low.

of using the resource at Ro as the unsustainable one.[6] Hardin (1968), on the other hand was talking about an open access resource regime in a different theoretical framework. He assumed that the costs of rearing sheep and using the fodder resources are zero. With zero cost of using the grazing land, the user would go up to Xc, a point of maximum sustainable yield, where the marginal productivity of the resource itself becomes zero. No rational user would go beyond this level of resource use when it pays negatively.

The main findings from this theoretical model are that: (i) CPR regime allows the management of large resources such as fishing lake, grazing lands, and protected forests having the characteristics of indivisibility; (ii) Total net benefits from CPR regimes are higher than those under private management, as CPR resource use is itself higher than that under a private regime; (iii) CPR regimes are superior to open access resource management (viewed from the point of view of sustainability); (iv) CPR management makes the exploitation of resources below the maximum sustainable yield rates. Because of these theoretical foundations, it can be said that CPR management can provide more benefits to the people who are dependent upon such resources. However, as argued by Dasgupta (1982) and Sengupta (1995), if the costs of governance, enforcement, and policing under a CPR regime become higher than the transaction costs under a private regime, or when CPR management fails to take note of market signals such as prices, the management of the resource under a CPR regime may become inefficient and may even collapse.[7]

CPR–PPR LINKAGE

The next major issue concerns the linkages between different common and private property resources. In a rural economic setting, households own PPRs such as cultivable land, livestock, agricultural equipment

---

[6]One can further show that the maximum sustainable yield (at which marginal productivity of the resource grassland is zero) is generally higher than the level $R_c$.

[7]One can cite several examples of such situations, as pointed out by Jodha (2000) in wastelands management. Chopra et al. (1990) give an example of the collapse of such CPR regimes in a village where private landowners had cornered all the benefits of a watershed development, leaving landless communities with no access to water.

(that is, capital), private wells, borewells, pump sets, seeds, fertilizers, fishing nets, boats, and so on. The productivity of these private resources depends not only on the quality and quantity of such resources but also upon access to a number of CPRs such as forest or village grass land, leaf biomass from forests, water harvesting and retaining structures, NTFPs, and the most important source of energy namely, fuelwood, and fishing from inland and marine sources. In other words, there is a very high level of production complementarity between common and private resources. Good livestock rearing is possible only with access to good grassland and pastures. Crop agriculture depends heavily upon the availability of water. Cooking in a rural setting depends immensely on the availability of fuelwood. Fishing is dependent upon the quality of the water resource and access to it.

Macro-level data on CPR and PPR land resources for Indian states are shown in Table 4.1. It is clear from the table and Figure 4.2, that there is a considerable degree of complementarity between these two types of resources. The estimated correlation coefficient between CPR and PPR is 0.8. As against the total CPRs of 74 million hectares among the major states in India, PPRs are 178 million hectares, comprising mainly operational holdings and current fallow lands.

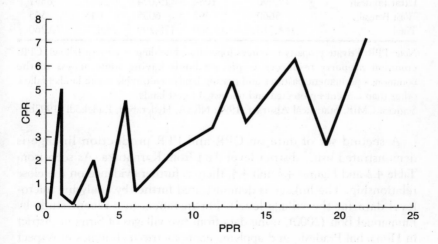

**Figure 4.2:** CPR–PPR Linkages, State Level ('000 Hectares)

Table 4.1
Private, Common Property, and Wasteland Resources, 1990–2

*('000 hectares)*

| State | Operational Holdings | Current Fallow | PPR | CPR | Wastelands |
|---|---|---|---|---|---|
| Andhra Pradesh | 14,460 | 2485 | 16,945 | 6286 | 5949 |
| Assam | 3160 | 88 | 3248 | 1984 | 1592 |
| Bihar | 10,900 | 1765 | 12,665 | 5348 | 2582 |
| Gujarat | 10,290 | 1039 | 11,329 | 3386 | 4580 |
| Haryana | 3710 | 169 | 3879 | 187 | 374 |
| Himachal Pradesh | 1020 | 45 | 1065 | 5019 | 3060 |
| Jammu and Kashmir | 1010 | 97 | 1107 | 525 | 7061 |
| Karnataka | 12,320 | 1290 | 13,610 | 3661 | 2712 |
| Kerala | 1800 | 44 | 1844 | 124 | 165 |
| Madhya Pradesh | 22,110 | 762 | 22,872 | 14,109 | 9186 |
| Maharashtra | 20,930 | 869 | 21,799 | 7196 | 7931 |
| Meghalaya | 300 | 59 | 359 | 732 | 973 |
| Nagaland | 970 | 118 | 1088 | 871 | 1032 |
| Orissa | 5300 | 119 | 5419 | 4547 | 2072 |
| Punjab | 4030 | 82 | 4112 | 359 | 378 |
| Rajasthan | 20,970 | 1814 | 22,784 | 14,196 | 11,017 |
| Tamil Nadu | 7470 | 1264 | 8734 | 2399 | 2298 |
| Tripura | 310 | 1 | 311 | 311 | 236 |
| Uttar Pradesh | 17,990 | 1084 | 19,074 | 2687 | 6557 |
| West Bengal | 5660 | 395 | 6055 | 646 | 505 |
| Total | 164,710 | 13,589 | 178,299 | 73,927 | 70,260 |

*Note:* PPR: Private property resources (operational holding + current fallow), CPR: common property resources = private lands having some access to the commons+permanent pastures and grazing lands+culturable waste lands+fallow other than current+protected and unclassed forest lands.
*Sources:* CMIE, Statistical Abstract, 1993; NRSA, Hyderabad; Kadekodi (1997b).

A second set of data on CPR and PPR production linkage is demonstrated using district level data from Karnataka. As seen from Table 4.2 and Figures 4.3 and 4.4, there is further evidence on the close relationship. The linkage is demonstrated further by analysing micro-level data (at the village level). For instance, in a recent study by Emmanuel Bon (2000), using data from two villages of Sirmour district in Himachal Pradesh, and applying econometric techniques in respect of land management, irrigation, and forest management, the strength of complementarity between private resources and common pooled resources is shown.

Such close links between the two types of resources is very characteristic in Indian rural settings. Then, there is the question of human labour inputs in managing both common and private resources together. While the cost of labour that goes into productive activities from private resources (for example, yield of fish, crop output, or milk yield) are payable as wages, the management of CPR generally does not prompt any wage payment or stipend for community labour (except for some national and state awards). There is an important question of recognizing (community) labour that goes into such activities.

Table 4.2
Districtwise  Data on CPR, PPR, and Wastelands in Karnataka

*(area in ha.)*

| District | CPR | PPR | Wasteland (1999) |
|---|---|---|---|
| Bangalore (Urban + Rural) | 141,471 | 468,364 | 152,825 |
| Belgaum | 137,950 | 1,010,674 | 144,939 |
| Bellary | 89,212 | 541,583 | 166,395 |
| Bidar | 231,762 | 465,561 | 40,554 |
| Chikmagalore | 231,427 | 305,133 | 83,204 |
| Gulbarga | 420,799 | 1,393,351 | 68,883 |
| Hassan | 172,682 | 431,644 | 57,135 |
| Kodagu | 66,397 | 169,869 | 11,720 |
| Kolar | 212,608 | 448,100 | 96,829 |
| Mandya | 156,059 | 326,100 | 46,737 |
| Mysore | 249,721 | 607,693 | 74,832 |
| Raichur | 356,222 | 1,142,362 | 94,583 |
| Tumkur | 315,259 | 688,625 | 277,039 |
| Uttara Kannada | 124,605 | 147,275 | 76,280 |
| Total | 4,643,601 | 12,321,315 | 2,083,928 |

*Sources*: Indian Agricultural Statistics, 1991–2; Annual Report 1998–9, Forest Dept, Government of Karnataka; Wastelands Atlas of India 2000, NRSA, Hyderabad.

The nature of the relationship between private and common pool resources is, however, dynamic and highly site specific. Where the link is strong, the people are likely to be more willing to invest time and resources in the rehabilitation of common resources, either voluntarily or on a nominal stipend basis. In such a context, common resources

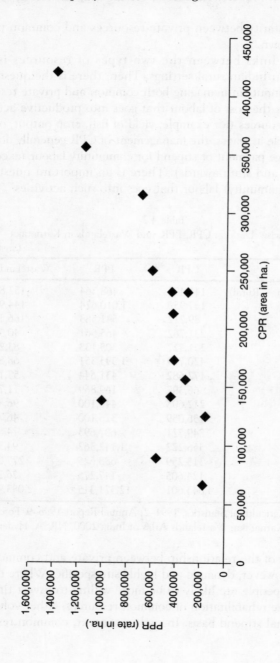

**Figure 4.3:** CPR–PPR Linkages in Karnataka

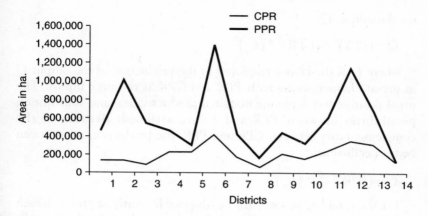

**Figure 4.4:** Districtwise Area under CPR and PPR in Karnataka

provide a focal activity around which communities can organize themselves. Examples are the emergence of water user associations, hill resource management schools, and so on. Where the relationship is weak or where the ratio of common pool resources to private resources is low, group action is likely to be more difficult to organize.

A MODEL OF CPR–PPR LINKAGE AND RECOGNITION OF COMMUNITY LABOUR

Keeping the above demonstrative data at the state and district levels in mind, a simple model of production linkage between CPR and PPR is developed here. The  model is also used to show employment (and hence income gains) from such a linkage.

The starting point is the complementarity between *PPR* and *CPR*.[8] This can be stated with a simple specification as:

$$CPR = (PPR)^d \text{ with } \partial CPR / \partial PPR, \text{ or}$$

The *PPR* and *CPR* together with labour are used to produce an output, designated as Q. A typical production function can be defined

[8]The CPRs, not only provide inputs for the productive use of PPRs, but also help in raising the productivities of PPRs through externalities. Examples of such links are improved water retention by good forest and grasslands, raising soil fertility of agricultural lands, or supply of fodder and leaf biomass for the cattle population.

for the output Q:

$$Q = (PPR)^a * (CPR)^b * (L_q)^g$$

where $L_q$ is the labour employed in the production of the output Q as private labour, along with PPR and CPR as resource inputs. The usual positive but declining marginal productivities, and substitution possibilities between PPR and $L_q$ are assumed. Because of the complementarity between CPR and PPR, the production relation can be re-specified as:

$$Q = (PPR)^{a+db} * (L_q)^g.$$

Let the total labour force (L) be disposable, partly as private labour ($L_q$) in the production of Q and/or as leisure (Lr). Under a profit maximizing condition, with given factor prices w and r for labour and PPR, respectively, the optimal rule of deploying the inputs is:

$$\frac{w}{r} = \left\{ \frac{g}{(a+db)} \right\} * \left\{ \frac{PPR}{L_q} \right\}.$$

Using this relation between optimal levels of labour and PPR, and the complementary relation between PPR and CPR, the derived demand for CPRs can be deduced as:

$$CPR = \left\{ \left[ \frac{(a+db)}{g} \right] * \left[ \frac{w}{r} \right] \times L_q \right\}^d.$$

Here, $L_c = (L_q)^d$ is the amount of community labour required, as complementary to private labour $L_q$, employable in order to maximize the output Q. Figure 4.5 shows the same diagrammatically. It, therefore, implies that community labour $L_c$ can be expressed as a function of CPRs:

$$L_c = h(CPR).$$

The derived demand for CPR and community labour are an integral part of the resource management to maximize the output Q. The marginal productivity of this derived demand for community labour can, therefore, yield the value of this labour for policy purposes. In the absence of this community labour input, the output Q will be sub-optimal.

Common Property Resources, Private Property Resources 101

CPR     Common property resources
PPR     Private property resources
PL      Private labour
CL      Community labour
$Q_1, Q_2$   Production functions
$CL_1, CL_2$  Derived demands for community labour

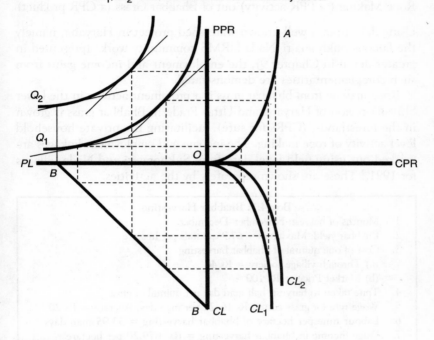

**Figure 4.5:** Derived Demand for CPR and Labour

In Figure 4.5, the complementarity between CPRs and PPRs is depicted by the curve $OA$. $Q_1$ and $Q_2$ are the two alternative production isoquants with inputs of PPRs and private labour. The line $BB$ represents the employment opportunity (or trade-off) between private labour employment and voluntary labour. The demands for community voluntary labour, $CL_1$ and $CL_2$, are accordingly deduced for the two alternative production relations.

CASE STUDIES OF CPR–PPR LINKAGES

The case studies presented here are taken from existing research studies. The purpose is to demonstrate the method of imputing values to the CPR–PPR linked employment and income generation.

Rope Making ( a PPR activity) out of Bhabbar Grass (a CPR product)

Using data from a well-known watershed project in Haryana, namely the famous Sukhomajri–Nada HRMS community work  (presented in greater detail in Chapter 9), the employment and income gains from such complementarities are demonstrated.

Rope making from bhabbar grass is a prominent activity in the lower Shivalik region of Haryana and Uttar Pradesh. Bhabbar grass is grown in the forestlands, (CPRs for sure), facilitating the private household level activity of rope making. The income and employment linkages are worked out using field level data from Sukhomajri and Nada villages for 1991.[9] These are shown separately by the activities.

---

**Box 4.1: Bhabbar Harvesting**

1. Months of harvest: November–December
2. Bhabbar yield: Maximum— 67.9 quintals per hectare
3. Cost of one quintal of bhabbar harvesting
   (a) Through village society = Rs 40
   (b) Market Price = Rs 100
4. Time taken to harvest: half man day per quintal of grass
5. Wage rate for grass cutter: Rs 16–22 per man day; Average = Rs 20
6. **Labour time per hectare of bhabbar harvesting = 33.95 man days**
7. **Wage income in bhabbar harvesting = Rs  679.20 per hectare**

---

**Box 4.2: Rope Making**

1. Yield of rope: 70 kg per quintal of  bhabbar
2. Yield of rope from one hectare of bhabbar: 47.53 quintals
3. Price of rope: Rs 4.5 per kg of rope
4. Labour time: 8 hours or one man day for 10 kg of rope
5. Rope Making charges if hired: Rs 3–4 per kg
6. **Employment in rope making per hectare of bhabbar: 475.50 man days**

---

[9]For a detailed account of the community based management of bhabbar grass, water harvesting, and dairying activities in these villages, see chapter 9.

The total employment and income from such an activity are deduced from the above data.

---

**Box 4.3: Total Employment in Rope Making**

A1. Total employment per quintal of rope (man days)
= employment in bhabbar harvesting (0.5)
+ employment in rope making (10.0)
+ marginal employment in marketing (1.0) = 11.5 man days

A2. Total employment per hectare of bhabbar grass (man days)
= employment in bhabbar harvesting (33.95) + employment in rope making (475.5) + employment in marketing (47.55) = 557 man days

A3. Average wage income or cost per quintal of rope
= Rs 230 if managed by the household
= Rs 444.28 if rope making is hired out

A4. Wage income from one hectare of bhabbar grass activity = Rs 11,140

B1. Costs in rope making per quintal of rope
(a) Cost of bhabbar = Rs 57.14 (b) Imputed capital charges = Rs 1.00 approx. Total: Rs 58.14 per quintal

B2. Wage income as shown in A3

B3. Profitability: Rs 161.86 per quintal of rope if managed by the household

B4. Profitability: Rs 7533 per hectare of bhabbar grass, if rope making is managed by the household

B5. Total income per  = wage income + profit income
quintal of rope    = Rs 230 + Rs 161.86 = Rs 391.86

With a yield of about 47.55 quintals of rope per hectare, the net income from this activity is of the order of Rs 18,000–19,000 per hectare.

---

## Income benefits of CPR based irrigation

Using the community based watershed development in the Nada and Sukhomajri villages, irrigation benefits are estimated which are attributable to the CPR linked agricultural activity: Essentially, the watershed development has added to the employment in agriculture and has changed crop productivities.

---

### Box 4.4: Irrigation Linked Employment and Income

**A. Employment potential per hectare per year:**

| | |
|---|---|
| i) Under rainfed agriculture: | 23 man days |
| ii) Under irrigated agriculture per hectare (additional): | 20 man days |
| iii) Additional time to be spent on irrigation management: | 4 days |
| iv) Employment per hectare total: | 47 man days |
| v) Employment per hectare incremental: 47–23 = | 24 man days |
| vi) Maintenance of irrigation system: | 34 man days |

**B. Yield Benefit Per Hectare:**

i) Yield rates before irrigation: Wheat—9 quintals per hectare;
   Maize—8 quintals per hectare
ii) Yield rates after irrigation:  Wheat—20 quintals per hectare;
   Maize—12 quintals per hectare

**C.** i) **Employment Potential in Dam Construction:** 247 man days per hectare metre of water storage capacity.

ii) Water conveyance system: 77 man days per hectare of command area

---

## Employment and Income Changes from CPR–PPR Based Dairying

Once again the data and information from Sukhomajri–Nada are used here. With stall feeding in practice, and community protected grazing lands, the livestock population could increase, as much as an increase in milk yield due to better water and fodder availability. An account of income and employment changes attributable to this CPR linked dairying is discussed.

As a consequence of the preservation of respective watersheds and the introduction of the institution of stall feeding the economics of, cattle rearing activity underwent a change in both the villages. The yield of fodder grass per hectare of forest land increased to above 10 quintals. Composition of cattle population changed (both quantitatively and qualitatively), more so in Sukhomajri, where the institution of stall feeding came to be established on a more permanent basis. Cows were replaced by buffaloes and a net surplus of milk and milk products emerged in Sukhomajri for marketing, whereas they were just enough to sustain local consumption in Nada. This was, in part, due to CPR resource endowments. Forest area per head of cattle was 2.62 hectares in Sukhomajri as against 1.1 in Nada. An increase in employment took place in both situations. The components of this increase are indicated in Box 4.5.

---

**Box 4.5: Employment Implications of Dairying Activity**

A. Stall feeding:
7 person days of labour time additionally required annually per hectare of forestland. This labour time also reduces time for fuel collection, as dung collected can be converted into dung cakes.

B. Changed composition of animal population:
Increase of one standard unit per hectare: 708.1 person days of labour time for rearing, milching, and sale of milk products.
Animal population stabilized at 2.6 per hectare of forest land required annually (for rearing, milching, and sale) : This amounts to 1841.06 person days of labour time per year.

C. One time initial employment:
708.1 person days per hectare for building cattle shed etc.

---

CPR–LIVELIHOOD LINKAGES

One of the most commonly talked hypotheses is about the linkage between CPRs and livelihood. The starting point, once again, is sustainable development. In this context, how should CPRs be viewed? Two distinct types of CPR–livelihood linkages can be recognized here. The first is at the level of the present generation to meet its basic needs, dignity, and quality of life. The second is over generations, on sustenance of livelihood with resilience, equity, and growth. In other words, going by the characterization, sustainable development is required to maintain CPRs in the interest of all sections of the present day society and the generations to come. It is this 'livelihood sustenance' which alone can act as a catalyst in maintaining CPRs as a production complement to PPRs in rural settings and not the other way round.

Talking of the livelihood and equity of the current generation, there is a revealing linkage between CPRs and the poor in India. Poor people often significantly depend upon the products of CPRs. Good examples are collection of fuelwood, fodder, and NTFPs, water (mainly public) and even public utilities such as public toilets and bathing places. The poor are not only the beneficiaries of CPRs but are also the providers of inputs such as local knowledge and community labour. According to Jodha (1986) about 30 per cent of landless labour and small farmers in Rajasthan consume only CPR food items. In Madhya Pradesh this dependency is 50 per cent. In Rajasthan, about 42 per cent of households' income is derived from CPRs only. According to him, about 80 per cent of rural poor depend on CPRs for food and almost 100 per cent for fuel, fodder, and fibre. Jodha also finds that in the case of small farmers (land holding less than 2 hectares), in absence of common pool resources to support livestock, 48 to 55 per cent of crop lands will have to be diverted to fodder crops, with an accompanying 68 to 76 per cent loss of draught power and a 35 to 43 per cent fall in available farmyard manure. The same has also been seen at the all-India level from NSS data (presented in Chapter 3) on annual consumption expenditure and collection and consumption of CPR products.[10]

As far as development is concerned, according to the World Resources Institute (1990), nearly 500 million people in India depend upon on NTFPs for their livelihood. The collection of NTFPs generates about 1063 million man days of employment in India (Khare et al., 2000). In other words, CPRs provide a significant component of income and growth for the masses.

Finally, CPRs provide livelihood support and resilience when regular crop or other forms of income fail to materialize (due to droughts, floods, earthquakes, or other natural calamities). During the periods of major droughts, the poor tribals of Chhotanagpur plateau depend on local roots and tubers (locally called *ghitti*, a CPR product) grown in the forests and survive. During the 1987–8 drought, grasslands (and not crop residues) saved millions of livestock in India. The livelihood link between CPRs and the people is much more fundamental and often non-substitutable than the production linkages between common and private resources. Unlike the production linkage between them (as discussed in the sections entitled 'CPR–PPR Linkage' and 'A Model of CPR–PPR Linkage...'), the poor have a higher degree of dependency upon CPR to meet their minimum needs. These resources provide the basic needs such as fuel, fodder, fallback livelihood, and a certain degree of social security.

Because of the nature as direct or home-grown or collected consumption and income in kind, CPR products enjoyed by the rural poor do not show up in their incomes. However, if one accounts for these, they amount to a significant portion of the incomes and consumptions, thereby making their livelihood income respectable.

[10]A number of tables in Chapter 3 substantiate this.

Among the rural population, therefore, the actual disparity in consumption is much less than that reflected in the official statistics of income and consumption.[11] Jodha (1994, p. 341) writes:

Certain inferences can be drawn from this table (reproduced here as Table 4.3). The rural poor receive the bulk of their fuel supplies and fodder from the commons, which make them important sources of employment and income, especially when other opportunities are non-existent. Income from common lands is likely to be significantly underestimated. Nevertheless, products of the commons account for 14 to 23 per cent of household income .....More importantly, if income from the commons is included in total household income, the gap between the rich and the poor groups is reduced.

Jodha also lists a large number of possible links between CPR and livelihood, at the all-India level. Apart from livelihood requirements such as food, fodder, and fuel etc. he also lists the gains from CPRs and the ecological benefits from protecting them (Table 4.3).

What if the livelihood is not to be derived from CPRs? Associated is the question on the extent of pressure from population growth in a CPR dependent region. Situations of this kind are quite normal in high CPR dependent regions such as Rajasthan. Chopra and Gulati (2001) show that both population pressure and non-availability of CPRs lead to reduced carrying capacity of the CPRs. This in turn leads to either permanent out–migration or seasonal migration.

The second type of livelihood linkage is over generations. Several scholars have looked into the inter-generational aspects of resource management (Hartwick, 1977; Howarth and Norgaard, 1992). From the Indian perspective and experience, it is generally found that the elder generation in a village society takes more interest in managing the village CPRs (say, common lands, water tanks, forests, etc.), sometimes with marginal support from the younger generations.[12] The specific livelihood related question is about the relative pay-offs to the younger and older generations, so as to make the whole village economy manage the CPRs as the most relevant resource .

[11]This fact is also revealed through various NSS surveys on consumer expenditures, already discussed in Chapter 3.

[12]This observation is purely empirical. The reasons may be many. First, younger people in general, have very little exposure to or idea about the role and relevance of

Table 4.3
Contribution of Common Pool Resources to Livelihoods

| Contribution | Collectively Managed Common Pool Resources | | | | | |
|---|---|---|---|---|---|---|
| | Community forest | Pasture/ wasteland | Ponds/ tanks | River | Watershed drainaged | River/ tank beds |
| **Physical Products** | | | | | | |
| Food/fibre | ✓ | | ✓ | ✓ | | ✓ |
| Fodder/fuel/timber | ✓ | ✓ | ✓ | | | ✓ |
| Water | | | | ✓ | ✓ | |
| Manure/silt | ✓ | | ✓ | | ✓ | ✓ |
| **Income and employment gains** | | | | | | |
| Off-season activities | ✓ | | | | ✓ | ✓ |
| Drought period sustenance | ✓ | ✓ | | ✓ | | ✓ |
| Additional crop activities | | | | | ✓ | ✓ |
| Additional animals | | | | | | ✓ |
| Petty trading and handicrafts | | | | | | ✓ |
| **Larger social/ ecological gains** | | | | | | |
| Resource conservation | ✓ | | ✓ | | | |
| Drainage/recharge ground water | | | ✓ | ✓ | ✓ | |
| Sustainability of farming systems | ✓ | | ✓ | ✓ | | ✓ |
| Renewable resource supply | ✓ | | ✓ | ✓ | | |
| Better micro-climate, environment | ✓ | | ✓ | ✓ | | |

Source: Jodha (1992).

We analyse this inter-generational livelihood sustainability with a model. Consider a village economy with a mix of two generations of people, broadly termed as 'younger ones' and 'elders'. The resources of the village are grouped broadly as PPRs and CPRs. Today's elders were

CPRs and indigenous knowledge. Second, they always look for more and more wage employment.

Table 4.4

Extent of Dependence on CPRs in Dry Regions

| No. of districts and villages by state | Household by income categories[b] | Fuel[c] (%) | Animal grazing | Employment[e] days | Annual income[f] (Rs) | Per cent income from CPRs | Gini coefficient on income from[g] All sources | All sources except CPRs(%) |
|---|---|---|---|---|---|---|---|---|
| Andhra Pradesh | Poor | 84 | – | 139 | 534 | 17 | 0.41 | 0.50 |
| | Others | 13 | – | 35 | 62 | 1 | 0.41 | 0.50 |
| Gujarat | Poor | 66 | 82 | 196 | 774 | 18 | 0.33 | 0.45 |
| | Others | 8 | 14 | 80 | 185 | 1 | 0.33 | 0.45 |
| Karnataka | Poor | – | 83 | 185 | 649 | 20 | – | – |
| | Others | – | 29 | 34 | 170 | 3 | – | – |
| Madhya Pradesh | Poor | 74 | 79 | 183 | 733 | 22 | 0.34 | 0.44 |
| | Others | 32 | 34 | 52 | 386 | 2 | 0.34 | 0.44 |
| Maharashtra | Poor | 75 | 69 | 128 | 557 | 14 | 0.40 | 0.48 |
| | Others | 12 | 27 | 43 | 177 | 1 | 0.40 | 0.48 |
| Rajasthan | Poor | 71 | 84 | 165 | 770 | 23 | – | – |
| | Others | 23 | 38 | 61 | 413 | 2 | – | – |
| Tamil Nadu | Poor | – | – | 137 | 738 | 22 | – | – |
| | Others | – | – | 31 | 164 | 2 | – | – |

*Notes*: a. CPRs include community pasture, village forests, wasteland, watershed drainage, river and stream banks, and other common lands. Data indicate average area per village.

b. The number of sample households from each village varied from 20 to 36 in different districts. 'Poor' households are defined as agricultural labourers and small farmers (< 2 ha dry land equivalent). 'Others' includes large farm households only.

c. Fuel gathered from CPRs as proportion of total fuel used during three seasons covering the whole year.

(Contd.)

d. Grazing days per animal unit on CPRs as a percentage of total grazing days per animal unit.

e. Total employment from CPR product collection.

f. Income derived mainly from CPR product collection. The estimation procedure underestimated the actual income derived from CPRs.

g. A higher Gini coefficient indicates a higher degree of income inequality. Calculations are based on income data for 1983–4 from a panel of households covered under ICRISAT's village level studies (Walker and Ryan 1990). The panel of 40 households from each village included 10 households from each of the categories, namely large, medium, and small farm households, and labourer households.

*Source:* Jodha (1986).

the younger ones in an earlier time block (say, twenty years ago). Two specific questions are raised here. First, with a view of inter-generational and inter-temporal sustainability, how are the income and consumption streams of the elders and the younger ones related? This is a question of livelihood sustainability. Second, what could be the rate and range of population growth that can be sustained, given the CPR–PPR linked production technology? This is a question of inter-generational carrying capacity.

Let the common and private resources be denoted by R and P, respectively. The young and elder population classes are denoted by y and e, respectively and the corresponding available labour force or time are denoted by $L_y$ and $L_e$. The total output of the village economy, Q, is assumed to depend upon both types of resources, and the two kinds of labour force. The younger people earn wage income either within the village or by working on their own PPRs, or earn wage income outside the village. The elders are assumed to refrain from being in the active wage-based labour market, but are more dedicated to looking after CPRs. Their labour time is spent in looking after their village CPRs, ensuring participation, proper distribution, co-operation, and enforcement of rules of CPR management. Their labour time should in fact be called 'participatory labour' (Chopra and Kadekodi, 1991).

The output of the village is presented in Equation 4.1. It suggests that both PPR and CPR together with the young labour force produce the village output; whereas the elders' participatory labour input is complementary to CPR maintenance and management.

$$Q = f\left(P, R, L_y; L_e\right) \qquad \qquad ... (4.1)$$

The output is distributed as returns to the two resources and as wage payment to the young labour force. The young ones, having the option of working either within the village or outside, expect a wage rate of w. The elders' time spent in the management of CPRs is rewarded in the form of royalty or welfare payments. Such payments are related to the level of CPR activities (in addition to any other welfare benefits such as pension which they may enjoy). Let $r_e$ be the welfare or royalty payment per unit of CPR and r be the rate of return per unit of PPR. Assuming that the returns or incomes from PPR are shared between the young and elderly population according to their size, the income shares of the two groups are specified as:

Income of younger generation: $Y_y = w. L_y + \alpha. r. P$        ... (4.2)

Income of elders: $Y_e = r_e. R + (1-\alpha). r. P$        ... (4.3)

where $\alpha = \dfrac{L_y}{(L_y + L_e)}$ :proportion of youth population.

In other words, the younger generation earns both a wage income and a share of incomes from PPRs. Apart from their share of the income from PPRs, the elders receive a royalty or welfare income for looking after the CPRs. To keep the model simple, it is further assumed that the rural folk spend their entire income on consumption, denoted as $C_e$ and $C_y$.[13] Implicitly this also means that the resources do not depreciate and no investments are made out of village PPR and CPR related incomes.

Now, population changes are introduced in the village situation, to make the inter-generational livelihood question more explicit. For this, some simplifying assumptions are made. Today's elders are treated as the same as last period's younger generation. Therefore, the only change in population is because of changes in younger generation (due to births). The population change is, therefore, linked only to the younger generations in two periods, with a net growth rate of n.

$$L_y(t) = (1+n). L_y (t-1); L_e (t) = L_y (t-1)        ... (4.4)$$

The dynamics of population is therefore obtained as:

$$L(t) = L_y (t) + L_e (t) = (2+n). L_y (t-1)        ... (4.5)$$

The value of $\alpha$ (in Equation 4.3) then becomes equal to $\dfrac{(1+n)}{(2+n)}$.

The livelihood sustainability condition is the most difficult to define. To begin with, two operational conditions are conceived. First, on equity grounds, per capita consumption of the overlapping young and elder population groups is equal in each period. Second, a more

---

[13]This is not too unrealistic as most of the farm and dairying incomes are consumed directly at home. Savings, if any, emerge out of non-farm incomes including incomes earned outside the village.

ambitious condition would be that the per capita consumption of the elders today be equal to their consumption rate when they were young. These two conditions will be denoted as weak and strong livelihood conditions, respectively. They are stated mathematically as:

$$\frac{C_y(t)}{L_y(t)} = \frac{C_e(t)}{L_y(t-1)} \quad \text{:Weak sustainability} \qquad \dots (4.6)$$

$$\frac{C_e(t)}{L_y(t-1)} = \frac{C_y(t-1)}{L_y(t-1)} \quad \text{:Strong sustainability} \qquad \dots (4.7)$$

The implications of weak sustainability (Equation 4.6) are evaluated first. The question before us is about distribution and sharing rules so as to fulfil this sustainability condition. Using the definitions of incomes and consumptions (Equations 4.2 and 4.3) and the population factors (Equations 4.4 and 4.5), one can show that the weak sustainability condition requires that:

$$r_e(t).R = w(t).L_y(t-1) \qquad \dots (4.8)$$

Two important policy implications follow from the Expression (4.8): first, welfare income earned by the elders from CPR management today should be the same as their wage income when they were young (or equal to wage income that they would have continued to earn, had they also been in the current potential labour force). Given the fact that incomes from PPR are shared according to the respective population sizes, the weak sustainability condition in Equation 4.8 will ensure equality of consumption between the younger and elder groups. Second, since the population of the younger group is itself growing at a rate 'n', the above also implies that over time the wage/royalty ratio will have to be adjusted downwards at the rate -n (unless the CPR gets augmented at the same rate as n).[14] This sets the limits and ranges for the distribution parameters $r_e$ and w. Only under the conditions of zero population growth (that is, n = 0) would the wage/royalty ratio remain constant, which incidentally is the condition of stationarity.

Now we take up the strong sustainability condition 4.7. Applying Expressions (4.2) and (4.3) with appropriate two time blocks, Differential Equation (4.9) is satisfied.

[14]Assuming R to remain constant, this is implied by the time rate of change of $w/r_e$.

$$r_e(t).R - w(t-1).L_y(t-1) = \frac{P}{(2+n)\left[(1+n).r(t-1)-r(t)\right]} \quad \dots (4.9)$$

Among the many possible solutions, the one of interest is the case corresponding to the weak sustainability condition.

Common property resource based welfare income of the elders today (that is, $r_e(t)$. R) would remain the same as their wage income when they were young in the previous time block (that is, $w(t-1)$. $L_y(t-1)$), provided the (4.10) holds:

$$r(t) = r(t-1).(1+n) \qquad \dots (4.10)$$

In other words, the rate of return on PPRs over time should grow at the same rate as the youth population. It further implies that the PPR based income of the elders today should be the same as their PPR based income when they were young.[15] The implications of this strong sustainability condition are rather rigid. Not only do the returns from PPRs over time have to grow (at the rate n), the wage/royalty ratio $\left(\dfrac{W(t-1)}{r_e(t)}\right)$ has to decline at the rate n (unless the CPR is augmented at the rate n). In any case, the stationary conditions of constant rates of return on PPR, CPR, and the wage rate would hold if the population growth rate is zero. The relevance of such a model for the Indian situation is demonstrated in the next section.

A CASE STUDY ON CPR–LIVELIHOOD LINKAGE AND INTER-GENERATIONAL EQUITY

Are there any real life situations in India with such a CPR management, strongly linked to inter-generational livelihood balance and equity? Let us take a look at the case of Sukhomajri village along with few other villages with varying degree of CPR–PPR and livelihood linkages in Haryana (Chopra *et. al*, 1990). The details of this case study are given in Chapter 9. The story of these villages as a case of participatory development is not repeated here, except to mention that a large number of CPR developmental activities have been undertaken in Sukhomajri and other adjacent villages (with varying degrees of success).

[15]This follows from the definition of $\alpha$ and $(1-\alpha)$.

Coming to the issue of livelihood, a crucial question is on  the agreement on the division of household labour between household PPR based activities (say, in livestock rearing and land related activity) and CPR conservation and management. As far as CPR management is concerned, one member from each family (by and large the elders, and often some women), took responsibility for looking after the village nursery; supervising forest protection, stall feeding, organizing community grass cutting, collecting fuelwood, and so on. The younger generation took the main responsibility for crop agriculture, dairying, and marketing. Over the years, a large number of villages have taken to this new institution of linking PPR–CPR with community participation.

The livelihood conditions of three of those villages, namely Sukhomajri, Jattanmajri, and Dhamala in Haryana, have shown a high degree of resource linkages. These villages shall be called 'participatory'. For purposes of comparison, two villages that have not moved in this direction, namely Prempura and Tanda, are also looked. They will be called 'non-participatory'. Tables 4.5 to 4.7 show various attributes of these villages.[16]

Some of the major observations based on these tables (and many more contained in Chopra *et al.* 1990) can be made on the villages with better CPR management linked with private resources.

1. Livestock population has increased in the villages  with better CPR–PPR linkages. Increased availability of fodder has led to greater income from dairying.

2. Soil erosion has come down significantly in villages that opted for stall feeding.

3. Land productivity has gone up with increased water supply that is equitably distributed.

4. Fuelwood availability has increased significantly and the forest cover has improved with higher survival rates.

5. Livelihood gains differ between villages depending on the degree of CPR–PPR linkage, and demographic structure (composition of elderly and younger population, growth rate, etc.).

Over the years it has been observed in the participatory villages that the elderly population alone is taking the prime interest and

[16]For details of ecological and environmental changes, see Chapter 9 of this book, and Chopra *et al.* (1990).

responsibility in the management of CPRs. They are generally unemployed or perform low key tasks within the households. The younger people on the other hand, either work on household private resources or seek wage employment elsewhere (mainly in Chandigarh). This division of labour and responsibility for resource management has implications for their livelihood conditions.

There is an overlap of elderly and younger population in each of these villages. Given the fact that they have different abilities and preferences, the experience from these villages suggests that private and common resources can be better managed by taking advantage of this overlap of two generations. The sharing of incomes or returns from the two types of resources should be worked out to keep the consumption rates balanced between the young and old. Such a management system can lead to livelihood sustainability. Table 4.7 shows the components of income streams for younger generation in terms of wage incomes, share in PPR income as well as the elders' income from CPR management in the three participatory villages.

Validation of even a simplified theoretical model is not easy.[17] The royalty or welfare income from CPRs is imputed as savings from the costs of fodder purchase (attributed to better forest management) plus imputed value of manure (attributed to stall feeding of animals), plus value of incremental fuelwood. The returns on private resources comprise crop and dairy net incomes. The wage income is defined as the total for 60 days of agricultural and other tasks at a wage rate of Rs 25 per day. Major observations on these estimates are:

1. The return from CPRs to the elder generation is just about half of the wage income of younger generation. Therefore, unless some more CPR based activities are linked with income generation (such as rope making with bhabbar grass), conflicts and social tensions within village societies may arise. The elders may refuse to look after the CPRs and the younger generation may not be interested in their management at all.

---

[17]The model developed here assumes no capital depreciation and no capital formation out of income from PPRs referred here (such as land, livestock etc.). Moreover, no discounting is used between the two time periods for any generation. But as argued by Howarth (1991), such simplifications do not bias the conclusion from the model. Rather, a zero discount rate is justifiable in inter-generation terms, but not necessarily for the same generation.

Table 4.5
CPR–PPR Resource Dimensions in Five Villages

| | Unit | Sukhomajri | Jattan Majri | Dhamala | Prem Pura | Tanda |
|---|---|---|---|---|---|---|
| **Private Property Resources** | | | | | | |
| Total cultivated land | Acres | 109.80 | 66.40 | 100.60 | 24.60 | 39.20 |
| Av. size of operational holding | Acres /hh | 1.34 (116) | 1.66 (106) | 1.48 (155) | 0.88 (119) | 0.67 (96) |
| HHs owning land | % | 90.40 | 62.30 | 41.20 | 75.00 | 77.60 |
| Buffaloes | 1977 | 136 | 82 | 111 | NA | NA |
| | 1986 | 182 | 116 | 161 | 18 | 67 |
| Cows | 1977 | 28 | 2 | 21 | NA | NA |
| | 1986 | 6 | 2 | 12 | 26 | 23 |
| Goats | 1977 | 89 | 2 | NA | NA | NA |
| | 1986 | 10 | 2 | 5 | 0 | 0 |
| Draught Animals | 1986 | 89 | 37 | 44 | 29 | 62 |
| Av. No. of Milch Animals | No./hh | 2.32 | 2.95 | 2.16 | 1.54 | 2.06 |
| HHs owning Milch Cattle | % | 94 | 90 | 74 | 93 | 90 |
| Workforce working outside the village | % | 32 | 19 | 25 | 29 | 31 |
| Total workforce | No. | 321 | 200 | 305 | 112 | 172 |
| **Common Property Resources** | | | | | | |
| Forest Land | Acres | 1219 | 597 | 517 | NA | NA |
| Storage Capacity of Irr. Tanks | Ha. Mt. | 9.16 | 3.96 | 6.67 | 0 | 0 |
| Command Area | Acres | 92.70 | 59.30 | 131.00 | 0 | 0 |

*Notes*: NA=not available; HH=household; Irr.=irrigation; Av.=average.
*Source*: Kadekodi, 1995.

2. Per capita returns from CPRs are comparable to those from private resources. This indicates that both PPR and CPR management are equally important in the context of village development.

3. The wage income within village is quite low as compared to income earned outside the village. Therefore, there are strong possibilities of migration of the young workforce, the leaving the management of both types of resources only to the elders. Such a tendency will have effects on the livelihood sustainability in the long run. Therefore, it is extremely important to maintain a balance

Table 4.6
Resource Linkages and Livelihood Conditions

| | Units | Sukhomajri | Jattamajri | Dhamala | Prempura | Tanda |
|---|---|---|---|---|---|---|
| **CPR–PPR Linkages** | | | | | | |
| Operational Holdings | % | 23.60 (129) | 2.50 (275) | 12.10 (191) | 0 | 0 |
| Irrigated by CPR Tanks | | | | | | |
| HHs receiving irr. from CPR tanks | % | 49 | 8 | 22 | 0 | 0 |
| Fodder from CPR forests | Kg./animal/day | 29.70 (66) | 20.00 (41) | 13.40 (67) | 19.80 | 21.00 |
| **Average Income Flows Attributable to CPR–PPR Linkages** | | | | | | |
| Income from operational holdings | Rs/acre | 2604 | 2050 | 1205 | 962 | 1849 |
| Dairy income | Rs/animal | 961 (73) | 762 (144) | 968 (114) | 374 (246) | 186 (314) |
| Income from rope making | Rs/hh | 0 | 0 | 0 | 2353 | 1891 |
| HH Income Total | Rs | 16,370 | 28,329 | 14,700 | 7454 | 5928 |
| Within village | Rs | 6138 | 17,695 | 4376 | 2659 | 2625 |
| Outside village | Rs | 10,232 | 10,634 | 10,324 | 4795 | 3303 |
| **Average Consumption out of all Income** | | | | | | |
| Food consumption | Rs/per cap | 2552 (34) | 2542 (29) | 2285 (40) | 2001 (43) | 2606 (29) |
| Fuelwood consumption | Rs/hh | 1247 (164) | 1451 (43) | 1036 (53) | 805 (92) | 798 (97) |

*Notes:* HH = household; cap. = capita; numbers in brackets are coefficients of variation
*Source:* Kadekodi; (1995).

118

Table 4.7
Implications for Sustainable Livelihood

|  | Units | Sukhomajri | Jattanmajri | Dhamala |
|---|---|---|---|---|
| PPR returns per workforce | Rs | 926 | 515 | 566 |
| CPR income per elder (=participating labour) | Rs | 685 | 916 | 507 |
| Wage income per workforce working on PPR (60 days*Rs 25 per day). | Rs | 1500 | 1500 | 1500 |

Notes: PPR returns=crop income + income from dairying-wage income of 50% of within village workforce.
CPR income=savings in fodder value from market purchase +value of organic manure attributed to stall feeding+ value of incremental fuelwood availability.
Participating labour=village total at the rate of one member per household.
Source: Kadekodi, (1995).

between incomes within and outside the village and between returns from CPRs that accrue to the elders and wage incomes to younger people.

Thus, models and case studies such as this ascertain the view that CPR management should be an integral long-term developmental strategy for raising income, employment, livelihood, and ecological sustenance.

On Sustainable Harvesting and Carrying Capacity of CPRs

Sustainability of CPRs is generally viewed on different theoretical platforms, first as a static situation, second as a dynamic situation, and third as an inter-generational issue.[18] The theoretical discussion is generally centered around 'looking for the amount of inputs or efforts to be used to extract the resource on a sustainable basis'. For example, how many fishermen should go for fishing in a particular water body such as a lake, or how much grazing land be devoted to raising fodder grass, or how many households should take up NTFP collection from a protected forest? All these are questions of sustainability of the resources. Any violation of these sustainability rates will amount to over or under exploitation harvesting of the resources.

[18]The inter-generational issues have already been referred and dealt with in the Sections 'CPR–livelihood Linkages' and 'A case study on CPR–livelihood linkage and inter-generational equity'.

To understand the conceptual framework, consider the example of fishing from a lake or a coastal zone. In this situation, the efforts can be measured in terms of the number of fishermen who go for fishing (or in terms of fishing hours). Let E stand for such a measure of efforts. Against this effort, the yield or harvest rate of fish is symbolically designated by Y. The stock of fishery resource, measured at any point of time is X. This stock of fish is subjected to two factors of change. First, there is the net growth of fish (positive by hatching and negative by natural death) in the absence of any fishing from the reservoir of fish. Let this growth rate be designated by G. Let the price of fish be a constant 'p' per unit, and the cost of a unit of effort be a constant 'c'. An example can be that of the wage rate of one person-power going for fishing (either actual or an opportunity cost).

How are the yields, growth rates, efforts, stock of fish, costs, and prices related? This question is first examined under a static model or condition. The static model of fishery economics was first examined in a systematic manner by Gordon (1954), followed by Anderson (1977), Dasgupta (1982), Conrad (1999), and several others. Let the net growth of fish G, depend upon the population or the stock X itself, which is a reasonable assumption to make. The most probable shape of the relationship is shown in Figure 4.6. It will rise till some increasing level of the stock of fish, beyond which the growth rate will decline. The reasons for such a shape are many. Basically, while the multiplication of fish stock depends upon the fish population size X, at a later stage, overpopulation may even become a curse for the growth, due to shortage of eutrophication (that is, nutrition) and oxygen, crowding and diseases, self-killing and preying by other aquatic animals and so on. Likewise, the yield of fish Y from catch is shown in Figure 4.6 as a function of efforts E. As E increases, the yield rate Y increases at a decreasing rate; ultimately, it also becomes a declining one. The declining yield rate is due to, once again, crowding and hence the emergence of negative externality, unfair exploitation, and so on. Finally, the yield rate Y itself depends positively upon the stock of fish X. As shown in Figure 4.6, the deduced relation between the efforts E and the growth rate is also a bell shaped curve. These are stated mathematically as:

1. $Y = H(X, E)$: Yield is a function of stock and efforts;

$$\frac{\partial H}{\partial X} > 0; \frac{\partial H}{\partial E} > 0 \text{ up to } E^*, \ < 0 \text{ after } E^*$$

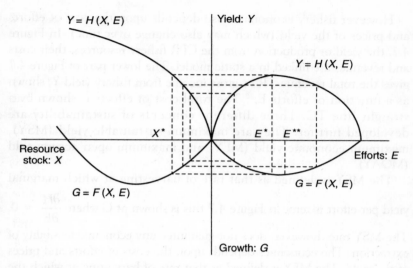

**Figure 4.6:** Linkage between Efforts, CPR Stock, Yield, and Growth

2. $G = F(X)$: Net growth is a function of stock of fish;

$G'(X) > 0$ up to $\chi^*$, $< 0$ after $\chi^*$

3. $G = B(E)$: Growth rate is a function of efforts:

$B'(E) > 0$ up to $E^{**}$; $< 0$ beyond $E^{**}$. Or the growth can be re-specified as $G = M(X, E)$

4. The changing stock of fish between two consecutive time periods can be now expressed as:

$x_{t+2} - X_t = M(X, E) - H(X, E)$: The change in stock depends upon both growth and yield rates. $X_0$ and $E_0$ are known.

If the functional specifications on M and H are made, the long-term implications of this fishery situation can be simulated. Under a condition of 'steady state' when the stock would remain the same (that is, the change in stock is zero), the net growth rate and yield or harvest rate should be equal. This condition itself can be defined as a steady state which is sustainable.[19]

---

[19]Equality of growth and yield rates is only the necessary condition, but it does not necessarily ensure a steady state. Because of this, such an equality may be one of low level or high level of stock equilibrium.

However fishery economics also depends upon the cost of efforts and prices of the yield (which may also change over time). In Figure 4.7, the yield or production from the CPR fishery resources, their costs and revenues are linked in a static model. The lower part of Figure 4.7 gives the total revenue TR or gross income from fishery yield Y, shown as a function of efforts E.[20] The total cost of efforts is shown by a straight line TC. Three different concepts of sustainability are developed further. They are maximum sustainable yield (MSY), maximum economic yield (MEY) and maximum open access yield (MOAY).

The MSY is defined as that rate of harvesting at which marginal yield per effort is zero. In Figure 4.7 this is shown at C when $\frac{\partial H}{\partial E} = 0$.

The MSY rate, however, does not guarantee any economic feasibility of extraction. The economics depends upon the costs of efforts and prices of the yield. The MEY is defined as that rate of harvesting at which the marginal revenue is equal to the marginal cost. In Figure 4.7 this occurs at K, when $\frac{\partial TR}{\partial E} = \frac{\partial TC}{\partial E}$. At this yield or harvest rate the total profit or net gain KP is maximum. Finally, the MOAY is that rate of harvesting at which total revenue is equal to total cost, or at which the net revenue or gain is zero. In Figure 4.7 this is shown at effort $E_{MOAY}$ and the corresponding yield rate is shown at Q.[21] Gordon (1954) calls this equilibrium as a binomic equilibrium. Generally, the MEY is lowest, and MOAY is the highest, with MSY falling in between.[22]

However, it is more important to look at the dynamics of CPR resource change. How will the stocks of resources change over time due to growth and harvest rates? One can visualize the reality that both the stock of fishery resources and the amount of efforts (say, in terms of number of families engaged in fishing) would change from

[20]Since the price of fish is assumed to be a constant, its shape will be the same as the yield function.

[21]This, however, depends upon the assumptions regarding the stock. If the total stock itself is exhausted prior to X then the MOAY will be lower, bounded by the total stock of the resource.

[22]This follows from the second order condition of optimality that the marginal revenue curve should intersect the marginal cost from above.

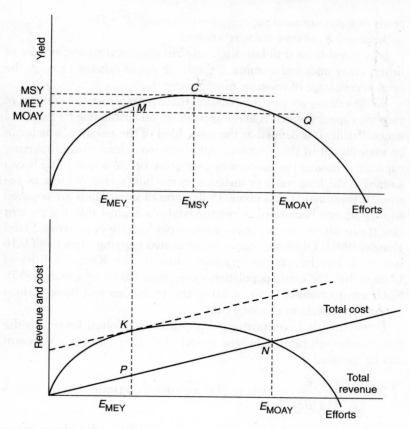

**Figure 4.7:** CPR Sustainability

time to time. Figure 4.7 shows that changes in efforts would change the yield or harvest rates. This in turn would change the stock of the resource. With a change in the stock of fish, the yield rates would change again and so on. The efforts are dependent upon the rate of net gain or profitability in fishing. The changes in the stock of the resource and the response in terms of efforts can be stated as being dynamically determined by the following equations.

1. $X_{t+1} - X_t = M(X, E)_t - H(X, E)_t$: The change in stock depends upon both growth and yield rates.

2. $E_{t+1} - E_t = \theta.\{p.H(X,E) - c.E_t\}$ : Efforts will be enhanced if the

profit or gains are positive; negative otherwise; $\theta > 0$.

3. $E_0$ and $X_0$ at time zero are known.

It is possible to simulate such an interlinked dynamic system of fishery economics and examine if the stock would exhaust to reach the open access stage of resource management.[23]

While talking about sustainability, there is an associated concept of carrying capacity which is also important in understanding CPR related issues. Briefly, it is defined as the stock level of the resource, which can be maintained in the long run. An alternative definition of carrying capacity is linking the amount of extraction or use a unit of CPR can sustain in the long run. For instance, in the hilly region of Uttaranchal state, it is estimated that about 15 hectares of forest lands are required to support one hectare of cultivated land. As against this, the present rate is just about two hectares of forest per hectare of cultivated land (Singh, 1992). Likewise, against an estimated carrying capacity of 0.16 livestock per hectare of grazing lands in the Kumaon hills of Uttaranchal, the cattle population varies from 1.6 to 3.3 (Shah, 1985). Such unsustainable rates of using the resources will have serious externality effects in the long run.

Usually, with a constant growth rate $G = r$ (often known as the intrinsic growth rate), a logistic model of CPR resource stock growth can be specified as:

$$X(t) = \frac{K}{\left\{1 + \beta e^{-rt}\right\}}, \text{ where } \beta \text{ is a positive constant. Under such a}$$

specification, one can see that as $t \to \infty$, $X(t) \to K$, which is the carrying capacity of the resource. Using such specifications, it may be possible to estimate the carrying capacities for CPRs such as grazing lands, marine fishery, NTFP collection, etc.

## A CASE STUDY OF ESTIMATING SUSTAINABLE RATES OF FISHING FROM KARNATAKA

Marine fishery resources are quite important for all coastal states in India. As reviewed in Chapter 3, India produces about 2700 million

---

[23]There are also other alternative ways of setting up the dynamic model, with certain optimization rules such as inter-temporal discounted profit maximization.

tonnes of marine fish products, of which about 6 per cent comes from Karnataka's coastal zones. Marine fishery is permitted in the EEZ of 200 nautical miles on all Indian coasts.[24] Karnataka is known for very rich marine biodiversity. It is estimated that around 310 different marine fish species are available in the coastal waters of Karnataka apart from other migratory aquatic animals. During 1998–9, the total fish production was 160,000 tonnes with a catchable potential of 270,000 tonnes and with a continental shelf of 27,000 sq. km.

From a list of species mentioned as commercially important by the Working Group of the Government of India, only certain species were selected for this case study from Karnataka. The selected species constituted 60 per cent of the total landings in 1998. Although laws in Karnataka provide for regulating open access fishery, the enforcement has been inadequate. Hence there are possibilities of over exploitation of certain species of fish. It is equally likely that some species remain under exploited as the fishing effort might be focussed on a few commercial species only.

Harvesting of marine resources depends upon the number of fishermen on the job and the number of fishing nets (normally called gears) and boats (commonly called as crafts). Bhatta and Bhat (2001) have made an attempt to estimate the MSY and MEY and compare them with the actual catch or landings for different species of fish for the year 1998.

In order to understand and estimate the sustainable rates of fish catch and the extent of over or under extraction, a modified version of Schaefer's model (Conrad and Clark, 1987) is used in this case study. A logarithmic relationship between catch per unit effort (Y/E) and fishing effort (E) is formulated as:

$$\ln\left(\frac{Y}{E}\right) = a + bE,$$ where $Y$ is total annual catch; $E$ annual fishing

effort; and $a$ and $b$ are constant parameters. The same can be re-written as: $Y = Ee^{a+bE}$.

Then (as explained in the previous section) the MSY and the effort

<hr>

[24]Ecologically speaking, 90 per cent of marine fishery resources are found in this EEZ only. This is mainly due to the availability of food and nutrition, conducive temperatures and vegetation.

corresponding to the MSY that is, $E_{MSY}$ are obtained as:

$$E_{MSY} = -\frac{1}{b}; \quad MSY = -\frac{1}{b}\left[e^{(a-1)}\right]$$

The estimation of MEY requires a little more complex modelling. A simple economic model introduced by Gordon (1954) is quite handy for this purpose. To begin with, in this model, fishery input and output values are expressed in terms of total cost and total revenue and as functions of the fishing effort. The total cost consists of two parts, fixed and variable costs of fishing effort. The fixed costs consist of costs required before any direct fishing effort is made. The variable costs consist of all the costs required directly to operate the fishing effort such as fuel, food, and labour. It is assumed that the per unit cost of fishing effort 'c' is constant. Hence, the relationship between the total cost and fishing effort would be linear. This means average and marginal cost would be identical.

The total cost of fishing (TC), marginal cost (MC), and average cost (AC) can be written as: $TC = cE$; $AC = MC = c$; where c is the cost of unit effort. Price in fishery economics can be considered either as fixed or variable depending on the type of product market. To keep the analysis simple and for want of better data, the output price (species wise) is assumed to be fixed. This assumption implies that fishermen in the study area are price takers and their supply will not affect the market price by any significant measure. Assuming a fixed price p, the total revenue (TR) and marginal revenue (MR) functions can be expressed as:

$$TR = pY = pEe^{(a+bE)}; \quad MR = p(bE+1)e^{(a+bE)}$$

The MEY occurs at the point of effort where the net profit from fishery is maximum. This happens when $MR = MC$. This implies that:

$$p(bE+1)e^{(a+bE)} = c$$

By further simplification, one can deduce the following:

$(bE+1)e^{bE} - \dfrac{c}{pe^a} = 0$. Using Newton's method of successive

approximations, an expression for the effort ($E_{MEY}$) and the corresponding MEY are obtained as:

$$E_{MEY} = \frac{1}{b}\left[-1 + \sqrt{\frac{c}{pe^a}}\right];$$

$$MEY = E_{MEY}e^{(a+bE_{MEY})}$$

Note that the MEY effort is generally lower than the MSY effort. On the other hand, the sustained stock associated with MEY is greater than the stock corresponding to MSY.

The next question is about estimating the stock of fish X. Here stocks are defined for each species with the same growth and mortality parameters. The historical and current stock estimates can serve as a benchmark for analysing the sustainability implications of current and future management policies. Though a large number of species exist in the coastal zone in Karnataka, only some species are of economic importance, and data are not available for all species. Therefore, only a selected few economically important species are considered here.

Following Conrad and Clark (1987), the annual harvest (yield) of a fishery can be expressed as a function of fishery effort (E) and stock (X) in each period. That is,

$Y = f(E, X)$; where Y and X are measured in the same unit. A stylized production function commonly used in the fishery literature is $Y = qEX$, where $q$ is the constant parameter, called catchability coefficient (Clark, 1985), representing the proportion of stock captured by unit effort. If the value of $q$ is known, with an initial period's annual catch Y and effort E, one can estimate the value of initial stock. Then for successive years, stock may be estimated using the dynamic equation of motion, $X_t = (1+\alpha)X_{t-1} - Y_{t-1}$

where $\alpha$ is the annual net biological growth parameter, and t is the time period.

The data for the description and modelling of Karnataka marine fisheries come from mainly two sources. The landings and effort data for the period 1994–8 were drawn from the Central Marine Fisheries Research Institute (CMFRI). The second set of data on costs and earnings, harvested price, labour share and income, and other economic parameters are based on a sample survey of the fishery vessels in coastal Karnataka, for two coastal districts namely, Dakshina Kannada and Udupi for the fishing season of 1999–2000. The costs of fishing trips, capital, and fixed costs of crafts and gear were compiled from 15–20 fishing units in each vessel class to estimate the economic efficiency of each selected vessel.

The model specified above has been estimated for a variety of fish species using regression techniques applied to time series data from 1990 to 1998.[25]

Table 4.8 shows the estimated parameters, cost and price norms used for the estimation of MSY and MEY. Table 4.9 shows the estimated sustainable yield rates, efforts, and the costs for a variety of selected fish species. There is significant over exploitation of species such as halibut, lizard fishes, pomfret, rays, sharks, soles, and thread fish beams. Additional sustainable yield potentials exist in respect of catfish and shrimps. Yield regulation through reduced number of fishing boats and gears are to be followed by entry tax and other such economic methods.

Table 4.8
Estimated Parameters of Yield Model, Average Cost/kg/effort
and Price/ kg of Demersal Species

| Species | Intercept (a) | Slope (b) | (R-square) | Catchability co-efficient | Cost/ kg/effort (in Rs) | Price per kg (in Rs) |
|---|---|---|---|---|---|---|
| Catfish | 6.55 | −0.00075 | 0.52 | 0.000131 | 9.32 | 17.85 |
| Halibut | 4.28 | −0.0005 | 0.20 | 0.000221 | 12.57 | 9 |
| Lizard fishes | 4.24 | −6.60E-06 | 0.28 | 7.56E-06 | 12.83 | 5 |
| Pomfret | 6.75 | −0.00012 | 0.57 | 1.95E-05 | 7.91 | 53.53 |
| Rays | 6.39 | −0.0004 | 0.68 | 0.000219 | 11.50 | 27.76 |
| Rock cods | 5.60 | −4.70E-05 | 0.50 | 3.93E-05 | 14.30 | 6 |
| Shark | 6.89 | −0.00048 | 0.71 | 0.000291 | 11.81 | 30.69 |
| Shrimp | 7.08 | −5.20E-05 | 0.78 | 4.06E-05 | 10.80 | 53.49 |
| Soles | 6.78 | −3.40E-05 | 0.67 | 1.36E-05 | 9.45 | 5.59 |
| Thread fish breams | 5.53 | −7.10E-06 | 0.52 | 7.6E-06 | 12.85 | 5 |

Source: Bhatta and Bhat (2001).

[25]For details of data, analysis and estimation see Bhatta and Bhat (2001).

Table 4.9

Yield and Effort at MSY and MEY Level, Cost at MSY, MEY of Selected Demersal Species in Karnataka

| Species | 1998 | | | MSY Level | | | ME Level | | |
|---|---|---|---|---|---|---|---|---|---|
| | Yield (tonnes) | Effort (AFH) | Cost ('000 Rs) | Yield (tonnes) | Effort (AFH) | Cost ('000 Rs) | Yield (tonnes) | Effort (AFH) | Cost ('000 Rs) |
| Catfish | 123 | 2510.96 | 1274.39 | 340.94 | 1329.97 | 3,532.49 | 338.02 | 1512.25 | 3,502.20 |
| Halibut | 2510.96 | 1346.36 | 723.28 | 53.43 | 2018.90 | 715.70 | 53.05 | 2272.01 | 710.52 |
| Lizard fishes | 9664.01 | 108,218 | 53,132.21 | 3834.48 | 150,788.98 | 52,468.31 | 3805.74 | 170,048.61 | 52,075.09 |
| Pomfret | 21,483.12 | 3634.35 | 9,697.49 | 2640.65 | 8425.90 | 23,049.21 | 2617.72 | 9588.12 | 22,849.11 |
| Rays | 3634.35 | 2260.30 | 4297.80 | 544.99 | 2495.40 | 6,730.65 | 540.29 | 2838.64 | 6,672.53 |
| Rock | 2260.30 | 52,462.13 | 24,825.36 | 2114.78 | 21,286.16 | 29,880.53 | 2097.05 | 24,169.16 | 29,630.00 |
| Shark | 3914.41 | 2516.31 | 7072.70 | 758.65 | 2102.53 | 9,809.35 | 752.12 | 2391.32 | 9,724.87 |
| Shrimp | 2516.31 | 19,719.70 | 60,747.54 | 8400.42 | 19,183.22 | 96,813.71 | 8327.48 | 21,829.52 | 95,973.03 |
| Soles | 19,719.70 | 22,479.40 | 54,379.59 | 9428.73 | 29,104.95 | 93,958.32 | 9348.36 | 33,081.16 | 93,157.41 |
| Thread fin breams | 15,732.56 | 38,1152.30 | 181,512.05 | 13,152.67 | 141,468.14 | 180,410.27 | 13,042.67 | 160,603.91 | 178,901.35 |

*Note:* AFH= Annual fishing hours.
*Source:* Bhatta and Bhat (2001).

# 5

# Theories of CPR Management: Collective Action, Participation, and Evolution

## COLLECTIVE ACTION: A CONCEPT

The 'collective action' approach is an amalgamated institution to manage private, public, or common property resources, based on a principle of collective decision and implementation. Collective action (often referred to as participatory management) is a group behaviour emerging as an alternative strategy to market, for managing rural, environmental, and natural resources.

How can collective action be described? It is a process, which takes place in five stages — appreciation, influence, consummation, action, and evaluation (Picciotto, 1992, p. 9). The appreciation phase involves listening, validating information, sharing perceptions and opinions, and collating lessons from the past. The influence phase is one in which consultation, persuasion, and exploration of options take place, leading to joint decisions or new relationships being established (between different sections of people or stakeholders) in the consummation stage. Consummation is also the stage in which the rules of responsibility and rewards are defined. The decision is acted upon in the action stage which is evaluated in the last stage with influence on future participation. Participatory management, therefore, implies sharing of information, mutual negotiations, collective decision making, and implementation.

The concept of collective action as a convergent institutional arrangement to manage common (and possibly also private) resources is pursued further. The basic social philosophy of collective action is participatory development as against individual development (Chopra et al., 1990). One is rather hesitant to give any rigorous definition of participation.[1] A definition, perhaps most acceptable is the following:

'Participation is a process of initiating and continuation of an active process by which beneficiary/client groups influence the direction and execution of a development activity with a view to enhancing their well-being in terms of personal income growth, self-reliance or the values they cherish including equity' (Paul, 1989).

There are a number of alternative definitions and views about the nature and content of participation: (i) participation as contribution by people in public projects (ECLA, 1973); (ii) participation as organization with new rules, regulations, and institutions (Pearse and Stiefel, 1979); and (iii) participation as empowering people in decision making, project implementation, and sharing benefits (Cohen and Uphoff, 1977; Paul 1989).

Is there a theory of collective action? This question has been viewed by economists, sociologists, historians, and political scientists in numerous ways, and hence it need not be tagged or labelled against any single theory (Richardson, 1983; Olson, 1965; Runge, 1986; Wade, 1987; Hardin, 1982; Murty, 1994; North, 1990). Economic theory normally takes the course of minimizing transactions costs, whereas sociologists use the logic of building social capital as distinct from man-made capital in a socially fragmented society (Ostrom, 1994; Steins and Edwards, 1999). Social capital as a building block includes harmony, mutual understanding, sympathy, and institutions of inter-dependency (Putnam, 1993). Historians treat this as an evolutionary process of learning and adaptation (Axelrod, 1990). Political scientists may treat it as a game between different stakeholders, arriving either at a co-operative or non-cooperative solution (Ostrom, 1990). A few of

---

[1]In the context of rural development in India, a further distinction between participatory management and participatory development is offered in Chapter 6.

these alternative theoretical frameworks are reviewed in this section, with some details of the models in the next section.

Consider the historical view first. Collective action is about people being able to influence the direction and outcome of activities, and participating in the action by themselves. There cannot be participatory approaches without room for learning over generations. Making learning feasible for participants may require the adoption of a long-term strategy, a sequencing of activities such that consequences of actions taken by the same generation or by an earlier generation become the basis for future action and further learning. Communities need to learn and so do organizations implementing programmes and schemes. Participatory approaches cannot be effective until there are changes in attitudes which are best brought about through a history of learning. Learning entails a continuous process of discovery wherein people can examine why they are not able to do what they want to do, identify ways of improving their action by questioning the fundamental approaches to their work, and adopting more promising actions.

How do economists view collective action? Two different economic arguments referring to costs and scale are offered here. First, theoretically speaking, the approach is to opt for such a strategy with a minimum of economic costs. For instance, the market as an institution minimizes transaction, search, or information costs in conducting any productive activity, be it agriculture or industry. When it comes to collective action in the management of CPRs, notable components of relevant economic costs are bargaining costs, monitoring costs, and enforcement costs. All these put together form a part of transactions costs. Under community action, both information and search costs are perhaps minimal, as the talents and skills within the community, knowledge about all the households and families of the community are known. However, unlike the market situation, in a collective action model the costs of bargaining, monitoring, and enforcement are the additional costs.[2] For this reason, alternative models of bargaining game, evolutionary game (Greenberg, 1990), and legal and social institutional strategies may be required. The second economic argument other than reducing the various costs is the case of economies of scale in resource management (referred to in Chapters 1 and 4), which would also reduce the transactions and information costs of managing the CPR.

[2]North (1990, p.68) calls these as hard to measure costs.

Other than the costs and scale issues, another major economic (or sociological) issue about collective action is about the size of group to take collective decision and action. Is there any optimum size of the members of the community that can be said to be ideal for collective action? For instance, if there is only one individual to take all the decisions and also to act, there does not seem to be  any logical problem. However, in a society with a large number of stakeholders and agents, collective action can follow only if there is a collective decision without conflicts.[3] In fact it was Olson (1965), and later on Runge (1986) who gave some theoretical flavour to the evolution of collective action and CPR institutions. Individual choices and preferences may be quite variant at each other. So, it is never easy, starting from individual behaviour, to arrive at any unique mode of collective action. One can build in a variety of incentives for the individuals in a collective action programme. But the gains from net incentive decline as the size of the group increases. As a classic case of collective action, consider the example of a water user association. As and when the user group is enlarged, the degree of uncertainty about the timely delivery of water increases. Inequities in distribution can emerge.[4] After examining all the options, Olson was of the opinion that no self-interested person would contribute to the production of a public good.

Unless the number of individuals in a group is quite small, or unless there is a coercion or some other special device to make individuals act in their common interest, rational self-interested individuals will not act to achieve their common or group interests (Olson, 1965: p. 2).

Some further  arguments can be advanced regarding the advantages and disadvantages of size groups. With smaller groups involved in a collective action, even some of the individual gains can be accommodated. Such gains may become larger than the cost of collective action. The larger the group, the individual gains are not to be counted. Also the costs of bargaining, monitoring, and enforcement

[3]This opens up a wider question about the existence of a social welfare function (Arrow, 1951; Sen,1970,1977), which is not dealt with in this book.

[4]Antia and Kadekodi (2002) have examined the logic for eight water user associations in Ralegan–Siddhi. Such an  arrangement  is more stable than having only one association for the village as a whole.

would rise and new costs of conflict resolution would arise. As against this situation, in a perfect market situation—where there are a large number of individuals or agents (with free entry and exit rules)—the sum total of all individual costs can be extremely high and individual gains may not give collective good.[5] Hence the sum of all individual net gains may be smaller than under the collective action situation. Thus the optimum size of the collective action group is important.

On the question of size of community organizations, two distinct economic arguments are generally made. The first is by Runge (1986) and also Olson (1965). It is based on a set theoretic logic, linking the net pay-offs from a community based CPR management with combinations of co-operators and defectors. The second is by Buchanan and Tullock (1965) and is based on the economic costs of collective decision making and the alternative cost of externalities. Runge, (as Olson also argues), considers the relative sizes of co-operators as one group and defectors as another group. Co-operators are collectively pooling and sharing the total gains from CPR management (as against their private benefits), whereas the defectors enjoy them as free riders, as an externality benefit. If out of 'n' number of agents or players in a CPR sharing game, 'k' of them decide to cooperate and 'n-k' of them defect, then depending upon the relative sizes of 'k' and 'n-k', the net pay-offs to the co-operators will emerge. In general, the externality gains to the free riders will increase elastically as the size of the co-operators' group increases (as they contribute positively to the growth of the CPR). Hence, the net benefits to the co-operators may not increase at the same rate as their pooling or increasing size. In such a situation, there will be a breaking point of $k=k^*$ at which the net pay-offs to the co-operators will be maximum, beyond which they will decline. Runge proposes that the limits of the CPR institution are governed by such a game between the two sets of players. The Runge–Olson framework is basically a static one. This argument also suggests that it is not necessary and possible that all members of a village community will be co-operators for the collective action.[6] Buchanan and Tullock (1965) also make a similar argument, but using an inter-temporal framework. The basic approach is to take

[5]In the situation of an imperfect market, additional problems of externality will arise, and further reduce the collective good.
[6]Runge identifies the case of $k^*=n$, as a situation of universal co-operation.

note of the long-term costs of collective action. Associated with the size of the co-operators 'k' and defectors 'n-k', are a variety of transactions costs (of collectivization, implementation, enforcing, etc.) and external costs (from the defectors or free riders). The present value of the sum total of all such costs will decline initially with an increasing size 'k' of the co-operators, but sooner or later it will rise. The co-operators group (basically the conditional co-operators, to use an expression from Ostrom, 2000) with the least present value costs is the most viable size for collectivization.

Finally, political science based developments on public life also provide several theoretical models and approaches to collective action. Recent experiments in public life and 'public good' management in many parts of the world have shown that the situation is not so hopeless in the management of natural resources, where people prefer to have CPR based institutional arrangements to manage public interests (Ostrom, 2000). In Chapter 4 it was found that it is logical to manage CPRs, purely in the private interest of people to get the best out of their private resources. The famous experiments and models of Sukhomajri (Chopra *et al.*, 1990) and Ralegan–Sidhi (Pangare and Pangare, 1992) have clearly shown that initially the private interests of dairying, crop agriculture, rope making etc., have been the catalysts for the people from those villages to agree to manage the buffer forest lands and water bodies in the villages.[7] Similarly, pooling of private lands to make a community managed land to get the best out of agriculture and other related economic activities in villages in  Palamau district (Chopra and Kadekodi, 1999) under the CVP is yet another example of pursuing self-interest or private interest for the common good.

Can there also be pure or mixed public interest in managing the commons through collective action? It is experimentally found and observed in many parts of the world that in about 50 per cent of situations people vote or participate for community action for some reason or the other (Ostrom, 2000). There are many reasons for people to choose or not choose community actions. First, as mentioned earlier, smallness and inability in getting involved individually in scale oriented resource management makes it necessary to collectivize. Examples are irrigation systems (Sengupta, 1991). Second, there may be various levels

---

[7]At a latter stage in collective action, the same villagers shifted away from pure watershed development to rural development (Antia and Kadekodi, 2002).

of information about the commons and their usability among the communities.[8] Because of such asymmetry of information and inequality between individuals, people trust the community rather than individual motivations and actions (Murty, 1994). The suspicion is that only the direct beneficiaries would benefit. In all such situations, pure public interest and action may be preferred by the communities. There can also be counter arguments. With the population around the CPR increasing, contrary to expectations, the returns from the resource decrease at the individual level. In such a case, people having alternative opportunities opt out of CPR participation. Finally, as argued earlier, because of complementarity between the private and common property resources, people may participate in CPR management to the extent that it adds to their private benefit and not beyond. So, the observed 50 per cent rule of participation is quite likely. With the background of individual gains and public interest, several theories have thus emerged.

How to initiate a collective action strategy? This is a question on which a large number of practitioners and theoreticians have a variety of suggestions. Practitioners such as the NGOs find it easy if there is some internal leadership in the community, atleast some degree of societal homogeneity among the people, and a minimal concern for the commons. In case the leadership does not emerge from within, then, the NGOs do provide this to some extent from outside. What the communities do not like about this external leadership is when it becomes a 'master', ignoring local knowledge, customs, and habits (typically known as the principal–agent problem). Therefore, care has to be taken to see that it emerges only as a catalyst, to be transformed into an internal leadership.[9] In theoretical terms, evolution of co-

[8]In many rural situations, the people may not actually know who owns the *dei shamlat* lands and who should reap the benefits, though the village accountant may have all the information in his records.

[9]A large number of examples can be given, wherein government agents have acted as such principal agents, and have failed to get any co-operation from the people for collective action. In the famous Sukhomajri example (see Chapter 9 for more details), when the officials of Central Soil Water Conservation and Training Institute initially started putting up typical soil conservation measures such as enclosures, check dams etc., without consulting the community, the people were indifferent towards these measures and often broke them.

operation requires certain pre-conditions (Axelrod, 1990). These, are robustness and initial viability. Moreover, whatever be the strategy for collective action, it should be simple enough for the community to view, to see the results, and trustworthy. The test of the strategy in the initial period is extremely important. Viability also requires that the actions should deliver some immediate returns to the communities. In India, several, very complicated technological strategies, or schemes that yielded returns after a long time, if and when introduced, did not stand these tests and were rejected by the communities. Examples are the introduction of eucalyptus plantation by communities (both on the common lands as well as their own private lands) in several states under social forestry or introduction of planting aromatic plants in place of bhabbar grass in the lower Shivaliks, and several others.

COLLECTIVE ACTION: SOME THEORIES

In the context of CPRs, there can be a number of stakeholders (and agents) with different preferences. An example can be cited from the forestry situation. The different stakeholders here are, say, the forest department, local communities, women, tourists, and scientists. The objective of the forest department may be maximizing revenue from the sale of timber and fodder. That of the locals can be maximizing fuelwood collection, of women water, of scientists micro-organisms and flora and fauna, of tourists recreation, and so on. In order to achieve their individual gains, they may opt for a particular strategy out of a fixed set. Examples of strategies are: to co-operate with the forest department; to opt for a market approach; to not co-operate with the forest department; to resort to stealing, trespassing or illegal encroachment, and so on. Then, each of them may prefer different strategies. Any strategy by one agent (say, the forest department) will have some pay-off to itself, and different pay-offs to others. It may even happen that a positive pay-off to one agent may install a negative pay-off to another. As stakeholders, all of them are allowed to opt for their own strategies (without compulsion or enforcement). The game that goes on in such a situation of diverse strategies and stakes can be conflicting, co-operating or even a 'tit-for tat'.[10]

[10]Briefly defined as one agent co-operating on the first move, and then doing whatever the other agent did in his previous move.

The question about different theories of collective action is pursued further now. Taking a clue from the selfish motives of different agents, the emergence of participatory institutions seems to follow one of the following two routes: (i) game theoretic approach and (ii) evolutionary approach.

Game theory is a branch of mathematics, which offers to model a behavioural situation and predict the outcomes (in both static and dynamic situations) based on several strategies that are open to different societal agents. Co-operative and non-cooperative games are normally talked about. The theory of evolutionary approach is an extended argument from the biological system for managing public goods and interests (Axelrod, 1990). Co-operation is adaptive (as seen in biological systems). Hence, its emergence is feasible only in the long run. In economic terms, this is generally feasible only with a very low discount rate in the collective decision making process.[11]

## Game Theoretic Approaches

The game theoretic approach has a rational basis of allocative efficiency. The evolutionary approach on the other hand follows a 'learning by doing' approach. It may be useful to take a quick look at these economic models. A game theoretic framework has four basic characteristics: there have to be 'players', their 'strategies' for the game, the 'pay-offs' from the strategies, and the 'rules' of the game. All these four entities are to be identified in advance. The set of these four entities (players, strategies, pay-offs, and rules) is said to be a game, for the reason that each player is assumed to maximize her/his gain through a choice of strategies. A participatory game is one in which the players are identified as participant stakeholders. A game can be defined between any number of players and with any number of fixed strategies. For instance, in the context of CPR management, the state (or government) and the village community can be treated as the two players. Then it is a case of a 'two person game'. With the government, the community, and an NGO as participants, it is a three players game.

---

[11]With a very low discount rate for all decisions regarding the benefits over a long time period, all parties involved in a collective action do not mind waiting for successive outcomes or gains over time. Axelrod (1990) puts this as a proposition.

If the players discuss their strategies and intentions, and reach a common agreement on the strategy, it is a case of a 'co-operative game'. This can also be viewed as a bargaining game between the different stakeholders till they come to an understanding and agreement. The agreements are fully binding on all the players, and are enforceable. Joint forest management with agreements on sharing rules and responsibilities between the forest department and village communities is an example of such a co-operative game. Otherwise, it is a 'non-cooperative game', in which the players, that is, the stakeholders take their independent stand and move on. A classic example of this was in Sukhomajri, when in the early 1970s the officials of the Central Soil and Water Conservation Research and Training Institute (CSWCRTI) kept constructing fences and check dams on the drainages of river Jhagger without consulting the villagers and the villages kept breaking them.

What is the meaning of a strategy? In the context of collective action, the strategies can be 'participate or co-operate' and 'defect or do not co-operate', say in forest management. There can also be situations of a variety of additional strategies, such as participate (or do not participate) for water management only, for fuelwood and timber sharing only, for fodder collection only, and so on. The pay-offs are the returns to each of the players (gains and losses, which are also known in advance), depending upon the strategy opted by them.

For instance, in the example of forest management, if the forest department and the village protection committee agree to participate, then the government and the village communities may share the forest produce. The sharing rules can be such that the forest department collects income from timber sale, and the village community collects fodder and fuelwood. If the village community decides not to co-operate or participate, it may indulge in cutting some timber illegally and get its value or market price, and the forest department may lose some income from timber sale. On the other hand, if the village community is to participate but not the forest department, then the forest department may collect all the forest produce and auction it, but the village communities will be the net losers. Finally, if both the forest department and the village community are not interested in participatory forest management, then the forest department may collect some timber and other forest produce, as well as fines and penalty from the people (at perhaps a very high cost of policing) and the communities may collect some forest produce by illegal methods.

A taxonomy of symmetric games is described first. Table 5.1 shows a typical two person, two strategy pay-off matrix of a game model. The pay-offs are symbolically shown in terms of a set P={x,y,a,b}.[12] Depending upon the values of the pay-offs, the game assumes different special features.[13]

Table 5.1
Typical Game Theoretic Model of Decision Making

|  |  | Defector | |
|  |  | Participate | Do not participate |
| --- | --- | --- | --- |
| Co-operator | Participate | x ; x | b ; a |
|  | Do not participate | a ; b | y ; y |

In this connection, the basic questions of decision making are:

1. Can the behaviour of two or more stakeholders involved in CPR management be modelled?

2. What are their strategies?

3. What are their pay-offs? In other words, can the set P={x,y,a,b} be estimated?

4. With such a game, is there a solution to come to a decision about the most acceptable strategy to manage the CPR?

An illustrative situation of such a forest management is shown in Table 5.2. If both players participate, then they share the forest produce equally at Rs 3 lakh each. If the community alone participates and not the forest department, then the forest department earns a forest revenue to a tune of Rs 5 lakh (and not a total of Rs 6 lakh), and the community gets nothing. If the community resorts to non-participation and indulges in forest theft etc., then it gets forest products worth Rs 5 lakhs and forest department is the net loser. Finally, if both do not participate, then, each gains revenues equal to just Rs 1 lakh. The low pay-offs to both in the last situation is due to the high costs of

[12]In Table 5.1, paired numbers are interpreted in the following manner: the first figure refers to the pay-off for the Co-operator and the second to the defector.

[13]In Appendix 5.1 based on the pay-offs, several well-known game models are listed.

policing by the forest department, and the high costs to the village community in collecting (stealing the produce). Incidentally, this pay-off matrix (as it is called in game theoretic language) represents what is classically known as the Prisoner's dilemma'.

Table 5.2

Illustration of Pay-offs in a Participatory Game between Forest Department and the Village Community

*(Rs lakh)*

|  |  | Forest Department | |
|---|---|---|---|
|  |  | Participate | Do not participate |
| Village Community | Participate | 3 ; 3 | 0 ; 5 |
|  | Do not participate | 5 ; 0 | 1 ; 1 |

A game of the kind described can be said to have been played once or repeatedly, depending on the rules of the game. When the game is played only once, it starts with one of the player declaring his strategy, say the forest department declaring its will wish to participate, and asking the community to set out the strategy next. In response to the strategy of the forest department, the community may choose either to participate or not to participate. Depending upon the move of the community, the government can then choose its next strategy; and the game can go on until there is no incentive to change the strategy for either of the stakeholders. In the example shown above, it can easily be seen that, no matter who makes the first move, the game comes to an end with both the community and forest department settling to a pay-off of Rs 1 lakh each. However, the best set of pay-offs could have been each getting Rs 3 lakh. This type of game is a classical example of the Prisoner's dilemma game (Luce and Raifa, 1957).[14]

As against a normal game, a repeated game is one in which the same game is played again and again, say over different points in time. Also, the pay-offs need not remain the same over different games. In the example of JFM, a repeated game situation can arise, when the

[14]Axelrod (1990) states that this type of game was first invented around 1950 by Merril Flood and Melvin Dresher. In a typical prisoner's dilemma game, the pay-offs are set out to be negative, as indications of penalties to the two prisoners, in the background of confessing and not confessing on a crime committed together, hence the name.

village communities and forest department intend to enter into an agreement on sharing rules every five years (say) again and again, depending upon the status of forest resources. For instance, initially no timber rights might have been given to the communities, but after 10–15 years, if and when the preservation rate is higher, the forest department may even agree to share timber with the village communities. Another example can be that of degrading CPR resources over time without any participation, because of which the pay-offs may fall over time. Case studies of a repeated non-cooperative game and a co-operative game are presented later in the chapter.

## An Illustration of a Non-cooperative Game as Applied to CPR Management

A non-cooperative repeated game model is formulated here with data from Haryana villages regarding the management of forests (followed by a co-operative game in the next section).[15] After the introduction of the JFM programme in Haryana, as many as 90 villages have taken up this programme in the lower Shivaliks (of the Himalayan range). Hill resource management societies have been established in these villages.[16] Households have the option of joining the society fully, marginally, or to stay away from it. The villagers have been experiencing a varied degree of benefits and losses from this programme, some having fully taken to this participatory management of the forests, some partially, many others staying away from it completely. The state government enabled JFM with building of dams to arrest soil run-offs, and inviting the villagers for nursery plantation, protection, and preservation activities on the hill slopes. The villagers took to social fencing, provided social protection, and preservation. In turn, they would gain from increased fodder, fuelwood, bamboo, and timber yields, at lower costs of maintenance and environmental restoration. The villagers also gain in terms of additional water from the dam, collection of fodder and fuel, share in bamboo and small timber, and access to fishing in the tanks.

A game theoretic model is formulated as follows.

[15]This case study is based on a detailed study by Lise (1997) and Chopra et al. (1990).
[16]Among these, a case study from Sukhomajri village is presented with more details in Chapter 9.

1. The Players: Among the households, two groups are identified: co-operators and defectors. Co-operators are current participants in JFM. The defectors are those who are currently not strictly participating in JFM (or more precisely participating at a low level).

2. The Strategies: Each group (of households) has two strategies namely, (i) to participate in JFM or (ii) to not participate. The current co-operators may also keep the option of giving up participation in JFM in due course, or to continue with participation. Likewise, the current defectors may keep the option of participating in future or continue to remain out of it. Hence the game is set out as a repeated game.

3. Pay-offs: The gains from JFM are in terms of incremental fodder, incremental fuelwood, fish catch, and bamboo and timber shares, etc. Obviously, the gains will differ across households, depending upon whether one is a member of the HRMS and hence a co-operator or not.

A survey in nine villages covering 127 sampled households in 1996–7 yielded information on (i) the attitudes of the individual households towards participation in the JFM of the HRMS, and (ii) the types and amount of gains or losses from participation (and non-participation) in JFM. As many as ten different attitudinal questions were posed to each of the sample households, regarding their interest and gains from participation in JFM activities.[17] Using their responses in a scalar form ranging from 1(standing for least) to 5 (standing for most), a composite index of participation is derived (as a sum of scores for each household). The sum of the scores are normalized to bring the index to range between zero and unity.[18] Based on these indices of participation, the households are grouped into four categories as (i) co-operators and participating in JFM, (ii) co-operators, but not willing to participation in JFM, (iii) defectors but participating in JFM, and (iv) defectors and also not willing to participate in JFM. The sample data at the household level are also used to estimate the gains from participation or non–participation. The corresponding average pay-offs for each group are estimated. For purposes of grouping the households into the four categories mentioned above, a statistical cluster method is used.[19] The

---

[17]The attitudinal questions are listed in Appendix A5.2.

[18]Define the normalized index $z_i^* = \{z_i - \text{Min } z\} / \{\text{Max } z - \text{Min } z\}$.

[19]For more details of econometric methods and assumptions, see Lise (1997, Chapter 4 and 5).

number of households falling in different categories, their average participatory index, and the pay-offs are shown in Table 5.3.

Table 5.3
Participatory Game  Model of HRMS in Haryana

(*Pay-offs* in Rs)

|  |  | Defector | |
|  |  | Participate (0.8236;55) | Do not participate (0.6406;8) |
| --- | --- | --- | --- |
| Co-operator | Participate (0.8236;55) | 3766 ; 3766 | 5366 ; 3528 |
|  | Do not participate (0.6777;57) | 3528 ; 5366 | 1583 ; 1583 |

*Note*: The figures in brackets stand for the average level of participatory index and the sample size used for those estimates.
*Source*: Field data base (Lise, 1997).

This pay-off matrix represents a typical Pareto game, where the choice by both the co-operators and defectors in the long run is to participate in JFM and earn the net incremental benefits of Rs 3766 each, which is also a Nash equilibrium. In other words, with a repeated game  rule, the villagers have no incentive to defect and not participate in JFM.[20]

An Illustration of Co-operative Game Theoretic Approach

As a demonstration of the logic and use of a co-operative game model as applicable to CPR management, a case of bargaining between the communities and the government to arrive at a  solution  to manage a grassland (that is, a CPR) is presented.[21]

The case study area is Sukhomajri and its surrounding villages in Haryana. It has been seen that over the years different types of contractual arrangements between the government and village societies in the study area have contributed towards improving the conservation of forest resources (Singh and Hegde, 2001). The notable one is the contractual arrangement between the Haryana forest department and

[20]Mathematically stated, under a Nash equilibrium, the critical discount factor is units the discount rate is zero.

[21]More details of the case study are available in Chopra et al., (1990, Chapter 6), from which  this section is based.

village societies for harvesting bhabbar and fodder grass from the forest land surrounding the villages.[22] For instance, the village societies of Sukhomajri and Dhamala had together obtained a contract for Rs 22,000 to harvest bhabbar grass from forest land in 1986, and the arrangement is continuing till today. Similarly, for harvesting fodder grass, the contract obtained in 1983 for one year initially, was later extended; the village societies were to pay Rs 9.50 per acre of fodder grass harvested.

What are the terms under which the village societies and the government come to an agreement on contracting bhabbar or fodder grasses? In this connection three specific questions are posed:

1. Out of the total forest lands, R, around the villages, how much should be contracted between the people and the forest department for managing the bhabbar and fodder grasses?

2. What is the contractual rental that the forest department should charge the village community for this arrangement?

3. What are the resultant pay-offs to the forest department and the village communities?

Such contractual arrangements are derived as solutions to a Nash bargaining problem in co-operative games (Nash, 1951; Friedman, 1986). The problem is posed as a case of a bilateral monopoly, with the village society as the single bidder for the CPR resource and the forest department as the single owner or supplier of the resource. The government owns the forest land and enjoys monopoly rights in leasing forest land to the village society. The village society is characterized as a monopsonist in hiring or renting a part of the forest land from the forest department for harvesting bhabbar and fodder grasses. Therefore, it is a case of bilateral monopoly. The conditions for optimal sharing of the CPR resource by the two parties—on the assumption that people's participation uniformly increases productivity of forest land—are derived. It is assumed that both the forest department and village societies agree to abide by the contract with a sense of commitment and complete knowledge about the gains from such an arrangement. They are also aware of the costs of breach of trust or non-existence of such a contract.

---

[22]The official document of contracting is shown in an extract form in Appendix 6.1.

The pay-offs to the two parties before and after bargaining are required to be estimated. What is the pre-bargaining situation? In the absence of a contract, villagers resort to free and illegal cutting of bhabbar and fodder grass, thereby earning some income. But this is not without any cost—when they are often caught by the forest guards they end up paying a penalty. The net income to the villagers, therefore, is the   income from illegal harvesting of grass, net of penalties paid when caught for free grazing and stealing. The income is termed as 'threat income or pay-off' to the village community in the pre-bargaining situation. On similar lines, the threat income (to be called as a 'pay-off') for the government is revenue in the form of penalties plus revenue from auction contracting, net of the policing cost through departmental personnel. The threat pay-off to the government and the people in the pre-bargaining situation may  be zero, positive, or even negative.  Let $s_g$ and $s_c$ denote the net per acre threat pay-off to the government (forest department) and village society, respectively.

The institutional arrangement after bargaining will be described now. The village society takes up part of the forest R  less than  or equal to R at a rental 'r' and harvests a total quantity Q of bhabbar grass.  It sells it in turn to individuals within the community or to outside buyers at a price P. While the government gets rental income from the leased out forest land, the village society gets a profit from the bhabbar grass operations.  The quantity of bhabbar grass that the society harvests depends  upon the amount of forest land it hires, as given by a production function.

$$Q = F(R); F'(R) \geq 0, F''(R) \leq 0 \qquad \text{....(5.1)}$$

The demand by households for bhabbar grass denoted by D, is assumed to be a function of the price, specified  as:

$$P = D(Q); D'(Q) \leq 0, D''(Q) \geq 0 \qquad \text{....(5.2)}$$

The monopoly profit that the village society makes and the rental income of the government due to the contract can be identified as :

Village Society's profit $= PQ - r R$        ....(5.3)

Government's rental income $= r R$        ....(5.4)

The bargaining problem is one of determining the optimal level of forest resource R to be leased to the community, and agreeing upon a rental, r.  In the light of the pre-bargaining and post-bargaining conditions, the net pay-off after the contract for the government $(T_g)$

and village society $(T_c)$, can now be identified as:

$$T_g = (rR - s_g R); \text{ and } T_c = (PQ - rR - s_c R); \qquad \qquad ....(5.5)$$

As a case of bilateral monopoly, the efficient production pattern is to be identified first. The Pareto efficient net total pay-off to the whole system is:

$$Z = T_g + T_c = PQ - s_g R - s_c R \qquad \qquad ....(5.6)$$

Maximal of this joint net pay-off with the option of bargaining the forest land R, is given by the first order condition:

$$\frac{\partial Z}{\partial R} = m - s_g - s_c = 0; \text{ or } m = s_g + s_c \qquad \qquad ....(5.7)$$

where, $m = \left[ P\left(1 + \frac{1}{e}\right) . \frac{\partial Q}{\partial R} \right]$ is the value of marginal revenue productivity of the bargained land and 'e' the price elasticity of demand for Q.

The Efficiency Condition (5.7) states that the post-bargaining joint net pay-off is maximum at a point of forest land bidding R = R*, at which the corresponding marginal revenue productivity m is equal to the pre-bargaining opportunity costs of the government and the society taken together. The corresponding joint net pay-off can be expressed as:

$$Z^* = P^* Q^* - s_g R^* - s_c R^* \qquad \qquad ....(5.8)$$

The bargaining process is complete only after the two parties agree upon a rental rate r. As can be seen from equation (5.5), the rental r is a distributional parameter to be determined during the process of bargaining. It depends on the trade-offs between the net pay-offs of the two parties. The distributional optimization is made possible by posing it as a solution to a Nash bargaining problem in co-operative games. The Nash objective function is defined as :

$$N = T_g . T_c \qquad \qquad ....(5.9)$$

Given the Pareto efficient set of production Z*, the maximal of N is determined by the choice of rental rate r. The optimality (first order) condition after some simplification is that: $T_g = T_c$ Then, from Equation (5.5) it follows that the optimal rental rate r is:

$$r^* = s_g + \frac{\{P^* Q^* - r^* R^* - s_c R^*\}}{R^*} \qquad \qquad ....(5.10)$$

Equation (5.10) states that the rental should be equal to the threat pay-off of the government plus the average net pay-off of the village society per unit of forest land bargained for; implying that it is at least equal to the threat income($s_g$) of the government. Furthermore, the net pay-offs of the government and the society are equal at the equilibrium. Both parties gain equally. It is this outcome and information that brings about a confidence on the  part of the government, and commitment on the part of the people to come together to participate in the management of such CPRs. There is, in the process, a degree of fairness in sharing the incremental gain (that is, joint net pay-off) equally between them. The equilibrium rental also implies that for increased threat income of the government $s_g$, the rental would be higher; and for increased threat income of the village society, it would be lower.  This is the consequence of bargaining in a co-operative way.

To illustrate this model, consider a quadratic output function Q, from the CPR land  R:

$$Q = a.R^2 + b.R + c, \qquad\qquad ....(5.11)$$

where a, b, c are constants with a $< 0$, and b$> | \ 2a \ R \ |$, and a constant elasticity demand function for the forest produce:

$$Q = dP^e \qquad\qquad\qquad ....(5.12)$$

where, $e$ is the price elasticity of demand, $d$ is a positive constant. From (5.7), Pareto optimality requires that:

$$R^* = \frac{\left\{ \left( s_g + s_c \right) e \right\}}{2aP(1+e) - \dfrac{b}{2a}} \qquad\qquad ....(5.13)$$

The optimal rental $r^*$ is given by equation (5.10).

One can interpret $(s_g + s_c)$ in (5.13) as the social opportunity cost of an acre of forest land available for a contractual agreement between the forest department and  the village society.

As a numerical illustration, consider two examples of $(s_g + s_c) =$ 1000 and 500, respectively.  Parameters of Equations (5.12) and (5.13) are also assumed within realistic ranges.  Table 5.4 presents the Pareto optimal amounts of forest land (R) leased out, forest output produced (Q), and monopoly price (P) charged by the village society for alternative opportunity costs of forest land.  As expected, for lower values of the opportunity cost, the forest department leases out more land to the village. As a result of this, the forest output increases and monopoly price for forest produce reduces as the opportunity cost of forest land falls. Table 5.5 presents solutions to the bargaining problem under different threat pay-offs for the forest department and the village society. The results show that the relative bargaining strengths of the two parties determine the optimum rent. The optimum rent increases as the ratio of threat pay-off of the forest department to that of the village society increases. For example, given the opportunity cost of an acre of forest land as Rs 1000, the optimum rent per acre of forest land increases from Rs 609 to Rs 1209 as the composition of threat pay-offs $(s_g, s_c)$ changes from (0, 1000) to (600, 400).

Table 5.4
Optimal Values of  Forest Lands Leased, Grass Production, and the Price

| R (acres) | Q (units) | P (Rupees) | $s_g + s_c$ |
|---|---|---|---|
| 920 | 416,493 | 4.90 | 1000 |
| 2113 | 835,310 | 3.46 | 500 |

Source: Chopra et al. 1990: p. 127.

Table 5.5
Bargaining Solutions under Different Pre-bargaining Situations

| $s_g + s_c$ | $s_g$ | $s_c$ | $s_g / s_c$ | R |
|---|---|---|---|---|
| 1000 | 0 | 1000 | 0.00 | 609 |
| | 400 | 600 | 0.67 | 1009 |
| | 500 | 500 | 1.00 | 1109 |
| | 600 | 400 | 1.50 | 1209 |
| 500 | 0 | 500 | 0.00 | 434 |
| | 100 | 400 | 0.25 | 534 |
| | 400 | 100 | 4.00 | 834 |

Notes: Parameters assumed: e =-2.0, a = -0.05, b = 500.0, c = 0.0, d = 10$^7$: The corresponding net pay-offs to the government and the community are Rs 560,280 each.
Source: Chopra et al., 1990, p. 127.

This illustration thus shows the use of  a game theoretic approach to resolve the issues of bargaining and arriving at the optimal rental to be paid  to the government, the amount of net pay-offs to the government and the community, and amount of grassland to be leased out to the community.

## THE EVOLUTIONARY MODEL

There is considerable similarity between the manner in which successful strategies in a non-co-operative game would converge leading to a cooperative game and the evolutionary process in biological sciences (Axelrod, 1990; Ostrom, 2000; North, 1990; Hirshleifer,1987). The theory of natural selection and inheritance is a clue to survival and the acceptance of successful strategies in social behaviour (Ostrom, 2000: p. 143). Therefore, one can also visualize the possibility of managing CPRs going through several experiments of defections, non-coordination, and learning. In fact, as noted by Axelrod (1990, p.62) defection itself is evolutionary, in the sense that it gives an opportunity to evolve a better strategy subsequently. A repeated game falls in the category of an evolutionary model, wherein the pay-offs keep on changing from time to time.

There are two distinct aspects of the evolutionary model, namely the evolution of social norms and the evolution of participatory institutions. The latter is, however, dependent upon the first. Evolving social norms of behaviour—away from the pursuit of self-interest—is a long-drawn-out process. It depends upon the level of understanding about the outcomes of collective action, obligations required, responsibilities to be delegated, and restrictions on individual behaviour. Furthermore, as argued by Ostrom (2000), they are more stable if and when evolved internally than when imposed externally. In terms of evolution of institutions, Sethi and Somanathan (1996) and Ostrom (2000) envisage the role of a third group of agents called 'enforcers' or 'willing punishers' who can be instrumental in stabilizing the emerging equilibrium collective action solutions to the management of the commons. Whether these should be external agents such as the state or evolved from within, is a matter of practical experience in different situations. For instance, in several irrigation water use situations, invariably the majority decision regarding water sharing rules is more stable than that imposed by the governmental agencies (Bardhan, 1999).

A related question about the evolution of social norms is the preference ordering of different perspectives, expectations about outcomes, responsibilities, and restrictions about CPR management. For instance, is there a preference ordering between economic relevance versus social relevance, as a case for survival of the CPR institution? This is a question about the strategy of an evolutionary process. Economic relevance would prompt gains from CPR management in terms of what the community gets in monetary terms or resource gains. Social relevance is attributed to concerns such as harmony, unity, mutual dependency, cultural and religious customs, and social security, etc.

The relative importance of economic versus social relevance in an evolutionary process is best illustrated with a case study by Lise (1997). In three different locational situations, Haryana, Uttarakhand, and Jharkhand, ten different attitudinal questions were posed to samples of households regarding participation in forest management. The questions are listed in Appendix 5.2. Using their responses (in a scalar form ranging from 1 to 5) a composite index is estimated using statistical factor analysis. The two extracted principal components are shown in Table 5.6.

Interestingly enough, in all the three situations, the first principal factor is dominated by participatory social indicators, whereas the second factors are dominated by participatory economic indicators. This suggests that communities have ranked societal matters as more relevant than economic matters in the management of CPR.[23]

How do institutions spread or replicate? This is an important issue of scaling up CPR institutions (Farington et al., 1999). The evolutionary process of CPR management is a Markovian one. The experience with community management in one situation can trigger similar institutions elsewhere. Therefore, the growth of participatory institutions itself can be evolutionary. Using time series data, Lise (1997) estimates the growth of such participatory institutions in Haryana and Jharkhand. The estimated regression models are presented in Box 5.1. Using prior probability in a Markovian process, it is then possible to predict the limits to growth of participatory institutions (depending upon site situations).

As seen from, Figures 5.1 and 5.2 in Haryana, there is a limit to expanding CPR institutions, whereas sufficient scope exists in Jharkhand to enlarge the scope of CPR institutions.

---

[23]Lise (1997) has also analysed the relation between incentives to participate (that is, social and economic taken together) and the levels of the resource (quality and quantity). He also shows that all of them exhibit a repeated Pareto game.

Table 5.6

Preference between Social and Economic Participation

| Attributes on participation | Factor 1 | | | Factor 2 | | |
|---|---|---|---|---|---|---|
| | Haryana | Uttarakhand | Jharkhand | Haryana | Uttarakhand | Jharkhand |
| *Economic Participation* | | | | | | |
| Nursery planting in the forest | 0.3828 ** | 0.0482 | 0.1721 | 0.0436 | 0.8675 ** | 0.6499 ** |
| Other contributions to forest development | 0.2262 | 0.1770 | 0.0978 | 0.6980 ** | 0.6175 ** | 0.8080 ** |
| Benefit from the forest | 0.0937 | 0.2327 ** | 0.1558 | 0.8319 ** | 0.1086 | 0.7056 ** |
| Agreement with the decisions | 0.0494 | 0.7708 ** | 0.8319 * | 0.8756 ** | 0.2386 | 0.1637 |
| *Social Participation* | | | | | | |
| Ability to influence decisions | 0.6812 * | 0.8096 * | 0.8678 * | 0.4156 | 0.1795 | 0.1222 |
| Frequency of meetings | 0.7920 * | 0.2754 * | -0.0198 | -0.1257 | 0.1432 | 0.0210 |
| Attendance of meetings | 0.7966 * | 0.5936 * | 0.7871 * | 0.1946 | 0.4214 | 0.3424 |
| Interest in meetings | 0.6400 * | 0.8422 * | 0.2919 * | 0.5306 | -0.0375 | 0.1408 |
| Gain from meetings | 0.6111 * | 0.8153 * | 0.2705 * | 0.5285 | 0.0055 | 0.2511 |
| Making suggestions during meetings | 0.5844 * | 0.4881 * | 0.2804 | 0.3951 | 0.4514 * | 0.4146 * |
| Variation Explained (%) | 45.1 | 35.4 | 36.0 | 14.4 | 11.9 | 12.3 |

*Note:* *stands for dominance of social variables in Factor 1 (over Factor 2); **stand for dominance of economic variable in Factor 2.
*Source:* Lise (1997, pp. 114, 158, 193).

---

**Box 5.1: Chronological Growth of Participatory Institutions**

Haryana: No. of HRMS (N)= 54 −50e−0.0119(T-1983)$^2$: T=time in calendar year; $R^2$ =0.977,

Jharkhand: No. of villages under CVP (N) = 22.2 T − 5.17 T$^2$ + 0.392 T$^3$: T = time in calendar year 1987; $R^2$=0.924

Note: All the estimated coefficients are statistically significant; $R^2$ stands for square of correlation co-efficient. CVP is, a participatory CPR institution.

Comments: As can be seen from the Figures 5.1 and 5.2, these depict growths of participatory institutions reaching saturation in a finite time period; e=mathematical exponent.

---

What is the evidence on the evolution of institutions in India? One can trace at least three broad strains of thought through which institutions to manage CPRs have evolved. First, traditional societies in India have evolved systems to manage them through a process of conflicts, learnings, and mechanisms to resolve them. The institution of 'sacred groves' reviewed in Chapter 6 is a case in example. This is how village republics have emerged in India and elsewhere (Wade, 1987). Basically, local convention has prevailed to guide the use patterns of such resources. The tribals of India have always dealt with this issue in this evolutionary manner. The institution of shifting

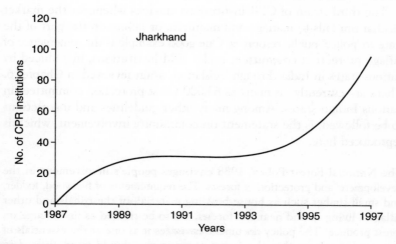

**Figure 5.1:** CPR Institutions in Jharkhand

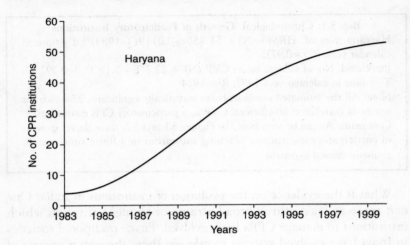

**Figure 5.2:** CPR Institutions in Haryana

cultivation in north-eastern India is another example to cite. Second, there is the process of customary laws recognized by the government, empowering the local communities to enjoy several CPRs. For instance, the Indian National Forest Policy document of 1988 clearly recognizes the rights and concessions to tribals and locals regarding grazing lands, collection of NTFPs, etc.

The third strain of CPR institutions emerges whenever the market mechanism fails to manage and maintain, or failure on the part of the state to 'police' public resources. One good example is the emergence of village protection committees under JFM institutions, introduced by various states in India through legislation, again reviewed in Chapter 6. There are currently as many as 63,000 forest protection committees in various Indian states. Among many other guidelines and instructions to be followed, is the statement on community involvement, which is reproduced here.

The National Forest Policy, 1988 envisages people's involvement in the development and protection of forests. The requirements of fuelwood, fodder, and small timber such as house-building material, of the tribals and other villagers living in and near the forests, are to be treated as first charge on forest produce. The policy document envisages it as one of the essentials of forest management that the forest communities should be motivated to identify themselves with the development and the protection of forests from which they derive benefits. Extract from Government of India letter dated 1 June 1990 (No. 6.21/89-F.P.).

Another example is the 73rd amendment to the Constitution of India in 1992, introducing Panchayat Raj institutions. Under this act, Panchayats are to be established by all the states as units of self-governance, covering a variety of activities, under the 11th schedule of the Constitution of India. They include the management of several CPRs in the rural setting.

CREATING INSTITUTIONS FOR POOLING PRIVATE RESOURCES

In Chapter 1, mention was made about the possibility of creating common management of PPRs, by creating CPPRs. In this section an attempt is made to formalize an analytical model, depicting the evolution of such social behaviour. The model itself is based on theorizing the observed situation in Palamau district of Jharkhand, with the concept of cyclic system of development (CVP), presented as a case study in Chapter 10. In doing so, certain specific questions are addressed.

1. Is a CVP type participatory approach of pooling private lands sustainable? The process is said to be sustainable provided the returns from resource management ensure a steady state income, which is much above the basic minimum attainable under any other private alternative.

2. The second issue is regarding the minimal effort required at the village level to sustain this process. In other words, how much of minimal community participation and land need to be pooled? This question is similar to the one raised by Olson (1965) and Runge (1986).

3. The third question is: how long will it take for a village to reach such a sustained growth and how far can this approach be stretched?

4. Finally, how to share or distribute the gains from participation?

A theoretical model is sketched here in the hope that it will provide some clues to formulate an operational policy for replicating CVP as an institution to manage CPRs. Several assumptions are made in developing the model. First, it is assumed that only degraded private lands belonging to village households are pooled, though in reality forest and revenue lands can also be pooled. Second, pooling and withdrawal of resources is permitted during the process of evolutionary development (*chakriya vikas*). Finally a leadership is assumed to exist to collectivize the resources and to introduce community based decision making on agro-forestry and sharing systems.

Initially at time zero, let $N(0)$ individuals (or households) referred to as 'students', some of who own land, come together to form a community. Let the owners of land decide to pool part or all of their land, initially totalling to $L(0)$. The land in question is either degraded or of low productivity. Let an initial one-time investment of $K(0)$ be made by the state as resource transfer to the community for village development.

The community decides to participate in the village development process on receiving a stipend at the rate of 'w' per student. The stipend rate may be much less than an acceptable minimum wage rate 'W' fixed on the basis of calories or other concepts of well-being. In any year 't', the participatory labour that the $N(t)$ individuals put in together on the pooled land $L(t)$ and accumulated capital $K(t)$, generates an annual village income $Y(t)$.

$$Y(t) = f\big[K(t), L(t), N(t)\big], \qquad\qquad ....(5.14)$$

with the usual assumptions of diminishing marginal productivities.

From the village income, after paying the 'stipendiary wages', the village community is left with a surplus income of $[Y - w.N]$. The villagers decide to distribute this surplus in three parts: The first part $\hat{a}_w$ goes to workers as 'participatory wage' income. The second part $\hat{a}_r$ is distributed among those who have agreed to pool their land. The third part $\hat{a}_v$ is retained as a net village fund for further investments or replacements towards village development. For obvious reasons $\hat{a}_w + \hat{a}_r + \hat{a}_v = 1$, that is, the income to be distributed is fully spread between workers, landowners, and village fund. The welfare and growth aspects of the village can be further specified now.

The wage earners, in a sustainable sense, expect a return or income at least as good as the minimum stipulated wage under any alternative rural development programme. In other words, the stipendiary plus participatory wage should be at least as good as the statutory minimum wage W. Stated algebraically,

$$w.N + \hat{a}_w[Y - w.N] \geq W.N \qquad\qquad ....(5.15)$$

Otherwise, the 'students' would withdraw from participation. This process of changing participation can be stated as:

$$\dot{N}(t) = \tilde{A}_w \left[ \hat{a}_w \left\{ Y(t) - w.N(t) \right\} + w.N(t) - W.N(t) \right], \quad ....(5.16)$$

where $\tilde{A}w$ is a positive constant.[24]

In other words, for an average return from participation, higher than any alternative wage pay-off, more and more people will continue to join CVP. The reverse situation would prevail if the average wage income from CVP is less than the alternative income stream. If ever the stipendiary wage rate is set equal to the alternative available W, households' participation in CVP is a bygone conclusion.

The owners of land who have pooled their land resources expect a minimum return out of the surplus as rental income.

$$\hat{a}_r \left[ Y - w.N \right] \geq r.L \qquad\qquad ....(5.17)$$

where r is the return on land under the non-pooled land use decision; otherwise withdrawal of pooled lands would take place. This decision process is specified as:

$$\dot{L}(t) = \tilde{A}_r \left[ \hat{a}_r \left\{ Y(t) - w.N(t) \right\} - r.L(t) \right] \qquad ....(5.18)$$

where $\tilde{A}r$ is a positive constant.

As long as the average income from land as rental under participation is higher than an alternative opportunity rental r, more and more land would be pooled. People would stop pooling their land whenever the returns become less than r.

The village fund is to be utilized exclusively for further investments including replacements. Therefore, the net addition to the community capital stock can be expressed as:

$$\dot{K}(t) = \hat{a}_v \left[ Y(t) - w.N(t) \right] - a'.K(t), \qquad ....(5.19)$$

where á is the depreciation rate.

One of the first questions in participatory development of CVP type is the minimum amount of land and labour to be pooled. As Runge (1986) argues, this depends upon the marginal gains at the time of pooling. These issues are analysed using the specified model.

The initiation of the process requires guaranteeing the beneficiaries that their minimum expectations will be fulfilled. The owners of land

---

[24]The dot (.) above any variable stands for change per unit of time.

who are willing to contribute some land must receive at least their alternative income. The landless labourers who will participate in the process should be guaranteed the minimum wage. These two conditions are stated mathematically as:

$$\hat{a}_r \left[ Y(0) - w.N(0) \right] = r.L(0) \quad \quad ....(5.20)$$

$$\hat{a}_w \left[ Y(0) - w.N(0) \right] + w.N(0) = W.N(0) \quad \quad ....(5.21)$$

The minimum condition for the participatory process should also include the need for growing village community assets. In other words, there is a need for net investment.

$$\hat{a}_v \left[ Y(0) - w.N(0) \right] - a'.K(0) > 0 \quad \quad ....(5.22)$$

These three conditions imply that:

$$N(0) = \frac{\hat{a}_w Y(0)}{\left[ W - w + \hat{a}_w.W \right]}$$

$$L(0) = \frac{\hat{a}_r (W - w).Y(0)}{r.\left[ W - w + \hat{a}_w.w \right]} \quad \quad ....(5.23)$$

$$\frac{N(0)}{K(0)} > \frac{a'.\hat{a}_w}{\hat{a}_v (W - w)} \quad \quad ....(5.24)$$

$$\frac{L(0)}{K(0)} = \frac{a'.\hat{a}_r}{r.\hat{a}_v} \quad \quad ....(5.25)$$

The required land/man ratio is given by Expression (5.23), whereas the minimum man/capital and land/capital ratios are given by Expressions (5.24) and (5.25). For any given values of $\hat{a}_w$, $\hat{a}_r$, and $\hat{a}_v$ and initial capital investment $K(0)$, the minimum initial pool of land and people are solvable.[25] The level of initial capital stock will, however, depend upon institutional requirements (as given in Expressions (5.24) and (5.25) as well as the ultimate objective of participatory development). The initial attributes of participation stated in Expressions (5.22) to (5.25) imply that participation depends upon (i) the level of initial resource transfer $K(0)$, (ii) the sharing or

[25]Mathematically speaking, given the Production Function (5.14) and Expression (5.22), it all depends upon the initial capital stock $K(0)$ and the type of sharing rules (that is, $\hat{a}_r$, $\hat{a}_w$, and $\hat{a}_v$) agreed upon by the participants.

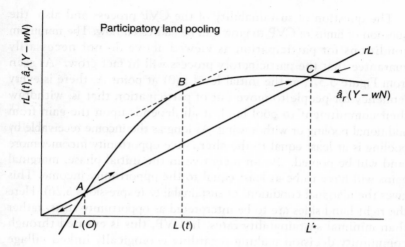

**Figure 5.3:** Evolution of Land Pooling

distribution mechanism decided by the participating villagers that is, $â_v$, $â_r$, $â_w$, (iii) the values of opportunity wage and rental incomes namely, W and r, and (iv) the depreciation rate á. The most crucial institutional factor is the agreement and understanding regarding the distributional mechanism.

Figure 5.3, shows that a minimum pooling of L(0) land is essential. For any pooled land less than L(0), the total return from land $â_r$(Y-w.N) is less than its threat pay-off r.L. Hence there is no reason why people should pool land. The total level of land pooling at this initial level L(0) is institutionally quite unstable; a marginal shift away from L(0) makes the participatory model either collapse (that is, L(0) declining to zero due to withdrawal of pooled land) or sets in motion participatory growth (that is, L(t) increasing).[26]

---

[26]It may be useful to illustrate such a participatory model with a numerical example. Using the data from a CVP village (Bhusadia of Palamau district in Jharkhand), the following parametric/ data specifications are made.

An initial investment K(0) = Rs 1 lakh

Equal sharing rule agreed by the community (that is, $â_i$= 0.33),

Land productivity before CVP = r = Rs 1000/acre

Stipendiary wage rate per day = w = Rs10

Alternative wage income = W = Rs 22.50

The question of sustainability of the CVP process and also the question of limits of CVP to grow can be addressed now. The minimum conditions for participation as viewed above do not necessarily guarantee that the participatory process will in fact grow. As seen from Figure 5.3.1, at the initial level L(0) at point A, there is every tendency for people to move out of participation that is, withdraw their commitment to pool land; it all depends upon the gain from additional pooling or withdrawing. As long as the income receivable by pooling is at least equal to the alternative opportunity income, more land will be pooled. As an incentive in the initial phase, marginal gains will have to be at least equal to the opportunity income. This gives the marginal conditions of sustainability (expressions 5.26). Here the right hand sides are to be interpreted as opportunity costs, rather than minimal sustainability rates. In CVP, this is ensured through community decision making regarding ecologically linked village development.

$$\hat{a}_r \left[ \frac{\partial Y}{\partial L} \right] > r$$

$$\hat{a}_v \left[ \frac{\partial Y}{\partial K} \right] > a' \qquad \qquad ....(5.26)$$

$$\hat{a}_w \left[ \frac{\partial Y}{\partial N - w} \right] > (W - w)$$

The process will then certainly expand up to point B at which the marginal gains are at par with the opportunity costs. But the inherent characteristic of the participatory model is internalizing the total gain. This makes the process grow beyond B but perhaps at a slower pace in the latter stages.

---

Discount rate = á = 0.10
Then the estimated initial values of Bhusadia CVP should be as follows:
Annual income = Y(0) = Rs 38,000
Land to be pooled = L(0) = 10 acres
Man-days of labour pooled = N(0) = 800 man days
Capital/output ratio = 2.63
Labour productivity = Rs 47.50 /man day
It may be useful to note that when Bhusadia CVP was started in 1987, the total land pooled was 25 acres and participation of labour was 1200 man days.

How long and how far this process can continue is the third most important analytical question. As seen in Figure 5.3, point C is of interest now. At this stage there are no incentives either to increase or reduce land pooling. It is a mature state in the participatory process. In fact, point C corresponds to the final equilibrium of the participatory process. The participatory process may be described as essentially moving away from the initiation at L(0) to L* through a CVP type   community participation programme, with the corresponding labour participation moving from N(0) to N*.

Sustainability is a long-run condition. In the long run, the participatory process is said to be sustainable provided the levels of activities stabilize at an equilibrium level which guarantee income benefits at a sufficiently high level depending upon peoples' preferences; and there are no incentives to move out of such a position. These steady state conditions can be obtained by equating Expressions (5.16), (5.18), and (5.19) to zero. They in turn imply that the long run village income will be,

$$Y^* = r.L^* + W.N^* + a'.K^* \qquad \qquad ....(5.27)$$

The steady state output Y* is equal to the opportunity rental income on land r.L* plus the opportunity wage income W.N* and the replacement capital investment á.K*.

The necessary and sufficient conditions for local stability of these solutions are that the trace of the associated Jacobean matrix be negative and its determinant non-negative.   The steady state conditions can now be written using (5.27) as:

$$\dot{L} = (\hat{a}_r - 1).r.L^* + \hat{a}_r.(W-w).N^* + \hat{a}_w.a'.K^* = 0 \qquad (5.28)$$

$$\dot{N} = \hat{a}_w.r.L^* + (\hat{a}_w - 1).(W-w).N^* + \hat{a}_w.a'.K^* = 0 \qquad (5.29)$$

The equation for $\dot{K}(t)$ is redundant. It can be seen that the trace of the above system of differential equations, $(\hat{a}_r-1)r + (W-w)(\hat{a}_w-1)$, is negative and the determinant (W-w) r.$\hat{a}_v > 0$. In other words, the steady state condition is a locally stable solution.

The long-run sustainable levels of resource (land) pooling and peoples' participation are given by:

$$L^* = \left[ \frac{\hat{a}_r}{\hat{a}_v} \right].\left[ \frac{a'}{r} \right].K^* \qquad (5.30)$$

$$N^* = \left[ \frac{\hat{a}_w}{\hat{a}_v} \right] \cdot \left[ \frac{a'}{(W-w)} \right] \cdot K^* \tag{5.31}$$

In other words, these in turn, depend upon the level of long-run capital formation.[27] The process of participatory development is said to be operational if one can make the levels of participation reach these sustainable magnitudes.

The last major issue that needs to be resolved in the analytical model is concerning distribution rules. Given the long-run objectives of sustaining the resources with participation, benefits from the development process should be so shared as to stabilize the participatory institution itself. Expressions 5.24 state the boundaries for $\hat{a}_r$, $\hat{a}_v$, and $\hat{a}_w$ so as to make the process a growing one. Steady state conditions (5.27), (5.30) and (5.31) indicate that in the long run, the levels of capital stock, land pooled, peoples' participation, and the resulting income gain depend upon the sharing mechanism and *vice versa*. This indeterminateness can be resolved only through a process of negotiations.[28] Here the role of leadership is extremely important. As long as the values of $\hat{a}_r$, $\hat{a}_w$, and $\hat{a}_v$ are adjusted at the margin but fulfil the expression (5.26), participation in the CPR development process may not have any major reservations. Revision of the sharing rules frequently is also generally not liked by people. If the per capita output and capital–output ratios are fixed, based on certain welfare and development dynamics, it is then possible to deduce the consistent values of $\hat{a}_r$, $\hat{a}_w$, and $\hat{a}_v$ under the steady state conditions. Assuming the per capita output $Y/N=a$ and capital–output ratio $K/Y=b$ at the study state situation as given, one can arrive at the estimates of the sharing or distribution parameters as:[29]

$$\hat{a}_w = \frac{(W-w)}{(a-W)}; \ \hat{a}_v = \frac{a.b.a'}{(a-w)}; \ \hat{a}_r = 1 - \hat{a}_w - \hat{a}_v \tag{5.32}$$

[27]Equations (5.25), (5.28) and (5.29) being homogeneous in $Y^*$, $L^*$, $N^*$, and $K^*$, one of them will have to be specified from outside. We choose $K^*$ to be chosen from outside, based on other criteria.

[28]There are precisely five equations to be solved for seven variables namely, L, N, K, Y, $\hat{a}_r$, $\hat{a}_w$, and $\hat{a}_v$. The five equations are (5.14), (5.27), (5.30), (5.31) and the identity $\hat{a}_w + \hat{a}_v + \hat{a}_r = 1$. Hence the indeterminacy.

[29]For the illustration presented, with a=4 and b=3, the estimated values of $\hat{a}_w$, $\hat{a}_v$, and $\hat{a}_r$ are 0.4, 0.4, and 0.2, respectively. However, in Bhusadia and many other villages, the gains are distributed in three equal shares of 0.33.

In other words,  the sharing rules ought to depend upon the long-term objectives of CPR development,  viewed in terms of  (i) returns from CPR on per capita basis, and (ii) the level of investment required. The first condition is a livelihood sustainability requirement. The second is a strategy on CPR developments, a question that will be addressed  in Chapter 7. This model is tested using data from about 40 villages in Jharkhand presented as a case study in Chapter 10.

## APPENDIX

APPENDIX 5.1: Taxonomy of Symmetric Games

A game is said to be completely specified when the set of players $N = \{1,2,....n\}$; set of strategies $S = \{s_1, s_2, ....s_k \}$; and the pay-offs $P_{ij}$, for each player i under each strategy $s_j$ are completely pre-specified. In a two-person, two-strategy game, the pay-offs can be represented by a set $P = \{x, y, a, b\}$, as shown in Table 5.1. Depending upon the relative pay-offs under the four possible groups of  the game matrix, certain well-known games are listed below.

Table A 5.1.1
Typology of Games

| S. No. | Name of the Game | Ordering of the Pay-offs |
|---|---|---|
| 1 | Prisoners' dilemma | $a > x > y > b$ |
| 2 | Pareto Game | $x > \max \{a, y\}; b > y$ |
| 3 | Assurance Game | $x > a > y > b$ |
| 4 | Co-ordination Game | $x > y > \max \{a, b\}$ |
| 5 | Non-coordination Game | $\min \{a, b\} > x > y$ |
| 6 | Chicken's Game | $a > x > b > y$ |
| 7 | Hawk–Dove Game | $x > y; a = x, b = y$ |

Source: Luce and Raifa (1957), Lise (1997)

APPENDIX 5.2: List of Participatory Information

1.  Are you undertaking tree plantation work?
2.  Are you contributing something like money or voluntary labour to the society to help in its functioning?
3.  To what extent are you benefited from the presence of the community organization in your village?
4.  To what extent do you agree with the decisions taken by the

management committee?
5. How frequent are the meetings of the management committee?
6. How frequently do you attend the meetings?
7. To what extent are you able to influence the decisions of the management committee?
8. To what extent do you find the discussions in the meeting to be of interest?
9. To what extent do you gain from the discussions in the meetings?
10. To what extent do you make suggestions in the meetings?

# 6

# Existing Institutions to Manage CPRs in India

## HOW ARE CPR RESOURCES MANAGED IN INDIA?

Theory apart, the existing and historically established institutional mechanisms in India say a lot about the manner in which CPRs are managed. To begin with, one can think of two extreme types of institutions to manage CPRs—either exclusively by the state or by individuals. As seen from data from India in Chapters 2 and 3, one recognizes instances of both private and public ownership in water (as wells, groundwater, etc.), fishery resources, forests, land, and in some cases, minerals.

However, in many countries the state has acted at some time or other, as the major custodian of CPRs. In India too for a variety of natural resources and CPRs the state has been acting as the custodian. A variety of land categories such as revenue lands, panchayat lands, railway lands, canal banks, PWD lands, are owned by central or state governments. Forests of all types (except for less than 1 per cent under private ownership) are owned by the state governments. All the rivers and irrigation and water supply systems are under the custody of individual states, central government, and public bodies such as municipal corporations. Some resources are retained as riparian rights and in many other cases they are governed by various state and central acts, such as Water Act, Forest Conservation Act, Mines Act, Coastal Zone Regulation Act and so on. Legally speaking, in the Constitution of India, under Article 246, several of the commons are either put under the exclusive responsibility of individual states (under the Seventh Schedule, as List II–State list) or that of the central government (under the Seventh Schedule, as List I–Union List), or under both the central and state governments (as List III Concurrent List).[1]

As a matter of governance and management, the state can act with three different objectives or motivations, namely, as a benevolent state, revenue maximizing state, or a policing state, the meanings of which are self-explanatory. The state may succeed or fail in managing the resources depending upon the socio-political climate. Often, it is also difficult to distinguish between motives and strategies. For instance, nationalization of coal (as was the case in both India and UK) can be considered to meet all the three motives.[2] In many actual situations, the state acts as a 'revenue maximizing state', as the case was with timber forestry by the states in India, to raise state revenues as well as to police and protect the natural capital. Experience, however, shows that in most situations the revenue objectives are not met at all by the forest management in the states, (Table 6.1).

At the same time, quite often, protection of such CPRs is treated mainly as a 'policing affair', the costs of which are quite high.[3] The failure of policing state, in managing CPRs such as forests and water

[1]For instance, the regulation of mines and minerals is the responsibility of the state governments; regulation and development of inter-state rivers and river valleys is the responsibility of the Central government, whereas water supply, irrigation, canals, drainage, development of ponds etc., are the responsibility of the individual states; land and fishery management are under state jurisdiction; forests and wildlife protection are in the concurrent list that is, the responsibility of both the central and state governments.

[2]At the time of nationalization of Indian coal, the main reasons were welfare oriented use of coal, proper pricing and conservation of energy, and minimizing the misuse of this precious primary energy source. Incidentally, the Coal Controller in his written evidence to the Estimates Committee of the Lok Sabha in 1954–5 put it bluntly as 'If the nationalization is postponed by 25 years and the industry is given a free hand, there will be little left at the end of the period for the country to takeover.'

[3]They are due to 'tragedy of the commons', leakages in the bureaucratic system, non-market exchanges, and many other reasons.

Table 6.1
Status of Revenue and Expenditure in Forestry in Selected States in India
*(Rs Lakh)*

| State | 1994–5 | | 1995–6 | |
|---|---|---|---|---|
| | Revenue | Expenditure | Revenue | Expenditure |
| Assam | 1692 | 5212 | 1726 | 5468 |
| Goa | 139 | 300 | 139 | 293 |
| Himachal Pradesh | 4711 | 8524 | 4494 | 9607 |
| Jammu and Kashmir | 1142 | 4861 | 3316 | 5945 |
| Karnataka | 9478 | 15,047 | 10,573 | 16,515 |
| Maharashtra | 14,786 | 22,403 | 13,729 | 23,165 |
| Meghalaya | 451 | 500 | 515 | 639 |
| Nagaland | 221 | 482 | 275 | 998 |
| Punjab | 525 | 1878 | 668 | 2147 |
| Rajasthan | 1338 | 3556 | 1318 | 3453 |
| Sikkim | 125 | 325 | 190 | 425 |
| Tamil Nadu | 6481 | 8653 | 5797 | 9367 |
| Tripura | 290 | 502 | 303 | 653 |
| Uttar Pradesh | 7760 | 13,162 | 9847 | 15,219 |
| West Bengal | 4498 | 8631 | 4352 | 9129 |
| All India | 144,153 | 173,091 | 169,028 | 199,340 |

*Note:* Few other states showing positive net revenues are not shown in this table.
*Source:* Forestry Statistics of India, 1996.

bodies, is quite well documented (Poffenburger and McGean, 1996; Bromley and Cernea, 1989; Meyer, 1996). The reasons are many. Basically it is due to failure of property rights and asymmetry in information between the government and people. After all, the government is the custodian and the people are the beneficiaries of CPRs (Hurley and Shogren, 1998). Thus arises a question of two different property rights regimes on the same property. Between these two property rights arrangements, conflicts and contradictions can arise. Being the owner, the government perhaps knows the most about the size and nature of the resource in term of its use and non-use values and the laws. However, it may exercise the management and exchange only in terms of its 'use value' for revenue maximizing. Treating forests for timber growth and sale by the governments is a classic example. An individual as a user may also know both these values, but because of unequal exchange, (s)he may also exercise the mind only for the 'use value'. The government has the policing power, which is not given to the people. People may want access to some CPRs (example water) free as a matter of right, but the government may ask for some responsibility. Perceptions may differ. The government may interpret preservation of CPR areas as complete evacuation of the people whereas the people may talk of social fencing.

Thus, for many such reasons, conflict resolution regarding the management of CPRs under state management is generally difficult (Chopra *et al.*, 1990; Ostrom and Gardner, 1993; Lise, 1997; Metrick and Weitzman, 1998; Singh and Hegde, 2001; Dasgupta, 1982). If anything, it may end up in a prisoners' dilemma type of solution (as discussed in Chapter 5). The expected outcomes are state governments losing revenue from forests, and people who are initially dependent on forests either resorting to illegal cutting or migrating out of the forest region, and degradation of forests (Sethi and Somanathan, 1996; Chopra and Gulati, 1997).[4] Thus, when the state fails to be a welfare state, or is unable to meet its revenue maximizing objective, or when it fails to police the property, there is a need to look for a switch of property rights away from state management. Such a move has already taken place in India in respect of a large number of CPRs.

The second extreme alternative for managing CPRs is to deal with them as PPRs. While some degree of efficiency in resource use may be the outcome, the social objectives of meeting everybody's requirements and equity are not at all ensured under such a scheme. Furthermore, there are several possibilities of conflicts between individuals due to the divergence between private values and social or collective values.[5] First, private interests may induce the individuals to ignore the total value of the CPRs. Consider the example of *betta* lands (village forest lands) given to individual areca nut plantation farmers in Karnataka (Nadkarni *et al.*, 1989). It was observed that the farmers then collect all

---

[4]In 1995–6, out of 31 states in India, 22 states reported revenue losses from state managed forestry (Government of India,1996) with total losses adding up to Rs 303 crores! This can also be interpreted as the government's concern to regenerate and protect the forests, rather than managing them to fulfil revenue objectives.

[5]The difference between private and social values can be seen from Figure 4.1. The CPR productivity is higher than private productivity and CPR costs are lower than private costs. Hence the net social gain from management as commons is higher than that under a private regime.

the leaf biomass as required for plantation farming (as manure), and ignore to protect or plant additional trees. Hence the total gain from that forest land as a CPR is not reaped. Second, due to acute poverty and lack of technical knowledge, or due to social insecurity, marginal farmers may find it difficult to manage their privately owned lands with social objectives. Frequent extortionist behaviour on the part of the administrators or exploitation by large landowners often forces them to leave their private lands uncultivated.

Having witnessed the problems in managing CPRs through either of the two extreme institutional arrangements, the need for a new institutional approach of collective action (as discussed in Chapter 5) is considered to be timely.[6] In the Indian context, collective action in respect of CPRs can be rephrased as participatory management. But, much of the resource management in the rural context (in India) is also development oriented and often referred to as participatory development. For instance, in watershed development or in community based forest management, there are elements of both development and resource management. Therefore, collective action in the context of CPR management in India can be referred to as participatory development in general, or as participatory management in particular.

The design, ground rules, and approach to collectivize and manage CPR resources have already been dealt with in Chapter 5. From the experience with a large number of existing rural institutions, one can say that collectivization is certainly not an easy task. One can list a number of limitations to such participatory actions, inherent due to the socio-economic conditions prevailing in the rural economies or resilience and frictions about the power structure that exists between the bureaucracy, politicians, and the people. Some of the apparent limitations are:

1. lack of bargaining skills on the part of the people;
2. the state (or government) acting as the owner of technology, finance, and law and not as their custodian;
3. difficulty in enforcement of rules and regulations due to short sightedness;

---

[6]The literature on this subject is quite rich. See Olson (1965), Commons (1950), Runge (1986), Freitag (1990), Ostrom (1990), Wade(1987), Hardin (1982), Murty (1994), Clague (1997), Nabli and Nugent (1989), Roy (1995), and North (1990).

4. existence of parallel programmes on CPR management with a focus on poverty alleviation; and

5. growing influence of market and consumerism.

Therefore, the success story of participatory institutions is to be gauged against such possible limitations. It is increasingly being revealed from the experience of different countries (and India) that the ultimate beneficiaries of many economic activities prefer to have themselves included as partners to the state and even market based machinery or development and implementation agencies rather than being left out as only the recipients.

Sengupta (1995) lists a large number of difficulties and weaknesses in promoting community based CPR institutions. The notable ones are uncertainties, persistent free rider problems, difficulty in co-ordination, and challenges from market based institutions. One can also add to this list, the problems of not finding leadership and social fragmentation of the society (based on caste and class). However, one can augment the role of the state to provide opportunities for external catalytic leaders, to promote internal leaderships, and also homogenize the social groups through awareness programmes, and education. Certainly, there are a number of essential design requirements before instituting any participatory CPR management (discussed in Chapter 7).

TYPES OF CPR INSTITUTIONS IN INDIA

In Chapters 2 and 3, the dimensions of CPRs in India under various property rights systems were presented. As much as precise estimates of CPRs are not available, no official data and information exist in India that would give a complete picture of community management and the institutions governing them. A variety of new local institutions have come up during the last thirty years (not referring to sources of funding), some under national and governmental framework, some jointly with NGOs and village communities, several others under region specific, individual initiatives and leadership totally outside the government. Apart from the emergence of local, community based institutions, there are a host of traditional institutions as well.

Among the broad categories of institutions to manage the commons, a macro review of three types of institutions (existing in India today) is presented in this chapter. This is followed by selected micro-level case studies later, in the book. They are (i) joint forest management, as an illustration of government and communities working together, with communities having a major role; (ii) watershed development, where the irrigation or soil-conservation department joined hand with the village communities, but with the government playing a major role; (iii) sacred groves, where traditionally only the village communities are involved without any involvement of the government.[7]

Joint Forest Management: A Community driven programme

India is one of the pioneering countries in the world where forest management regimes stressing on partnerships between the state forest departments and the local communities, generically known as JFM have been introduced. The driving force behind these innovative changes is the Forest Policy of 1988, which stressed on the management of forests for conservation and meeting the needs of local communities; and made commercial exploitation and revenue generation secondary objectives.

The involvement of local communities in the management of state forest lands was facilitated by the issuance of specific guidelines by the Central Government on 1st June 1990. In the following years, several state governments adopted this concept and issued state-specific orders and resolutions for its implementation. As of date, 27 states in the country have passed enabling orders and resolutions, and about 14.25 million hectares of forest area is under JFM, (some details in Table 6.2).[8] About 63,000 village protection committees have been registered

[7]Apart from these macro-level institutions, one can identify several micro-level institutions such as Pani Panchayats, Water User Associations, CVP, several NGO led programmes and institutions such as Seva Mandir, Participatory and Integrated Development of Watersheds (PIDOWL), Aga Khan Foundation, Deccan Development Society, PRADAN, MYRADA, Tarun Bharat Sangh, Ubheswar Vikar Mandal, and a large number of others. World Wildlife Fund (India) has brought out a compendium of all the NGOs (with their addresses) working, by and large, on soil, water, forest, and wildlife resources. But the actual involvements by activities or performance evaluation are not available. NGO based institutions are not reviewed as one category, because of their heterogeneity, and differential objectives and missions. Interested readers can get a glimpse of these from Kadekodi (1997b) and Singh (1994a). As a sample, CVP is reviewed as a case study in Chapter 9.

[8]As an example of the state level resolution, selected sections and paragraphs from a Notification on JFM from Haryana Government are shown in Appendix A6.1. It shows the precisely defined rules and responsibilities assigned to communities and forest departments. For such details from all the states see SPWD (1998).

all over the country. Joint Forest Management covers about 18 per cent of total forest area, or about 40 per cent of protected and unclassed area or about the same magnitude out of degraded forest area. One can, therefore, hope that very soon this programme will become a major community oriented programme. As can be seen from Table 6.2, states such as Orissa, Uttaranchal (because of van panchayats), Madhya Pradesh, Andhra Pradesh and Chattisgarh have taken a lead in JFM.

Table 6.2
Status of JFM in the country

| State | Area under JFM (000 ha.) | Number of FPCs |
| --- | --- | --- |
| Andhra Pradesh | 1679.08 | 7606 |
| Arunachal Pradesh | 5.81 | 13 |
| Assam | 6.97 | 245 |
| Bihar | 504.60 | 296 |
| Chhatisgarh | 3391.31 | 6412 |
| Goa | 13.00 | 26 |
| Gujarat | 138.01 | 1237 |
| Haryana | 65.85 | 471 |
| Himachal Pradesh | 111.25 | 914 |
| Jammu and Kashmir | 79.55 | 1895 |
| Jharkhand | 430.46 | 1379 |
| Karnataka | 185.00 | 2620 |
| Kerala | 4.99 | 32 |
| Madhya Pradesh | 4125.84 | 9203 |
| Maharashtra | 686.69 | 2153 |
| Manipur | 10.50 | 58 |
| Mizoram | 12.74 | 129 |
| Nagaland | 150.00 | 55 |
| Orissa | 783.47 | 12,317 |
| Punjab | 97.19 | 188 |
| Rajasthan | 309.34 | 3042 |
| Sikkim | 0.60 | 158 |
| Tamil Nadu | 299.39 | 799 |
| Tripura | 23.48 | 160 |
| Uttar Pradesh | 45.03 | 502 |
| Uttaranchal | 606.61 | 7435 |
| West Bengal | 488.10 | 3545 |
| Total | 14,254.85 | 62,890 |

Note: As on 1 June, 2001.
Source: Ministry of Environment and Forests.

Under the JFM scheme, village communities enter into an agreement with the forest department to jointly manage the forest land adjoining the villages, and to share responsibilities to protect and preserve the forest lands. In return, they receive benefits under agreed formulae framed from time to time. The village community is represented by a village protection committee (VPC) or village forest committee (VFC), which takes all the major decisions regarding the management of the resource.[9]

The essential economic and institutional features of JFMs are summarized in Box 6.1.[10]

---

**Box 6.1: Features and Experience with Joint Forest Management in India**

- Equal rights to all members of the community
- Changing attitudes of the communities and forest department away from one of suspicion and conflicts to one of co-operation
- Sharing of forest produce such as fuelwood, fodder, fruits, medicinal plants, and herbs, bark etc. by an agreed formula
- Improvements in forest protection from illegal felling, trespassing, poaching, and forest fires
- Enhanced regeneration and survival of plant and animal species
- Reduced encroachments
- Improved income and equity in the community

---

There are several emerging issues with JFM today. Invariably, JFM has been supported by certain bilateral donors.[11] With the withdrawals of such financial support, the state governments are unable to maintain the growth of JFM spreading to all the states and to all the villages. Second, communities continue to view them as employment schemes and not as participatory village development programmes. Third, by and large, JFM is still restricted to degraded forests only (with the

---

[9]Different names are associated with such VFCs, such as Vana Samrakshana Samiti in Andhra Pradesh, HRMS in Haryana, CVP in Jharkhand and so on.

[10]One can cite hundreds of case studies on the JFM experience. Some of these can be seen in Sundar. (2001), Ravindranath et al. (2000).

[11]During the period 1990 to date, about Rs 42,278 million have been invested by donor agencies with a target of covering 2,447,000 hectares in various forestry related projects in India, of which a substantial part is on JFM only. On average, a cost of Rs 16,900 per hectare has been spent, which is quite high.

exception of Madhya Pradesh). Fourth, in certain states such as Jharkhand, Orissa, and Nagaland, there are thousands of traditional tribal community groups that have been protecting the forests over generations. But they have been marginalized under JFM to some extent. Fifth, JFM has still not worked out proper marketing strategies or links with market based institutions, an issue raised by Sengupta (1995); because of this the poor collectors from the forests are still being exploited. Sixth, the participation of women is still very nominal, despite procedures established in the JFM guidelines. Finally, one of the major issues is about the link between JFM and Panchayati Raj institutions. While the latter have constitutional approval and regular flows of budgetary allocations, JFM has neither. Because of this, communities may ignore JFM programmes and be attracted by the Panchayat based programmes.[12] However, recent notifications from the Ministry of Environment and Forests have been trying to improve the performance of JFM. Moreover, the involvement of the corporate sector (for example, TVS–Suzuki in Tamil Nadu JFM) has emerged recently, which may help to bridge the gaps in JFM programmes (in marketing and pricing, etc.).

Sacred Groves in India

Since times immemorial, forests have served mankind by fulfilling needs such as food, fibre, shelter, medicine, security, and so on. Most traditional forest-dwelling societies, however, link forests, trees, animals, and other objects associated with forests, to deities and animistic beliefs, thus attaching a sacred connotation to forests. The concept here is that forests are the property of the Gods of the villages in which they are situated.[13] A sacred grove is a patch of vegetation, ranging in the extent from a few trees to several hectares, which is left undisturbed because of its association with a particular deity. Anthropological studies (Roy Barman, 1992; Malhotra *et al.*, undated) show that the village

[12]Under Article 243 G of the Constitution of India, it is possible to amalgamate these two local institutions.

[13]Buchanan (1870) who traveled through Uttara Kannada district of Karnataka wrote:

'The forests are the property of the Gods of the villages in which they are situated, and the trees ought not to be cut without having leave from the Gauda or Headman of the village, who here is also the priest to the temple of the village God.'

communities had protected and preserved the sacred groves much better than their own private land resources. Hence they have survived as commons for the village communities believing in their village deities. They have also been studied as biodiversity preserves and avenues for local participation (Godbole *et al.*, 1998). Sacred groves represent common property biodiversity resources, encompassing a large variety of tree and animal species, water bodies, and micro-organisms.[14]

The existence of sacred groves has been widely reported from the Western Ghats, spread over Kerala in the south (approximately 2000 groves), Karnataka in the central region and Maharashtra (over 1750) in the north. Studies have also been reported, from parts of Rajasthan, Himachal Pradesh, Uttar Pradesh, the hilly regions of the states like Bihar (particularly the Chhotanagpur region), Orissa, Assam, Meghalaya (especially the Cherrapunji region), Mizoram, Madhya Pradesh (particularly Bastar region), and Tamil Nadu, showing the inventory of wild and domesticated plants and animal species protected, the areas, the link with village communities and customary beliefs and worships of deities (Malhotra *et al.*, undated; Gadgil and Vartak, 1981).

| Box 6.2: Documented Sacred Groves in India | | |
|---|---|---|
| Location | No. of Sacred Groves | Area (ha.) |
| Andhra Pradesh | 750 | – |
| Maharashtra | 483 | 3570 |
| Karnataka(Kodagu) | 1214 | 5947 |
| Meghalaya | 79 | 26,326 |
| Kerala | 2000 | 500 |
| Tamil Nadu | 10 | 127 |
| Rajasthan | 9 | 241 |
| Uttar Pradesh | 1 | 5500 |
| Orissa | 322 | 50 |
| West Bengal | 7 | 2 |
| Total | 4875 | 39,063 |

*Note*: These reflect only the researched inventories of sacred groves.
*Source*: Malhotra *et al.*, (undated), p. 12.

[14]The tree species vary from evergreen to semi-evergreen, mangroves to deciduous types. Examples are food plants like mango, jackfruit, cashew, wild palm, and a variety of wild fruits; spices like pepper, nutmeg, curry leaf, and cinnamon; wealth of medicinal plants; and minor forest produce like honey, mushroom, and bamboo

The most probable rationale for the close and sacred association between mankind and forests in general, and sacred groves in particular, lies in the short and long-term benefits flowing from the forests. Sacred groves serve critical functions such as sheltering rare plants and protecting water sources. Being the only remnants of tree vegetation along the countryside they are also the main sources of leaf litter. They are of significant economic and climatic importance to the people who benefit from them (Gokhale *et al.*, 1998).

In the past, sacred groves survived, to a large extent, due to the existence of certain basic characteristics for their sustainable use. These include a small number of groups sharing the resource, repeated and long-term interaction between groups sharing access to the resource, equitable distribution of harvests, and reciprocal or kinship relations between parties. Inspite of being one of the world's top 12 mega diversity countries with traditions and enhanced efforts of biodiversity conservation, India's biodiversity reserves are being eroded rapidly. This can be attributed to the deficiencies in the current system of forest utilization and weakening traditions. One such factor is changing religious beliefs; for instance, the amalgamation of primitive deities into the pantheon of Hindu gods, often followed by the construction of temples. A major threat to their survival, which arose with the 'state' under the British regime, taking up control of forests including sacred groves, still continues. People's traditional rights over sacred groves have been reduced to minor concessions or privileges. With depleting resource availability, and curtailed rights and transfer of forest resources out of community control, they have virtually become open access resources from being CPRs. Contract systems and their exploitation by forest-based industries have only hastened their degradation. An important factor furthering such degradation is the

shoots. Besides these, a large number of wild relatives of cultivated plants have also been spotted. Sacred groves also provide shelter to numerous species of birds like drongos, swallows, flycatchers, and orioles; fish species; mammals like bats, primates, and minor mammals; and reptiles like cobras, vipers, kraits, and pythons (primarily in serpent groves). The above-mentioned and innumerable other mobile and immobile species have been spotted and documented by researchers. Studies of floral, faunal, and wildlife diversity have been made by Gadgil and Vartak (1981) in the Maharashtra region of the Western Ghats, Chandrakanth and Nagaraj (1997) in Coorg, and Chandran and Gadgil (1993) in Uttara Kannada district, besides several other studies.

narrowly focussed notion of protected areas, with the neglect of neighbouring areas no patch of vegetation can escape the effects of surrounding environmental conditions. One other societal factor is the exclusion of human use and on the use of force, particularly against local tribal and rural populations who are dependent on forests for their subsistence needs. A final factor is the recent phenomenon of emerging preference for modern scientific knowledge to traditional and tenable folk ecological knowledge.

Watershed Development Programmes (WDP)

Watershed development is a composite concept in which the management of soil, water, and plantations is integrated with the development of the people around them. Since all these resources are by and large 'common' in nature, it can also be construed that this is an alternative institutional mechanism to manage them. Hence, it may be useful to review it briefly.[15]

What is a watershed? Watershed is defined on the basis of water drainage basins. The smallest watershed is based on a single drainage (often called a first order watershed). As one basin joins another one, the size and concept of the watershed changes (hence, there are second, third, and higher order watersheds). Spatially speaking, a watershed can be defined at various levels, at a macro-level (district or regional levels), at a micro-level or village level (hundreds or thousands of hectares), at the farm level or even within the farm.[16] In general, a watershed development concept aims to establish an enabling environment for the integrated use, regulation, and treatment of water and land resources of a watershed based ecosystem to accomplish resource conservation and biomass production objectives (Jensen, 1996).

Experience all over the world reveals that although a micro watershed may be conceived as a sensible planning unit from a bio-physical perspective, an institutional framework based on community involvement is necessary for the protection and rehabilitation of PPRs

[15]There is a vast literature that exists on this subject in India and other countries. Some of the relevant, recent books in India are: Farington et al., (1999), Srivastava and Chundi (1999), Turton et al., (1998), and Singh (1995).

[16]For more a detailed, scientific definition of a watershed, see Kadekod et al (2000).

and CPRs. However, quite often the bio-physically defined watershed area does not coincide with the boundaries of the village or community-wise hamlets. Second, apart from land and water related activities, which are directly a part of watershed management, it is necessary to add on several other primary (livestock rearing, fishing) and secondary activities (rope making, fish canning, milk processing) as part of an integrated development programme of the area. Then WDPs may or may not strictly remain an institution for purely CPR management. But as discussed in Chapter 4, the links between such private and common property resources translate into management for better development. An important characterization of the watershed management programme in India today is to bring both the private and common property resources under one umbrella of development. This way the programme can enthuse the villagers to participate better (Farington et al., 1999; Chopra and Rao, 1996; Turton et al., 1998). Third, watershed management and development are also linked to the role of women in CPR resource management ( Lokur, 2000). In a large number of situations it has enabled the women to participate better and has also reduced their hardship.

| Box 6.3: Evolution of Watershed Programmes in India | |
|---|---|
| Year | Description of the programmes |
| 1974 | Scheme for soil conservation in river valley projects |
| 1982 | 46 model watershed development projects launched for the development of dry land agriculture |
| 1984 | World Bank initiated watershed projects in four states |
| 1986 | National Watershed Development Programme for Rainfed Areas(NWDPRA) in 16 states (under the Ministry of Agriculture) with 99 projects |
| 1989 | Integrated Watershed Projects (IWDP)initiated by National Wastelands Development Board (NWDB). |
| 1991 | IWDP in the plains, under taken by the World Bank in three states |
| 1994 | Watershed development programmes merged with various ongoing programmes such as DPAP, DDP, TWDP, JRY, and EAS of the Ministry of Rural Development. |
| 1995 | Growth of Donor agencies |
| 1997 | NABARD initiative |

Table 6.3
Growth of Organized Watershed Management
Programme in India: A Selected Sample

| Year of Start | Watershed Nos/area | Agency/Scheme | Investment (Rs in million) |
|---|---|---|---|
| 1956 | 42 | CSWCRTI | Experimental |
| 1961–2 (RVP) | 3.3 m ha up to 8th Plan | 29 catchments in 18 states | 6826 |
| 1974 | 4 | CSWCRTI | ORP |
| 1980–1(FPR) | 0.83 m ha | 10 catchments in 8 states | 2640 |
| 1983 | 47 | CSWCRTI & CRIDA | ORP |
| 1987 | .12,000 ha | PIDOW | 300 |
| 1991 | 2497 | NWDPRA | 11,285 |
| 1991 | 5 lakh ha | World Bank | 8210 |
| 1991 | 1.3 lakh ha | DANIDA | 600 |
| 1991 | 1 | Rel Majra, CSWCRTI | Experimental |
| 1993 | 2.42 lakh | EEC | 1065 |
| 1994 | 2.54 lakh ha | MRAE | 2157 |
| 1995 | Monitoring | KFW, GERMANY | 767 |
| 1995 | 0.35 lakh ha | SPWD | 203 |
| 1997 | 0.51 lakh ha | DFID (KAWAD) | 15  (in pounds) |
| 1997 | MERC | Aga Khan Foundation | 200 |
| 1997 | UP State | NABARD | Finalization stage |

*Source*: Samra and Dhyani (1998).

Almost starting from the recommendations of the National Commission on Agriculture in 1972, a large number of programmes on soil and water management were started in India, initially as purely government departmental programmes. Soon it was realized that unless the communities—for whom soil and water are commons—are not involved in the management of such resources, the programme cannot be a lasting one (Chopra *et al.*, 1990). Even after such a realization, the development of community based watershed development in India has been rather slow. This is partly because of conflicts between several other parallel land, forest, and water development programmes that have existed since the beginning of the planning era. However, some early initiatives in the late 1980s included 19 pilot community linked watersheds promoted by the Ministry of Agriculture and Co-operation and a further 23 watersheds under the DPAP of the then Department of Rural Development. The success achieved by these led to a larger effort in the Seventh Plan in the form of 99 watersheds under the National Watershed Development Programme for Rainfed Agriculture, later renamed the National Watershed Development Programme for Rainfed Areas (NWDPRA) in 1990. The Eighth Five Year Plan covered 2554 micro watersheds. The Ministry of Rural Areas and Employment administers the DPAP, the Desert Development Programme (DDP), which got merged with a watershed development programme as an approach under the Integrated Watershed Development Programme (IWDP), and Jawahar Rozgar Yojana (JRY). Then came the 1994 guidelines for watershed development issued by the Ministry of Rural Areas and Employment, wholly as 'participatory' and community oriented. The guidelines set up a norm of Rs 4000 per hectare as the necessary government investment for each watershed of about 500 hectares. The new guidelines have several major features: (i) An unprecedented devolution of decision taking power to the district and village level; (ii) Financial allocations from the central government directly down to the district level, and thence to people's organizations at the village level; and (iii) Creation of partnerships through co-ordination among the technical departments of the government, and also between the government, NGOs, and people's organizations.[17]

Box 6.3 and Table 6.3 show the chronological growth of watershed management programmes in India. Apart from this, the JFM independently emerged as another institutional approach in 1990.

A range of other government initiatives and incentives have also been added to supplement the watershed developments. Some serve a supporting role in improving the benefits to be derived from watershed resources, and include sectoral policies on markets and prices, policies and legislation on land, resource and water rights, and the reorientation of extension and research services in the agricultural, livestock, forestry, and wildlife sectors. For instance, one of the functions of the Department of Wasteland Development of the Ministry of Rural Areas and Employment is to administer a grant-in-aid scheme, in which funds are allocated from central government to registered voluntary agencies specifically for wasteland and micro-watershed development. The World

---

[17]An extract of the new guidelines is given in Appendix A6.2.

Wildlife Fund (WWF), 1995 reported that over 800 environmental NGOs and voluntary agencies with projects or programmes involving wasteland or watershed rehabilitation have been established in the last twenty years.

Reflecting on the success or failure of watershed development is not an easy one. When community based developments are taken up by an NGO, they are generally small in scale, with minimum costs, but with very intensive inputs of social and technical capital. Also there is every tendency that they are chosen with certain background and back-up of internal leadership, caste and class homogeneity of the community, and some common hardship at the community level (Kadekodi, 1997b). A sample of outcomes from watershed management programmes in India is provided in Tables 6.4 and 6.5. The success stories here invariably show quite high benefit–cost ratios and remarkable productivity changes.

Table 6.4
Watershed Management Impact on Productivity of Common Land

| Watershed | State | Fodder grass productivity (t/ha) | |
|---|---|---|---|
| | | Pre-project | Post project |
| Sukhomajri | Haryana | 0.10 | 2.10 |
| Bunga | Haryana | 0.20 | 3.20 |
| Bajra–Ganiyar | Haryana | 0.10 | 0.50 |
| Chajawa | Rajasthan | 0.10 | 1.60 |
| Kharkbun Kalan | Rajasthan | 0.10 | 0.20 |
| Mandvarsa | Rajasthan | 0.15 | 0.30 |
| Navamota | Gujarat | 1.00 | 2.00 |
| Shankarpura | Gujarat | 0.10 | 1.50 |
| Chinnatekur | Andhra Pradesh | 0.83 | 11.60 |

Source: Samra and Dhyani (1998).

Table 6.5
Watershed Management Impact on Productivity of Arable Lands,
Employment, and Economic Viability

| Watershed | State | Percentage increase in | | | B/C Ratio |
|---|---|---|---|---|---|
| | | Cropping intensity | Producti-vity | Employ-ment | |
| Sukhomajri | Haryana | 82 | 210 | 29.40 | 2.06 |
| Nada | Haryana | 78 | 165 | 18.60 | 1.97 |
| Bunga | Haryana | 110 | 170 | 28.20 | 2.05 |
| Rel Maira | Punjab | 32 | 52 | 24 | |
| Behdala | Himachal Pradesh | 17 | 12 | Neg | |
| Bajra-Ganiyar | Haryana | 21 | 58 | 16 | 1.58 |
| Siha | Haryana | 23 | 67 | 27 | |
| Kharkhan Kalan | Rajasthan | 17 | 15 | Neg | 6.07 |
| Kishangarh | Rajasthan | 10 | 12 | Neg | 2.35 |
| Chhajawa | Rajasthan | 32 | 45 | 36 | 2.24 |
| Mandvarsa | Rajasthan | 31 | 13 | 3 | 1.90 |
| Matatila | Uttar Pradesh | 41 | 21 | 4 | 3.80 |
| Tejpura | Uttar Pradesh | 97 | 180 | 40 | 3.40 |
| Gomti (Gyij) | Uttar Pradesh | 68 | 52 | 18 | 3.90 |
| Gomti (GK3a) | Uttar Pradesh | 41 | 24 | 6 | 2.00 |
| Rebari | Gujarat | 20 | 56 | 3 | 2.60 |
| Joladarasi | Karnataka | 18 | 56 | 5 | 1.50 |
| Chinnatekur | Andhra Pradesh | 25 | 62 | 7 | 1.80 |
| GR Halli | Karnataka | 12 | 42 | 3 | 1.50 |
| Shankarpura | Gujarat | 60 | 82 | 14 | |
| Ralegaon–Siddhi | Maharashtra | 62 | 185 | 21 | |

Note: Neg = negligible.
Source: Samra and Dhyani (1998).

# APPENDIX

Government of Haryana
Forest Department
Notification (3799-FTI-98/13358 dated 29.6.1998)
Extracts

In pursuance of the Government of India's letter no. (6-21/89-FP) dated June 1, 1990 from the Secretary (Environment and Forests) to the Forest Secretary of all states, it has been decided by the Government of Haryana to issue instructions for smooth implementation of the policy for Joint Forest Management in the state already approved by the government vide Financial Commissioner & Secretary, Forest & Wildlife Department memo No. 3373-Ft-I-90/15610 dated 13.6.90.

Preamble

The Joint Forest Management Policy of the Government of Haryana aims at tying the economic interests of villages, living within or adjacent to Forest areas, with sustainable management of those areas. This is to be achieved through motivating the villagers to organize themselves into registered societies for improving the productivity of forest areas by giving them a major share of the increased production, resulting from their participation. For the state government, there will be no loss in existing revenues (if any) from the concerned areas. The present levels of revenue will be maintained and in certain cases there will be increase over a period of time. Besides improving the economic status of villagers, the joint management approach aims to improve the environment of forest areas of the state.

Constitution and eligibility of Hill Resource Management Society

An HRMS shall be constituted by its members of their own free will and consent. For participation in HFD's Joint Forest Management programme, an HRMS shall satisfy the following conditions:

1. An HRMS may be constituted by a hamlet, village, or a group of villages located within or near forest areas.
2. All adult men and women from all households residing in above location and who have usufruct rights in the MA as per last forest settlement or have traditionally been collecting/using forest produce from there are entitled to become members of the HRMS.
3. Each HRMS shall annually elect a Managing Committee in a general body meeting to carry out its tasks. The managing committee shall have 7 to 9 members who should ideally be persons who go to collect produce from the forest themselves. At least one third of the total members shall be women.

Responsibility of the Haryana Forest Department

1. To give wide publicity to the governments Joint Forest Management policy among villages living in or near forest areas.
2. To follow the procedure outlined in Appendix - II while reaching Joint Management Agreements.
3. After signing each Joint Management Agreement, to inform different concerned wings (Production, Working Plan, Social Forestry, Kandi Project, etc.) of the Haryana Forest Department about it and ensure that any future work in the management area is done in accordance with the Joint Management Agreement in consultation with the HRMS. All JMAs shall be incorporated in working plans or the concerned DFO shall obtain the necessary deviation.
4. To redefine the duties of the HFD personnel to make these compatible with implementing the Joint Management Policy. This should bind them to take prompt action against any person(s) willfully causing damage or attempting theft of forest produce from MA brought to the notice of the staff by the HRMS and report the action taken to the concerned HRMS president.
5. To train HFD personnel to enable them to acquire the necessary skills for implementing the Joint Management Policy and to integrate the same in the regular training curricula for HFD personnel. In this, emphasis shall be given to practical methods for promoting women's equal participation in all aspects of HRMS decision making.
6. To provide administrative and technical guidance to HRMS's for

successful implementation of the programme.

7. To ensure that the most disadvantaged men and women members of the HRMS have access to forest produce for meeting their bonafide needs of firewood, fodder, fibre, etc. by promoting consultative and accountable decision making by HRMS office bearers.

8. To monitor changes in the conditions and productivity of forest areas brought under Joint Management with the help of baseline surveys and periodic studies.

9. To permit sale by HRMS(s) of only surplus biomass/grass not needed within the village by their own members.

10. Where a water harvesting dam is to be built under the Joint Forest Management programme, to involve villagers in site selection, pipeline layout and ensure that a dam system is completely functional before it is handed over to HRMS(s).

11. To authorize the Block Officer to be an ex-officio member of the executive committees and help the HRMS(s) in maintaining records including cash accounts.

12. To authorize the DEFO to ensure that the accounts are maintained properly by HRMS(s) and presented in the annual general body meeting in the month of April.

13. To facilitate resolution of conflicts within or between HRMS(s) related to forests.

14. To ensure equitable distribution of the usufruct which may be in cash or kind.

15. To ensure involvement of grassroots Non Government Organizations (NGO), knowledgeable individuals/activists, academics and researchers in the development of the programme.

## Responsibilities of the HRMS

1. To develop an MP through participatory microplanning with the assistance of HFD personnel. Bonafide domestic needs of the members regarding forest produce traditionally used by them shall be met on a sustainable basis from the MA before considering sale of such produce. Meeting the subsistence needs of the economically disadvantaged members and the raw material need of artisanal producers such as bamboo basket and rope makers shall be given priority over increasing the HRMS cash income.

2. To execute forestry works in accordance with the MP under supervision of HFD personnel. For this funds may be provided by HFD and/or obtained from independent sources such as NWDB, NAEB, CAPART, NABARD, etc. after due authorization by the Government.

3. To honour all its commitments made in the JMA and protect its MA from encroachment, cultivation, grazing, fire, and illicit felling or willfully causing death of trees by girdling. For this, it shall evolve a code of conduct for its members which may include specifying fines, the HRMS may levy, or prescribe penalties for those members violating the code. The HRMS shall make good loss caused due to above said activities.

4. To inform HFD personnel of any person(s), particularly non-members, willfully causing damage in its MA or attempting theft of its produce.

5. Where the HFD has built a water harvesting dam or a kuhl system, to manage water distribution from it on equitable basis and take care of minor repairs and maintenance through levying water charges on its members. During the rainy season, to keep a vigil on the dam and in case of any breach or chances of a breach in the dam, to immediately inform the beat Forest Guard and take all protective measures to save the dam. All members of an HRMS shall have the rights to claim an equal share of the water irrespective of whether they own land or not.

6. To assist HFD personnel in resolving conflicts with residents of neighbouring villages over competing claims in the MA.

7. In consultation with the concerned Range Forest Officer to evolve rules for its members for collection/harvesting of forest produce such as fodder, grass, dry and fallen wood, prunings, thinning, small timber, poles, etc. from its MA in a sustainable manner.

*Sharing of Forest Produce from Joint Management Areas with the Concerned HRMS*

All members of HRMS(s) may be permitted to collect dry and fallen wood, fencing material, limited numbers of bamboo, and poles free of cost from their respective joint management areas for their bonafide domestic use and not for sale.

Provide that, previously existing rights of members or non-members are not to be interfered with. The HRMS(s) shall regulate collection of the forest produce on a sustainable basis by framing rules for their members in consultation with the concerned Range Forest Officer.

*Annual Purchase of Fodder Grass by HRMS from HFD*

1.  As a part of its Joint Management Agreement, all fodder grass shall be given to the HRMS(s) at the average price obtained in open auction for the last 3 years proceeding JFM. Where such information is not available the price shall be settled between the DFO and the HRMS after taking into account the condition of the area and/or the price fetched by similar adjoining areas. Annual increment at the rate of 1 per cent of the above price is to be paid by HRMS after signing the agreement.
2.  Payment for the fodder grass shall be made in lump sum by each HRMS every year.
3.  In case of an exceptional drought or other natural disasters, the DFO may reduce the price to be paid.

*Annual Purchase of Bhabbar*

As a part of Joint Management Agreement an HRMS shall have first right over collection and use of bhabbar grass from forest areas on an annual lease basis. The price of bhabbar grass shall be determined as under:

1.  The average price obtained in open auction for the last three years preceding Joint Forest Management Agreement will be treated as the base price. When such information is not available, price will be settled between DFO and HRMS on the advice of the state level working group.
2.  The EFO may permit an HRMS to pay for the bhabbar in three instalments in exceptional cases.
3.  For the existing HRMS(s), which dispose off surplus bhabbar grass after fulfilling their own requirements, there will be no increase in price for subsequent years.
4.  In case of HRMSs which use bhabbar harvest for *ban* making, the lease amount will increase at 7.5 per cent annually for every subsequent year.
5.  Those HRMSs which dispose off surplus bhabbar through an open bidding shall do so in a general body meeting and in the presence

of the concerned DFO of his representative.

6.  The net income made from the sale of bhabbar shall be divided between the Government and the HRMS in the ratio of 25:75. The HRMS shall contribute 30 per cent of its share towards plough back fund for further improvement of the MA and another 10 per cent towards Kalyan Kosh.

7.  Other terms and conditions for the sale of bhabbar and grass are given in the Joint Management Agreement.

*Bamboo*

HRMS(s) of bamboo makers shall continue to get permits to cut a specified number of bamboos per household per month for 9 months (October–June) every year as per the terms specified in the existing notification of the Government of Haryana on the matter.

*Share of HRMS from Sale of Timber from Joint Management Areas*

After ten years of Joint Forest Management to the satisfaction of Conservator of Forests of that area, the HFD shall share the income from timber, at the time of final harvest and after deducting the expenditure incurred on felling, transportation and auction, with the HRMSs in the following manner:

70 per cent to the Government

30 per cent to the HRMS

Provided that HRMS shall contribute 30 percent of its share towards plough back fund for further improvement of the MA and another 10 percent towards *Kalyan Kosh*.

*Benefit Sharing with Existing HRMS Participating in Joint Forest Management before Notification of these Instructions*

The registered societies already in existence prior to the notification of these Instructions shall be considered eligible for their share of income from timber from the year in which they were registered.

Management and Utilization of Funds of HRMS

The income accruing to the HRMS(s) from various sources would be managed and utilized as separate funds in the following manner;

*Kalyan Kosh*

1. The Kalyan Kosh would be set up from contributions available from each HRMS: an annual contribution of 10 per cent from the net proceeds of sale of surplus bhabbar and another 10 per cent from the net proceeds of sale of timber.
2. The contributions by the respective HRMS(s) will be pooled into Kalyan Kosh at the Divisional Level. The concerned DFO will maintain this fund as Personal Ledger Account, to be operated with due concurrence of the PCCF/Chairperson of the SWG as authorized to do so by the SWG till a federation of societies comes into existence.
3. The Kalyan Kosh would be utilized for the promotion of the activities of the HRMSs and for expansion of JFM Programme in the State of Haryana.

*Forest Resources Development Fund (Plough-back Fund)*

1. This fund would help in recycling a part of the income generated from the forest (under joint management) into the asset itself.
2. This fund would be se-up at the HRMS level from the contributions made by an HRMS; an annual contribution of 30 per cent of the HRMS share from the proceeds of sale of surplus bhabbar and 30 percent from the share of timber.
3. This fund would be retained by each HRMS as separate bank jointly operated by the DFO and the concerned HRMS functionary (according to the byelaws) with due approval by the General Body of the HRMS.
4. This fund would be used for the improvement and development of the Joint Management Area according to the prescriptions of the Management Plan.

*Village Development Fund (HRMS Fund)*

1. The HRMS fund is to be used by the village community.
2. This fund would consist of the income of the HRMS from the various sources, including that available from the HRMS share of proceeds from sale of surplus bhabbar, from timber, and all other sources.
3. This fund would be maintained by the HRMS as a separate bank

account to be operated by the cashier and any of the other two office bearers, with due approval of the General Body, according to the procedures stated in the bye laws of the society.

4. This fund is to be used for village development and community welfare as decided by the General Body.

5. This fund is to be used strictly on nonreligious and apolitical activities.

## Dispute Arbitration/Termination of Agreement

1. If any member of an HRMS fails to comply with any of the general conditions laid down above or the specific conditions laid down in a Joint Management Agreement between HFD and HRMS, the HRMS may terminate his/her membership and inform the HFD accordingly.

2. If an HRMS as a whole fails to comply with any of the conditions laid down above, despite at least two warnings in writing by the Forest Officer, the DFO shall be entitled to terminate the agreement with the HRMS after due enquiry.

3. If HRMS intends to terminate the agreement due to the non fulfillment of its obligations/commitments by the Government/HFD as specified above and in the Instructions, the HRMS shall give one months prior notice to the DFO.

4. In case of any dispute arising out of any action taken at any level, the matter will be referred to an Arbitration Committee comprising of concerned territorial Conservator and two non forester members of SWG which will be appointed by the PCCF. Majority decision of the Arbitration Committee shall be final.

APPENDIX 6.2

Guidelines for Watershed Development, 1994
Some Major Extracts and Features

## Administrative Arrangements

1. District rural development agencies (DRDAs) and zila parishads have overall responsibility for programme planning and implementation in the district.

2. The DRDA (or zila parishad) appoints a 'watershed-development advisory committee' with multi-source membership of officials and

non-officials. This committee advises the DRDA on the selection of project implementing agencies, watershed-development team members, watershed-development planning, training, community organizing, etc.

3. The DRDA appoints project implementing agencies, which are responsible for appointment of the watershed development teams, recommending villages for watershed programmes, planning, implementing and reviewing of watershed programmes through village-level organization, and maintenance of accounts of funds to be spent by the implementing agency and through watershed committees.

4. A watershed development team has a minimum of 4 members representing relevant disciplines such as agriculture, engineering, life sciences, animal husbandry, and social work. The team shall work exclusively and full-time for the watershed programme. The team is to be located close to project villages.

5. In each village, the watershed association shall be registered under the Societies Registration Act. The association will appoint the watershed committee, which will consist of representatives of user groups, self-help groups, gram panchayat and watershed development team.

6. Each watershed committee shall have a secretary, who will be a paid employee of the watershed association and will be responsible for maintaining records and accounts of the watershed programme.

Financial Provisions

7. The funds will flow directly from the national and state governments to the DRDA or zila parishad. Depending upon the region, Rs 3000–5000 of funds are allotted per hectare. The average and most common provision is Rs 4000 per ha. Each micro-watershed will consist of about 500 ha; at the rate of Rs 4000 per ha, this means about Rs 200,000 will be available. This should be spent over four years in the following manner:

- Entry-point activities, 5 per cent;
- Community organization, 5 per cent;
- Training programme, 5 per cent;
- Administration of project implementing agency and watershed association, 10 per cent;

- Watershed works, 75 per cent.

The DRDA or zila parishad will make 25 per cent of the funds available to the implementing agency. It will make the remaining 75 per cent available directly to the watershed committee on the advice of the implementing agency, depending upon the capability of the watershed committee and the progress of implementation.

8. People's participation is to be assured through voluntary donations and contribution in terms of labour, raw materials, cash etc., for developmental activities as well as for operation and maintenance. The minimum norms prescribed are:
   - 5 per cent for community works;
   - 10 per cent for work on private property. This will be 5 per cent in case of scheduled castes or tribes and persons identified as below the poverty line.

9. Maintenance fund: Against such contributions from the community, an equal amount in value will be withdrawn from the watershed works budget and deposited in a separate fund for the future operations and maintenance of community assets (but not for private property). The users shall operate this fund themselves.

Planning Process

10. Participation of the village community and groups is central to the watershed programme. The Guidelines therefore lay down a detailed process to be followed for ensuring participatory planning.
    - Participatory rural appraisals. The watershed development team has to conduct various participatory rural appraisal exercises to identify potential programmes and the concerned user groups.
    - Basic Surveys. Collection of various details through surveys (engineering, socio-economic) by the watershed development team and volunteers.

11. This process will lead to the development of a watershed plan and will contain the details of various activities, a list of user groups, fund requirements and user contributions. The watershed-development plan will be approved by the watershed association, and then submitted to the DRDA through the project-implementing agency (para 86).

12. This project plan will be prepared by the watershed development team in consultation with the watershed committee, according to

the schedule of rates approved by the DRDA.

13. Implementation starts after the plan is approved by the DRDA. There is no need for formal technical approval.

Technical Parameters

14. The watershed approach gives significant benefits through various treatments intended to arrest soil erosion, restore soil fertility, and recharge ground water by harvesting rainwater. According to the Guidelines, the planning unit has to cover all lands, irrespective of ownership, including forest, revenue, panchayat and private lands.

15. Since the watershed development programme plans for development of all resources within the watershed, including land, water vegetation, animals and human resources, in an integrated manner, an organizational structure at the village level is conceived, which has to be developed in a participatory way. The project implementing agency has overall responsibility for the programme and for institutional arrangements at the village level. The agency will employ a multi-disciplinary team to implement the watershed programme in an integrated manner.

16. Each micro-watershed will be about 500 ha. If a village is larger, it can be allotted an additional area, to be brought under the programme after the watershed association has shown its capacity for promoting people's institutions, and for planning and implementing a watershed programme covering (particularly) the public lands.

17. Each project implementing agency is expected to handle 10 micro-watersheds, totally 5000-6200 ha.

18. Through a participatory process, the user groups and watershed committee, with the support of volunteers, will prepare a watershed development plan, which will have appropriate programme activities depending upon the agro-climatic situation of the watershed. Para 42 indicates the variety of activities that can be taken up under watershed programmes are also listed.

19. Works and activities should be low-cost, simple, easily operated and maintained. The watershed development plan should be based on local technical knowledge and solutions related to specific problems, supported by expert knowledge of the watershed team, district officers and research organizations. Around 80 per cent of works and activities should be based on local knowledge.

# 7

# Political Economy of CPRs Investment and Design of Management and Legal Strategies

The relevance of CPR development came in to the domain of Indian planning in 1974 when the National Commission on Agriculture came out with its report. The report had then estimated the extent of waste and degraded lands of the order of 175 million hectares, of which 85 million hectares were cultivable lands, 35 million hectares degraded and barren lands, and 55 million hectares common and revenue lands. The Commission then touched on various strategies of wastelands developments and regeneration. Within the framework of Indian planning, these were incorporated under various programmes such as the DPAP, DDP, Integrated Area Development Programmes (IADP), Integrated Rural Development Programme (IRDP) and many others. In a sense, managing the commons and wastelands were then treated essentially as being the responsibility of the government reversing the process of degradation—through technical assistance, official (or bureaucratic) administration, and financial assistance through the plans (Jodha, 2000). These strategies can be categorized as: pro-active approach of the government, equating state authority with knowledge, and over-reliance on technology (often based on western technical know-how).

The fall-out of such a mix of strategies was: (i) the burden of high costs of subsidies on the government in such programmes, (ii) poor deliverables due to inefficient administrative machinery, (iii) lack of stakeholder involvements, and (iv) a deep rooted signal in the minds of people that the state owns the CPRs and it should manage them alone.[1] In 1984, it was felt by the government, that with massive urbanization, and rural transformation, the extent of wastelands was increasing in the country (as seen in Chapter 2) and some new intervention strategies were immediately required.[2] The NWDB was set up, as part of Ministry of Rural Development. Several wastelands and watershed development projects were initiated, with additional support and programmes from external donor agencies. Non-governmental agencies and federations such as the Federation of Tree Growers Co-operatives (TGCF) were formed and encouraged to undertake land regeneration programmes. The approach turned towards community participation. Corporates such as Indian Farmers' Fertilizer Co-operative (IFFCO) were also encouraged in this process of wastelands development. Specialized research institutions such as the Central Arid Zone Research Institute (CAZRI) in Jodhpur, Central Soil and Water Conservation Research Institutes (in several places) with its headquarter at Dehradun, Society for Promotion of Wastelands Development (SPWD) were set up to identify technological approaches to deal with the problem. A large number of NGOs (numbering over 5000) came up all over the country, working on various aspects of land, water, and forest resources. With the setting up of the National Afforestation and Eco-development Board (NAEB) in the Ministry of Environment and Forests, and WDPs under the umbrella of the Ministry of Rural Development and Agriculture in 1992, an institutional approach of community and NGO involvement was introduced.

[1]Random opinion surveys conducted in various parts of the country reveal that when people are asked as 'to whom the forest belongs', the standard answer is that it belongs to the government.

[2]A recent CAG report on DPAP indicates that the drought prone area has increased from 55.3 MHA in 1973 to 74.6 MHA in 1995.

At present, there is a multiple set of agencies implementing various programmes on commons and wastelands (see Box 7.1).

| Box 7.1: Multiplicity of Agencies in CPR–Wastelands Development | |
|---|---|
| Ministry/Department | Programmes |
| Ministry of Agriculture and Co-operation | National Watershed Development Projects for Rain-fed Areas (NWDPRA) |
| Ministry of Environment and Forests | Integrated Afforestation and Eco-development Scheme |
| Ministry of Rural Development | Drought Prone Area Programme (DPAP), Desert Development Area Programme (DDAP), Integrated Watershed Development Programme (IWDP), and many others |
| Planning Commission and the state governments | Special Area Development Programmes (such as Western Ghat and Eastern Ghat Development Programmes, Hill Area Development, Tribal Area Development), Integrated Rural Development Programme, and many others. |

Apart from those mentioned in Box 7.1, several other rural development programmes also have some elements of CPR–wastelands management, for example, JRY. It was pointed out, time and again, (and also specifically by the High Level Committee headed by Mohan Dharia, which recommended a Land Use Authority), that it is essential to have a co-ordinated land, water, and forest linked programme to monitor all the programmes under one institution. Finally, in April 1999, a Department of Land Resources was created in the Ministry of Rural Development merging various watershed, soil conservation, social forestry, and other area development programmes.

All these institutional developments to make programmes of regenerating the wastelands and the commons amenable to the people have had various degrees of success and effectiveness. The major limitations that are common to all strategies are summarized in Box 7.2. Briefly stated, they can be grouped into financial, institutional, and technological limitations.

## Box 7.2: Barriers and Limitations in CPR Development Programmes

| Major Limitations Observed | Policy Options |
|---|---|
| **Institutional** | |
| 1. Little participation of the local communities | Stakeholders must be identified first; They should be involved in design and planning and monitoring the programmes (as discussed in Chapter 5). |
| 2. Too many agencies operating with different guidelines | This has been the problem for a long time in all spheres of development, because of which even the villagers suspect the motivation of the departments. It is better to merge all land and water related CPR programmes under one umbrella. This was also the recommendation of the Dharia Committee. |
| 3. Neglect of conflicts | The implementing agencies must attend to local conflicts first, before propagating any technical or developmental alternatives. Examples are transparency in distributional rules. Also the conflicts between NGOs, governmental agencies, and people should be first solved. |
| 4. Lack of market avenues for CPR products | The programme should also include a well-defined and practical approach to processing of CPR products and marketing. |
| 5. No built-in scheme to sensitize and reduce gender gaps | Because of this, the pay-offs are uneven between men and women. There is a need to introduce a gender perspective as a part of stakeholder analysis. |
| 6. Lack of leadership | There is no built-in mechanism to develop leadership, as part of the programmes. This is very essential and the education system also needs to be geared to this requirement. |
| **Financial** | |
| 1. Insecurity of flow of funds | The programmes should be part of a long-term perspective plan (as recommended by Dharia Committee) |
| 2. Low financial allocations | A separate fund in the form of corporate funding should be created for the programmes, which can be circulated from one project to another. Also it is time to encourage private corporate and local financing for these programmes. |
| 3. No monitoring or appraisal of implementation | Most of the programmes are good starters but without any monitoring and appraisal. Impact assessments are to be built into the programmes. |

(Cont.)

(Box 7.2 Contd.)

| Major Limitations Observed | Policy Options |
| --- | --- |
| **Technical** | |
| 1. Ignoring local knowledge | The indigenous knowledge of the communities should be fully utilized. |
| 2. Lack of proper techniques of land and water management | The projects should link the agro-climatic and agro-ecological characteristics of the region (as suggested in Chapter 7, Section 'Design of CPR Revival Programmes'). |
| 3. Limited training and human resource capabilities | The education system at the rural level needs to be attuned to CPR resource management as well. There is a need for training the locals, demonstration with successful programmes, gender sensitization, developing leadership qualities, demonstration of replicability, etc. |
| 4. Replication and extensions are often not built-in | It is necessary to make the land and water development programmes extendable, as and when the village economy grows. For this, some kind of inter-generation approach (as discussed in Chapter 4) needs to be built into the programme. |
| 5. Lack of adequate database: because of this, most of the programmes are faulty in their design | Data on village micro-plan, demographic status, flow of funds, participation rate, livelihood linkage etc., are necessary in advance. |

The most needed are well-defined distribution rules (as stressed in the Design Principles further in this Chapter), methods of promoting leadership, and creating employment and income opportunities from CPR management for all sections of people.

INVESTMENT PATTERNS OF CPR AND WASTELANDS PROGRAMMES

On reviewing the allocation of public resources for CPR management in India, one finds that the actual investment on revival of these over the first seven plan period is about Rs 1217 per hectare (GoI, 1989). Since the 1980s, several donor agencies have started investing on land, water and forestry projects in India as part of social forestry programme. For instance, between 1990–1 to 1998–9, the total of such investments on forestry and related land development programmes other than social forestry is Rs 42,278 million, amounting, on average, to Rs 16,911 per hectare. On average, investment on social forestry programmes by external donor agencies were of the order of Rs 4806 per hectare. Social forestry was unfortunately treated purely as the programme of the Forest Department. During the Ninth Plan period, a special allocation of funds on wastelands development, and enhanced allocation on rural area development programmes were made. The investment outlays on wastelands development during the Ninth Five Year Plan was raised to Rs 6000 crore, of which Rs 2778 crore were spent during 1997–2000. Likewise, under rural development, covering revenue and other wastelands, programmes such as National Rural Employment Programme (NREP), Rural Landless Employment Guarantee Programme (RLEGP), JRY, and several others have set aside about Rs 10,000 crores to regenerate the lands via creating rural employments.

Evaluation reports from several states such as Gujarat and Orissa (Kohlin, 2001) have made it clear that for want of community participation, such forestry regeneration programmes did not yield the desired results. Basically, the two issues of poverty and sustainable development got mixed up. Table 7.2 shows that many of the recent donor driven forestry projects were also either directly addressed to forest regeneration, or to poverty elimination and rural development (Ninan, 1998). Recently, the UNDP and the World Bank, through their capacity building programmes in environmental management, enabled a large number of NGOs and officers from departments dealing with land, water, soil, and forests to come close to each other, and to view the development of the commons in a participatory manner. This should considerably bring down the overall investment cost, and the programmes can become truly participatory. Table 7.1 shows the budgetary allocations at the central government level on various forest and environment related matters, partly to bring back the commons and partly to revive the lost forest cover and environmental richness in general. But, considering the fact that land, water, forests, and biodiversity are basic resources, with more than 50 per cent falling under various categories of the commons, the resource allocation for this sector is just about 3.5 per cent of the total budget.

Unfortunately, till today, most of these investments are concentrated on degraded forest lands only. Second, the involvement of the locals and village communities is very minimal. The high

## Table 7.1
## Major Budget Allocation for MoEF at 1993–4 Prices

(Rs crores)

| Major Head | 1986–7 | 1987–8 | 1988–9 | 1989–90 | 1990–1 | 1991–2 | 1992–3 | 1993–4 | 1994–5 | 1995–6 | 1996–7 | 1997–8 | 1998–9 | 1999–2000 | 2000–01 |
|---|---|---|---|---|---|---|---|---|---|---|---|---|---|---|---|
| **Ecological and Environment** | | | | | | | | | | | | | | | |
| Botanical & zoological survey | 15.355 | 10.090 | 15.411 | 16.389 | 16.801 | 15.281 | 15.343 | 14.930 | 15.298 | 14.965 | 14.458 | 17.710 | 17.370 | 16.914 | 16.549 |
| Env. education/training/ extension | 2.309 | 3.434 | 3.128 | 1.758 | 4.044 | 3.891 | 5.636 | 6.400 | 5.924 | 5.601 | 5.410 | 4.552 | 4.230 | 4.598 | 4.733 |
| Conservation programme | 0.885 | 1.239 | 3.194 | 5.568 | 3.063 | 4.152 | 3.830 | 7.000 | 5.933 | 5.039 | 5.441 | 4.736 | 4.220 | 5.370 | 8.004 |
| Environmental planning and co-ordination | 5.888 | 4.125 | 4.422 | 5.574 | 5.609 | 4.627 | 5.198 | 7.180 | 4.856 | 4.845 | 5.612 | 4.994 | 5.450 | 5.486 | 5.187 |
| research & ecological regeneration | 13.758 | 11.471 | 11.300 | 7.014 | 9.421 | 10.974 | 11.753 | 12.700 | 12.066 | 10.254 | 9.802 | 10.090 | 9.260 | 10.869 | 11.018 |
| International co-operation | 0.635 | 0.584 | 0.540 | 0.324 | 0.749 | 0.914 | 1.094 | 1.350 | 1.552 | 1.629 | 1.531 | 1.449 | 1.480 | 1.518 | 1.436 |
| Prevention of pollution of Ganga/national river | 49.644 | 80.545 | 93.351 | 74.175 | 84.411 | 64.658 | 53.940 | 60.000 | 34.456 | 35.186 | 94.986 | 78.672 | 72.940 | 128.626 | 78.964 |
| Prevention of air and water pollution | 15.220 | 17.083 | 17.900 | 12.752 | 24.125 | 21.521 | 36.047 | 46.250 | 19.168 | 45.180 | 75.150 | 64.566 | 62.680 | 51.386 | 47.241 |
| Impact assessment | 0.539 | 0.354 | 0.655 | 0.925 | 0.817 | 1.910 | 4.355 | 4.950 | 4.965 | 2.511 | 3.187 | 5.501 | 1.870 | 4.624 | 2.504 |
| Total prevention and control of pollution | 65.403 | 97.982 | 111.906 | 87.565 | 109.353 | 88.089 | 94.342 | 111.200 | 71.166 | 82.877 | 173.323 | 148.739 | 137.500 | 184.636 | 128.709 |
| Other programmes | 0.000 | 1.894 | 2.653 | 0.672 | 3.717 | 4.971 | 5.373 | 30.840 | 55.705 | 16.720 | 29.732 | 24.682 | 11.550 | 64.602 | 35.474 |
| Capital outlay on ecology and env. | 0.000 | 0.460 | 2.358 | 7.689 | 2.900 | 3.381 | 4.848 | 5.570 | 5.805 | 3.737 | 4.508 | 4.523 | 6.700 | 6.528 | 6.875 |
| Total—Ecology and Environment | 104.426 | 135.351 | 154.913 | 208.888 | 155.657 | 136.280 | 147.417 | 197.170 | 178.304 | 145.667 | 249.817 | 221.475 | 197.810 | 300.521 | 254.816 |

(Contd.)

(Rs crores)

| Major Head | 1986-7 | 1987-8 | 1988-9 | 1989-90 | 1990-1 | 1991-2 | 1992-3 | 1993-4 | 1994-5 | 1995-6 | 1996-7 | 1997-8 | 1998-9 | 1999-2000 | 2000-01 |
|---|---|---|---|---|---|---|---|---|---|---|---|---|---|---|---|
| Forestry and Wildlife | | | | | | | | | | | | | | | |
| Research | 4.810 | 11.489 | 14.494 | 12.073 | 16.079 | 28.841 | 30.072 | 35.070 | 43.510 | 48.665 | 53.517 | 49.835 | 57.630 | 52.833 | 37.321 |
| Education and training | 13.392 | 8.037 | 7.403 | 3.869 | 8.877 | 6.086 | 7.135 | 8.030 | 8.844 | 7.457 | 7.765 | 7.987 | 9.690 | 9.673 | 8.379 |
| Survey and utilization of forest resources | 5.157 | 5.682 | 5.241 | 2.583 | 4.221 | 3.168 | 4.049 | 9.950 | 9.073 | 10.035 | 3.521 | 4.391 | 4.890 | 4.759 | 4.794 |
| Forest conservation and develop. regression | 6.446 | 4.072 | 7.042 | 9.598 | 5.882 | 6.228 | 8.777 | 6.900 | 5.203 | 6.004 | 5.791 | 5.589 | 8.300 | 8.875 | 6.507 |
| Wildlife | 14.989 | 18.729 | 16.885 | 12.189 | 28.496 | 31.629 | 20.103 | 25.560 | 27.254 | 26.176 | 24.710 | 383,347.000 | 43.010 | 68.564 | 49.979 |
| NWDB/NAEDB | 100.981 | 106.798 | 133.48 | 90.051 | 103.458 | 144.133 | 116.174 | 98.030 | 94.907 | 88.117 | 69.810 | 55.049 | 50.320 | 62.319 | 60.469 |
| Capital outlay on forestry and wildlife | 0.000 | 0.690 | 2.457 | 5.626 | 3.000 | 2.930 | 1.379 | 1.650 | | | | | | | |
| Total—Forestry and Wildlife | 146.700 | 156.506 | 165.657 | 118.157 | 176.310 | 223.526 | 210.000 | 198.750 | 201.899 | 197.010 | 173.012 | 172.406 | 184.500 | 216.966 | 179.854 |
| Grand Total | 254.474 | 295.008 | 323.649 | 327.045 | 335.126 | 362.795 | 360.440 | 398.980 | 383.288 | 345.902 | 426.242 | 397.977 | 386.760 | 521.886 | 439.414 |
| | | | | | | | | | | | | | 111,220.0 | | |

*Source:* RBI Bulletin, various issues; Expenditure Budgets of MoEF.

Table 7.2

Involvement of Donor Agencies in Forest Conservation and Restoration

Projects under implementation

| S. No. | Name of Project | Funding Agency | Project Cost (million rupees) | Duration of the Project (years) | Physical Target ('000 ha.) |
|---|---|---|---|---|---|
| 1. | Maharashtra Forestry Project | World Bank | 4315.10 | 8 | 369 |
| 2. | Andhra Pradesh Forestry Project | World Bank | 3539.20 | 6 | 355 |
| 3. | Tamil Nadu Afforestation Project | OECF (Japan) | 4992.00 | 6 | 405 |
| 4. | Capacity Building Project for Participatory Management | SIDA (Sweden) | 85.00 | 2 | 19 |
| 5. | Dungarpur Integrated Wastelands Development Project | SIDA (Sweden) | 282.10 | 7 | 47 |
| 6. | Rehabilitation of Common Lands in Aravalis | EEC | 481.50 | 10 | 33 |
| 7. | Afforestation & Pasture Development along in | | | | |
| | Indira Gandhi Canal | OECF (Japan) | 1075.00 | 10 | 61.5 |
| 8. | Afforestation of Aravali Hills | OECF (Japan) | 1766.90 | 7 | 115 |
| 9. | Western Ghat Forestry Project | DFID (UK) | 842.00 | 7 | 61 |
| 10. | Forestry and Eco-development Project in Changer | GTZ (Germany) | 187.00 | 5 | 11 |
| 11. | Forestry Project Kullu–Mandi | DFID (UK) | 139.20 | 6 | 7 |
| 12. | Uttar Pradesh Research Project | World Bank | 2720.00 | 4 | 160 |
| 13. | Madhya Pradesh Forestry Project | World Bank | 2459.40 | 5 | 235 |
| 14. | Rajasthan Forestry Project | OECF (Japan) | 1391.80 | 5 | 55 |
| 15. | Integrated Gujarat Forestry Development Project | OECF (Japan) | 6085 | 6 | 230 |
| 16. | Eastern Karnataka Afforestation Project | OECF (Japan) | 5655.40 | 6 | 171 |

(Contd.)

## Projects under implementation

| S. No. | Name of Project | Funding Agency | Project Cost (million rupees) | Duration of the Project (years) | Physical Target ('000 ha.) |
|---|---|---|---|---|---|
| 17. | Punjab Afforestation Project | OECF (Japan) | 4420* | 8 | 59 |
| 18. | Kerala Forestry Project | World Bank | 1830 | 4 | 54 |
| 19. | Capacity Building Project for Rehabilitation of Degraded Forests through Landscape Participatory Programme | AUSAID (Australia) | 11.70 | 3 | |
| | Grand Total | | 42,278.30 | | 2447 |

*Note:* Invariably these are the projects funded in the 1990s; *Loan amount has been provided for four years only in the first phase.
*Comment:* The average plantation cost of external agency funded projects is about Rs 16,911.32 per ha. as compared to Rs 4806 per ha. for social forestry projects by external agencies in the 1980s.
*Source:* MoEF.

203

investment rates in the externally funded projects made the people feel that the beneficiaries do not necessarily have to be 'participatory'.

## DESIGN OF CPR REVIVAL PROGRAMMES

By now it is clear that the design of land regeneration programmes should be based on both (i) the kinds and extent of CPRs and wastelands available in different pockets in the country, and (ii) the types of institutions to manage them. The extent of land, forest, and water resources available in India that qualify to be categorized as CPRs have already been viewed in Chapters 2 and 3. To the extent that these programmes fall in the domain of CPRs, they can be brought under alternative collective action programmes. With the 73$^{rd}$ and 74$^{th}$ Amendments of the constitution and the enactment of Panchayat Act and JFM programmes in several states, it should be left to the village communities to decide upon the kinds of land development programmes that they think are best. These decentralized democratic institutions are yet to find their roots in the economy on a large scale. The reasons are many; the major ones are:

1. Land, water, and forests being on the concurrent list under Article 246 of the Constitution of India, many states have not done anything towards enactment and implementation.

2. The sharing rule of gains from community participation have not been worked out satisfactorily. For instance, in Haryana the HRMS (the village societies) will have the first right on fodder grass, but the price of fodder will be the average of the past three years contract rates prior to JFM! In other words, there is no additional share or gain for stall feeding, or nursery protection and development, or forest protection being carried out by the village community. Further, there is no transparency, in the sense that the basis of the average contract price has not been explained to the communities.

3. Many of the JFM programmes are still long timber oriented, whose benefits do not reach the local communities even after 15 years!

4. JFM is still restricted to degraded forests only.

5. Under the cover of stall feeding, local communities are made to go out and fetch their fuelwood and other NTFP needs from elsewhere, which is actually self-defeating.

It is becoming increasingly clear from different countries and from within India that the ultimate beneficiaries prefer to be included as partners with the state and even market based machinery or development and implementation agencies of such programmes, rather than being left out only as simply recipients (Ramachandran, 2002).

Evolution of participatory institutions, (discussed in Chapter 5), is not easy, and not instantaneous either. Ostrom (1990) develops a set of eight 'Design Principles' for the management of common pool resources under a participatory institution (Box 7.3). These principles can be used as generalized self-governance rules. In this case, the state need not claim ownership. In a way, it is a characterization of the resource between open access resource and CPR. On the basis of the Indian experience, one may augment these principles to operationalize them (Box 7.4).

---

**Box 7.3: Design Principle for Pooled Common Resources**

1. **Clearly defined boundaries**: Individuals or households with rights to withdraw resources from the common pool resource and the boundaries of the common pool resource itself are clearly defined.

2. **Congruence**: (i) The distribution of benefits from appropriation rules is roughly proportionate to the costs imposed by provision rules; (ii) Appropriation rules restricting time, place, technology, and/or quantity of resources are related to local conditions.

3. **Collective-choice arrangements**: Most individuals affected by operational rules can participate in modifying the operational rules.

4. **Monitoring**: Monitors, who actively audit common pool resource conditions and appropriator behaviour, are accountable to the appropriators and/or are the appropriators themselves.

5. **Graduated sanctions**: Appropriators who violate operational rules are likely to receive graduated sanctions (depending on the seriousness and context of the offence) from other appropriators, from officials accountable to these appropriators, or from both.

6. **Conflict resolution mechanisms**: Appropriators and their officials have rapid access to low-cost, local arenas to resolve conflict among appropriators or between appropriators and officials.

7. **Minimal recognition of rights to organize**: The rights of appropriators to devise their own institutions are not challenged by external governmental authorities.

For common pool resources that are part of larger systems:

8. **Nested enterprises**: Appropriation, provision, monitoring, enforcement, conflict resolution, and governance activities are organized in multiple layers of nested enterprises.

---

*Source*: Ostrom (1990).

> **Box 7.4: Operationalising cf Participatory Rural Institutions to Manage Wastelands and CPRs**
>
> • Self-governance by the communities be permitted by the state, preferably by their ethnic and anthropological identities
> • Clearly defined boundaries of CPRs
> • Sharing rules and rights with weightage for current benefits
> • Rules for contributing or pooling private resource along with CPRs and also for withdrawals
> • Rules to be evolved from within the system by the members
> • The agreed rules are to be monitored properly
> • Sanctions are proportionate to the kind of violation
> • Existence of conflict resolution mechanisms
> • Over time the CPR regime needs to be linked to a larger system in which market and other institutions operate.
> Among these, operationally the most relevant ones are those pertaining to sharing rules among the users, power to effect sanctions, and existence of a conflict resolution mechanism.

With all the design principles and development rules based on past experience a basic question arises again and again. How to initiate a participatory process in the Indian context? Since India began the development process under the umbrella of a planned economy, it was then logical to bring all land, water, and forest development programmes under the planning system. However, it is now increasingly felt that land regeneration programmes should be transferred in a phased manner to community based organizations, with the official agencies of the states overseeing their performance and progress. The Panchayats, JFM, Tree Growers Federations, HRMS, and many such institutions are already in operation in several pockets in the country. Some of them require amendments in their structure and targets, broadly following the charter as given in Box 7.4. Though in the initial stages, the role of the state agencies has been quite significant in monitoring the activities, sooner or later, a cadre of land army should be promoted to take over the functions substantially out of 'state' control.

Next to the design of an institutional mechanism, is the scheme for covering various types of wastelands and CPRs. Only a broad methodology is mentioned here. A three-way classification of the relevant regions needs to be made based on: (i) type of wastelands, (ii) levels of CPR, and (iii) geographical configurations. The wastelands can be grouped as water eroded, usar lands, culturable waste, misc ellaneous tree crop areas, and forest areas. The CPRs can be grouped as below 10 per cent, between 10–30 per cent, and more than 30 per cent and so on (Box 2.1 in Chapter 2). The geographical grouping of the regions can be made as tribal areas, predominantly agricultural plain areas, and coastal areas. Overlaying of these three types of classifications would lead to 36 possible clusters of problem areas or pockets in the country for which programmes of regeneration need to be developed. In several of these cluster areas and regions, a large number of successful experiments and programmes are already going on. They should be studied and specific models of replicating the regeneration programme on a large scale need to be worked out for each of these pockets.

Finally, it is equally important to develop the necessary data bank on a sample basis in each of these cluster areas, on matters such as geo-physical accounting of the extent of commons and wastelands and their recoveries over time, socio-economic changes, and regeneration programme related information. Such a data bank should be used to monitor the programme on an all-India scale.

LEGAL STATUS OF COMMON PROPERTY MANAGEMENT IN INDIA

With large land, inland, and marine water resources in the country, India has introduced various legal structures to protect and preserve them; most of these have to do with the commons. The Environment (Protection) Act of 1986, Wildlife Protection Act of 1972, Water (Prevention and Control of Pollution) Act of 1974, Water Cess Act of 1977, Forest Conservation Act of 1980, Air Act of 1981, and Land Acquisition Act of 1894 are only some of the major ones. Many of them are relevant in respect of CPRs. Several of the international regulations coming from World Trade Organization (WTO), General Agreement on Tariffs and Trade (GATT), Convention on International Trade in Endangered species (CITES), and Trade Record Analysis of Flora and Fauna in Commerce (TRAFFIC) etc., also become applicable to the Indian situation. India is also a signatory to the International Convention on Biological Diversity of 1992. The National Biodiversity Strategy Action Plan was prepared in 2002 and the Biodiversity Conservation Act has been passed by the Parliament in 2002.

As far as land related CPRs are concerned, the oldest relevant act is the 1894 Land Acquisition Act (amended on several occasions upto 1999). The 'state' in this case is supposed to act as the 'eminent domain' in acquiring private lands in public interest to protect, preserve, and develop them. Whenever any land is acquired by the government under this law, several rehabilitation and compensation packages for the affected locals are worked out on the basis of many recently amended sections of the Act. But unfortunately, apart from the problems of justice for the affected people ( in terms of right to live in one's own desired place), injustice is often meted out in terms of rate of compensations. In the context of common property land resources, it is more important to note that the state has invariably failed to revive such acquired wastelands and other degraded lands (discussed in Chapter 2). Thus, the concept of eminent domain of the state versus the local community has come to the fore of the discussion in the wider legal and  political economic debates (Fernandes and Paranjape, 1997).

The 1980 and (further amended) 1988 Forest (Conservation) Act is the most relevant forest law in India today. Under this Act, the government attains its eminent domain on the management of forest area in India (except for the cultivation of tea, coffee, spices, rubber, palms, oil bearing plants, horticultural crops, and medicinal plants). The main component of the Act is restriction on the state governments to allow the use of forest lands for any non-forest purpose without the approval of the central government. One of the greatest drawbacks of this Act is the failure of the government to recognize the customary and traditional rights of the people to use forest resources as commons. On top of this, failure of the state governments to protect, preserve, and develop forest lands has been noticed very widely (Poffeberger and McGean, 1996). Then came the 1990 Forest Policy Statement followed by orders by individual states to honour and respect the traditional rights (SPWD, 1998). In the light of recent statistics, the good intention of protecting the commons has become a matter of contention. Table 7.3 shows that during the last 45 years about 4.7 million hectares of forest lands have been diverted for different developmental uses.

Table 7.3
Diversion of Forest Lands to Other uses in India

| Land use | 1951–80[a] | | 1980–90[b] | | 1991–95[c] | | 1951–95 |
|---|---|---|---|---|---|---|---|
| | Area (million hectares) | % of diverted area | Area (million hectares) | % of diverted area | Area (million hectares) | % of diverted area | Total minimum area diverted (million hectares) |
| Agriculture | 2.623 | 60.60 | > 0.103 [c] | NA | 0.038 | 49.30 | 2.764 |
| River valley projects | 0.502 | 11.60 | NA | NA | 0.016 | 20.80 | 0.518 |
| Industries and townships | 0.134 | 3.10 | NA | NA | 0.007 | 9.10 | 0.141 |
| Transmission lines and roads | 0.061 | 1.40 | NA | NA | NA | NA | NA |
| Miscellaneous | 1.008 | 23.30 | > 0.012 [d] | NA | 0.016 | 20.80 | 1.036 |
| Total | 4.328 | 100.00 | 0.291 | 100.00 | 0.077 | 100.00 | 4.696 |

Notes: [a]Forest Survey of India 1988 and Indian Council of Forestry Research and Education 1995; [b]Derived from National Forestry Action Plan, unpublished data; [c]Regularization of encroachments in Madhya Pradesh in 1990; [d]Clearance for Field Firing Range in Madhya Pradesh in 1990.

Source: Looking Back to Think Ahead: GREEN India 2047, TERI, New Delhi, 1998.

The Wildlife (Protection) Act of 1972 empowers the government to declare areas as sanctuaries, national parks, and closed areas. Once forest areas are declared under this Act, the management of the area rests exclusively with the concerned authorities, such as forest department, sanctuary, national park, and zoo authorities. By 1996, as many as 80 national parks and 441 wild life sanctuaries have been declared. The Act prohibits hunting of wild animals and trade in wild animals and articles specified in the Schedule. For instance, ivory is declared as a property of the state. The Schedule includes wild animals as well as protection of specified plants (Schedule 6).

The basic flaw in the Wildlife and Forest Acts is the identification of the 'state' as the singular stakeholder. With all its good intentions, the 'state' is unable to manage the protected areas under this act, due to various conflicts with the people. In such conflicting situations, it is difficult to provide any justice under the law. The basic lacunae in the Act is declaring the state as the only exogenic manager of this CPR, whereas local communities inhabiting the forest areas have lost their traditional rights and roles. Thus, the act is quite against the local communities and does not envisage of any role for them in the process of protection. For instance, there is no provision for local communities or any NGO to participate in such declared areas, except for the recently declared eco-development programme in different national parks in the country.[3] The Eco-development Programme coined a new concept of peoples' participation. The local communities are asked to contribute 25 per cent of the total eco-restoration costs. The programme did not take off due to the fact that, the villagers argued that they were traditionally contributing a lot more than this monetary contribution. Ultimately, the programme took away all the rights of the local communities, and they were asked to leave the park areas. In several instances, such as the famous Rajaji Park in Uttaranchal, this attitude of the government has antagonized the nomadic Gujjar people, and has led to several agitations. The people of Nagarhole National Park have been fighting for their rights to minor forest products (such as, honey and gooseberry) from the park area. In

[3]During the much revaged forest fires in Kumaon and Garhwal hills in 1995, the villagers refused to co-operate with the forest officials in putting out the fires. Subsequently the Forest department in the then Uttar Pradesh state thought of buying specially designed airplanes to drop water.

some other situations such as Buxar Tiger Reserve area, when the forest authorities came up with the suggestion of providing smokeless *chulhas*, the local communities refused to accept them.

In addition to the eco-development programmes, with community participation, the other major forestry programme that has come under a collective action framework is JFM.

At present, the two most powerful water related acts are the Water Act of 1974 and the Water Cess Act, 1977. They pertain to ground water, surface water, water pollution, and drinking water rights. The legal framework for the management of groundwater in India *de facto* links land-owners' rights on their land to the groundwater underlying it. Laws such as the Easement Act and the Land Acquisition Act of 1894 view groundwater essentially as a chattel attached to land. The non-specification of limits to groundwater extraction (by land owners), along with power subsidies to farmers, has resulted in over exploitation of the resource. The Groundwater Bills of 1970 and 1992 focussed on the creation of a groundwater authority to approve the installation of water extraction mechanisms, but failed to factor in the unutilized potential of localized and participative options of management. In the absence of well-defined limits to groundwater withdrawal and no clear-cut systems of property rights on groundwater, developments such as the significant growth of the groundwater market in Gujarat could be catastrophic for the aquifers in the long run.

As far as surface water in the country is concerned, it has been a story of under-utilization of irrigation potential as well as wasteful use. The Command Area Development Programme introduced in 1974 has not been very successful in realizing the irrigation potential of surface water mainly due to lack of provisions to effective participation by farmers (Saleth, 1996). Supply of cheap water has led to its wastage through over watering (Mitra, 1996). Despite recommendations of the Second Irrigation Commission (1972) that water charges should be at least 5 per cent of the gross income from food crops and 12 per cent from cash crops, state governments have invariably succumbed to powerful lobbies and toed a path of appeasement by grossly under-pricing water. Another reason behind the failure of the policy leading to under-utilized irrigation potential is the neglect of traditional water harvesting methods (example tank irrigation) and local level institutional arrangements.

Identical maladies of under-pricing and wastage affect drinking water provisioning by the government in the country. The National Drinking Water Mission launched in 1986 aims at expanding the availability of drinking water in rural areas. It is only in the National Water Policy of 1987 and the recently approved policy of 2002 that drinking water was assigned top priority in the allocation of water among alternative uses.

Legislation on water pollution can be traced as far back as the Indian Penal Code of 1860 in which Section 277 provides for punitive measures for polluters of public sources of water. The earlier legislation of the post-independence period with some bearing on the issue follows the same approach of providing for punitive measures. Examples may be cited of the Damodar Valley Corporation Act of 1948, the River Boards Act of 1956, and the Northern Indian Canal and Drainage Act of 1973. However, a comprehensive 'command and control' regime was sought to be established by the 1974 Water (Prevention and Control of Pollution) Act through the establishment of pollution control boards, both at the centre and state levels. The Act, an offshoot of the 1972 Stockholm Declaration, aimed at laying down a uniform set of standards (source-specific and ambient concentration) to which all polluters must conform. The legislation does not take into account differences in either their preferences or their opportunity costs of compliance, thereby creating avenues for non-compliance or deviation. A better approach characterizes the Water Cess Act of 1977 in which the effort is to induce rather than enforce adoption of pollution abatement measures by polluters through fiscal incentives for sewage treatment, trading effluent, etc.

The National Water Policy of 1987 laid down priorities for allocation of water—drinking water at the top, followed by irrigation, hydropower, navigation, and industrial uses. The thrust areas of the policy related to (i) setting up of a standardized nation-wide information system; (ii) resource planning on the basis of a hydrological unit; (iii) transfers from one river basin to another; (iv) improved project planning; and (v) development of groundwater sources. Though water is recognized as a major natural resource, access to water has not yet been declared a human right. The recent National Water Policy 2002 document is also totally silent on this matter, except for adding that communities will have more opportunities to manage water collection and distribution on a participatory basis.

Fishing is another activity, which has come under various legal frameworks (both at the national and international levels). Deep sea fishing is a CPR based activity which has strict international and national laws for its sustainable management. In India, the Murari Committee set up in 1995 came out with a set of 22 recommendations. From the point of view of CPR management, the most important ones are listed here. They clearly indicate the concern about the use of the marine CPR resources in a sustainable manner.

1. All licences and permits for fishing be made public documents.

2. The areas already being exploited by fishermen operating traditional crafts or mechanical vessels below 20 metres size, or areas which may be exploited in the medium-term future, should not be permitted for exploitation by vessels above 20 metres length, except for Indian owned vessels currently in operation, which may be given three years time to move out.

3. Deep sea fishing regulations should be enacted by the Parliament.

4. Fishermen and fisherwomen need to be trained in handling new equipment, larger vessels, and new fishing techniques, besides fish handling and processing aspects.

In most states with coastal zones, two specific acts become applicable. They are the Coastal Zone Regulation Act (at the all-India level), declared under the Environment (Protection) Act of 1986, and the individual state level Marine Fisheries (Regulation ) Acts. Under Coastal Regulation Zone (CRZ) regulations, each of the concerned states is expected to demarcate the areas within CRZ I, II, and III, and notify coastal stretches of seas, bays, estuaries, rivers, and backwaters which were influenced by tidal action up to 500 metres from the high tide line, and the land between high tide line and low tide line, as regulation zones. Various restrictions are imposed with regard to setting up of industries and processing operations (example, fish storage, drying, etc). Yet, due to persistent free rider problems, several industries have been established just outside these CRZ areas,—degrading the coastal commons. The state level regulations are meant to regulate fishing by fishermen communities. Apart from licensing of vessels, there are restrictions on the use of mechanized boats·to fish in monsoon season (it being the breeding season), restriction on fishing from certain areas, number of vessels, etc. Various international laws under WTO and GATT, and CITES also restrict trading in several endangered species and corals. For instance, in 1982, the Indian government put a ban on export of sea cucumber (Beche-de-mer) below the size of 7.5 cm. Likewise in Andaman and Nicobar islands fishing of sea cucumber is totally banned. However, unless the coastal communities are fully made responsible, the laws alone cannot bring about any major preservation or conservation of such rare CPR resources.

It may also be recalled that  preservation of biodiversity has attained the highest importance in recent years. As a party to the 1992 United Nations Convention on Biological Diversity (known as the Rio Declaration), India is committed to providing for the conservation of biological diversity, its sustainable use, and equitable sharing of the benefits arising therefrom. Article 8(j) of the Convention takes cognizance of the importance of involving local and indigenous communities in conservation and sustainable use of biological resources, and utilization of traditional knowledge, practices, and innovations in such efforts. The proposed Biological Diversity Act envisages the establishment of biodiversity management committees at the local levels that will be responsible for conservation and development of areas from where resources are accessed. As part of the process of stakeholders' involvement, biodiversity management committees are to be consulted by the national-level authority and state boards on matters related to use of biological resources and associated knowledge within their jurisdiction. Even then, the institutional aspects of ensuring effective community involvement and equitable benefit-sharing require a range of supplementary legislative measures relating to granting of ownership rights on biogenetic material to local communities, protection of traditional knowledge, modes of resource use, and conflict resolution. Current Intellectual Property Rights (IPR) regimes, particularly the Trade Related Intellectual Property Rights (TRIPs) Agreement, need to be appropriately amended to protect the rights of indigeneous and local communities.

## POLITICAL ECONOMY TO MANAGE CPRs

The 73$^{rd}$ and 74$^{th}$ Amendments to the Constitution of India, popularly known for bringing Panchayat Raj institutions to the grassroot level, brought some hope for managing CPRs on a national scale. The Act confers certain powers to the Panchayats including (i) powers to prepare and implement plans for economic development and social justice; (ii) implementation of schemes entrusted to them by the central and state governments; and (iii) exercise of powers as delegated in the subjects listed in the Eleventh Schedule of the Constitution. They include maintenance of community assets, forestry, fuel and fodder, fisheries, animal husbandry, water management, watershed development, drinking water, agricultural extension, land improvement, soil conservation, food processing industries, distribution of electricity, non-conventional energy sources, health and sanitation, and so on. Clearly many of these activities fall under CPR management.

The effect of the Structural Adjustment Programme, started in India in 1991, on the management of CPRs is another important political–economic question. To a large extent, both agriculture and the resources associated with it do not have any direct effects. Indirectly, however, trade liberalization and marketization have been affecting the value systems such that much of CPRs are being converted to such activities to cater to global, rather than local needs. Examples are growth of floriculture in CPR lands, or prawn aquaculture in lakes, rivers, and oceans for export purposes (Kadekodi and Gulati, 1999). Growth of mining in several CPR lands has been also reported. All such human interventions can distort the biodiversity and ecology of the region, in addition to making the locals dependent on external support for their livelihood.

The role of external agencies in the early stages of CPR regeneration is important. Apart from several bilateral donor agencies, under the Global Environmental Facility (GEF) of UNDP and Capacity Building Programmes of the World Bank, there are a number of opportunities to formulate land regeneration programmes with the involvement of stakeholders. At present, much of the focus is on regeneration of degraded forestlands only. For instance, out of 19 ongoing bilateral donor agency aided projects, thirteen are exclusively on forestry, one each on pasture land development, rehabilitation of common lands, wastelands development, and capacity building on participatory development.

A high power committee (Dharia Committee) was set up in 1994 to advise the Ministry of Rural Development on how to deal with commons and wastelands. In addition to suggestions to make the Zila Parishads and Gram Panchayats the nodal agencies to implement the CPR–wastelands programmes, it also stressed on the need to create a central (as well as state level) Land Use Authority, to prepare long-term (15–20 years) plans and  to enhance the role of National Bank for Agriculture and Rural Development (NABARD) to take up these programmes. With a micro-watershed approach and the decentralized Panchayat Raj institutions, the CPR and wastelands development programmes can be  made  a  peoples' programme, a *mantra* one always heard from late P. R. Mishra.

# 8

# Revenue Land as Commons
## The Case of National Tree Growers
## Cooperative Federation

## INTRODUCTION

This chapter illustrates—with an approach of creating CPRs—how village level institutions, particularly co-operative societies, can be catalytic in the sustainable management of natural resources and regeneration of wastelands. As discussed in Chapters 2 and 3, a substantial proportion of wastelands in India (almost one-third of the geographical area) comprise common property land resources. There are many reasons for the degradation of land. But the growth of wastelands can be attributed basically to the lack of institutions to revive these lands into productive and livelihood supportive assets. Can a co-operative approach be a feasible institution then?

In Chapter 4, the link between proper management of common lands, particularly wastelands and the livelihood of the people was examined theoretically. It was with this vision to restore the ecological security of village communities in eco-fragile and marginalized zones and to set in place the processes of collective management and governance that the National Dairy Development Board (NDDB), at the instance of the NWDB, set up the National Tree Growers Co-operative Federation (NTGCF) in 1986. The pilot project was funded by the NDDB from 1986 to 1991 in five states of the country, namely, Gujarat, Karnataka, Andhra Pradesh, Orissa, and Rajasthan. Later, assistance from the Swedish International Development Authority (SIDA) since 1991, and the Canadian International Development Agency (CIDA) from 1993 enabled the Federation to scale up its activities from five to seven states. A status review of the existing co-operative institutions under the umbrella of NTGCF is presented in this chapter to highlight the role of such institutions in the management of CPRs.

The NTGCF institutions follow a two-tier principle: one, creating community based co-operative institutions and two, converting wastelands (irrespective of the ownership or property rights systems) into CPRs for the common good and promoting regeneration activities. Apart from providing some basic information about NTGCF, two specific case studies are also reviewed in this chapter.

GENESIS AND GROWTH OF TREE GROWERS COOPERATIVE SOCIETIES IN INDIA

The guiding principles of NTGCF in the management of common wastelands are equity, sustainability, collective action, ecological integration, transparency, openness and trust, and honesty and integrity. Guided by these principles and aiming towards re-vegetating severely degraded lands, the Federation has been following these strategies:

1. facilitate the development of village level institutions;
2. catalyse the development/diffusion of appropriate technology and experiments; create information centres, financial services (village funds, etc.), and local networking;
3. build the capacity of teams;
4. develop methods (tools, techniques, models) for efficiency;
5. set up management systems;
6. ensure flow of financing;
7. network with other similar organizations;
8. influence policy makers; and
9. create consciousness and educate the public.

Till March 2000, there were a total of 476 registered tree growers' co-operatives in India, spread across seven states, Andhra Pradesh, Karnataka, Gujarat, Madhya Pradesh, Orissa, Rajasthan, and Uttar

Pradesh. The NTGCF not only facilitates the formation of tree growers' co-operatives but also works through other village institutions like van panchayats, VFCs, panchayat institutions, and the like. The total number of such linkages supported by the Federation till March 2000 was 241. These institutions are located across 722 villages and involve 56,075 members. They have helped in the re-vegetation of 14,249 hectares out of 35,700 hectares of common land made available to them and planted over 11 million trees on the common lands as well as the private lands. This work generated an employment of about 2.25 million work days in these villages. Table 8.1 gives a picture of the spread of these institutions across the country.

Table 8.1
Statewise Number of NTGCF Institutions

| Andhra Pradesh | Karnataka | Gujarat | Madhya Pradesh | Orissa | Rajasthan | Uttar Pradesh |
|---|---|---|---|---|---|---|
| 87 (TG) | 56 (TG) | 79 (TG) | 25 (TG) | 58 (TG) | 75 (TG) | 27 (TG) |
| 2 (VC) | 12 (VC) | 3 (VC) | | 20 (GJC) | 18 (CVS) | 54 (VP) |
| | | 15 (FDCS) | | 43 (VC) | | |
| | | 2 (PI) | | | | |

Notes:  TG: Tree Growers Co-operative Societies
VC: Village Committees
FDCS: Forest Development Co-operative Societies
PI: Panchayat Institutions
GJC: Gramya Jungle Committees
CVS: Charagah Vikas Samitis
VP: Van Panchayats

How does Institution Building take place at the Village Level?

In its endeavour towards regeneration of degraded lands, the approach of the NTGCF has primarily been based on principles of community action. The efforts are to secure and transfer tenancy of degraded wastelands such that open access regimes are transferred to common property regimes, to build up rules and regulations to manage and govern CPRs through a process of collective decision making, and safeguarding and strengthening the diverse usage practices. Using CPR management and governance as an entry point, the process of localized collective decision making is extended to other spheres of village life as well.

The vehicle that NTGCF uses in its work is a tree growers' co-operative society (TGCS). Typically, a TGCS acquires 30 to 40 hectares of revenue wasteland on a long lease from the state with complete freedom to plant, regenerate, and utilize its biomass. A Memorandum of Understanding (MoU) is signed between NTGCF and the respective state governments. The government issues orders authorizing the district collector to lease out land to the TGCS on a nominal fee of Re 1 per acre per annum. For tree growing, common and revenue wastelands as well as marginally productive private lands are selected.

Generally, small and homogeneous villages associated with common lands are selected. Once a geographic location is found viable, the staff of the state unit of the Federation gets involved in building up a rapport with the village community. The process of rapport establishment, besides understanding the people and processes in the village, comprises dissemination of information on the principles and advantages of co-operatives as people's institutions and in the management of wastelands. The teams try to generate discussions among community members regarding the need for such a project. Villagers are also made to visit, observe, and study an existing functional TGCS to enable them to clearly understand the project and its objectives. This is generally a time consuming stage in the formation of a TGCS. Several rounds of discussions are required before the village community is convinced of the usefulness of such an institution. Once the co-operative is registered, the focus shifts to training on land development techniques, maintenance of records and accounts, nursery raising, causes of soil erosion, soil and water conservation techniques, and the like. The staff of spearhead teams help in making decisions regarding the species to be planted, income generation options, and in the development of rules and regulations. The staff give due considerations to aspects such as the collective needs of the people, strengthening trust amongst members, putting in place mechanisms that facilitate harnessing people's repository of indigenous knowledge, practices, attitudes, and beliefs.

When the Federation started functioning initially, the only form of collective institutional set-up envisaged was the co-operative form of organization. With the varied experiences over time, however, the teams have explored the appropriateness of other institutional arrangements for their governance. Table 8.1 shows the various alternative organizational forms that have been used for re-vegetation of wastelands—van panchayats, village committees, forest protection committees, etc. Thus, their institutional forms and designs are now not restricted to co-operatives alone as foreseen at the outset of the process. The communities decide the design and form of their institutions based on the user group pattern, and formulate their own byelaws, that is, the village institutions mature into corporate bodies in the process.

Initially, to address the essential fodder and fuelwood needs of the communities, the project had restricted itself to villages with the number of households not exceeding 350, land availability per household being at least half an acre and the land not being too distant from the village. In other words, the sole criteria of village selection was availability of land. To enlarge the scope, the Federation has now included many other factors like village size and land availability ratio. This helps in overcoming the disproportionate creation of resources. Wherever resources have not been sufficient to satisfy the needs of the villagers, or where surplus resources have been created, it is observed that the community is not able to manage their protection efficiently and sustainably.

The most important activities of TGCS over the years have been:

1. to lease-in village wastelands from the government and grow trees and grasses on them under co-operative ownership;

2. to adopt suitable soil and water conservation measures on the leased-in wastelands to improve their quality;

3. to provide incentives for nurseries and planting trees and grasses on private lands;

4. to provide proper marketing facilities for the surplus produce of the leased-in wasteland as well as tree produce of the private lands;

5. to facilitate installation of bio-gas plants, construction of smokeless *chulhas* and use of solar and pressure cookers for energy conservation; and

6. to arrange awareness and skill building programmes.

## BRIEF HISTORY OF NTGCF GROWTH

Common property lands can be of various types such as revenue lands, *gomal* (grazing) lands, land under forests, and so on. The NTGCF has generally resorted to re-vegetating revenue wastelands rather than the other types of CPRs. As pointed out earlier, however, this approach is slowly undergoing changes; and the rejuvenation of other categories of CPRs is also being explored.

A brief view of some select projects in some of the states would facilitate better appreciation of the actual field level situation. An account of a few of the Federation's project activities at the state level are presented here.

In 1987, the organization began work with village communities in Andhra Pradesh to form institutions for accessing and managing revenue wastelands leased to them by the state government. The district administration of Chittoor delineated eight contiguous blocks of approximately 28,000 hectares in the catchment areas of the two tributaries of Papagni river. Comprising 154 hamlets of 40–50 households each, the area is surrounded by two forest hill ranges of approximately 8000 hectares—a total of 36,000 hectares to be addressed in the watershed. The Federation team focussed on the commons constituting 61 per cent of the area. Work expanded to communities living along the catchment area of Chinneru and Pennuru and progressed to other categories of land besides revenue wastelands. In addition, the district administration of Anantpur further delineated watershed areas in 12 revenue villages comprising 120 hamlets that adjoin the Chittoor catchment area for NTGCF intervention in the same year. The Federation team has so far organized 105 village level institutions in the state.

In Karnataka, the project began with organizing TGCS on scattered revenue wastelands in 1988 with the support of NDDB; and with the assistance of CIDA since 1993, it has moved on to working in the contiguous uplands of the catchment area of Papagni river. It thereby complements the work of the Federation team in Andhra Pradesh, which is also working on tributaries of the same river. The TGCS programmes in the state had spread to 29 TGCS by March 1996 with a total membership of 3059. From working only on revenue wastelands through the single institutional form of TGCS, the team has now begun to work on different categories of lands such as grazing and forest lands along the river in a holistic watershed development approach with Panchayats and VFCs. Following meetings and discussions, an (MoU) was signed between the State Government of Karnataka and NDDB. The state approval for working on one lakh hectares of land covering 179 villages in the Papagni catchment—for undertaking institution-building, land development and revegetation efforts on gomal and degraded forest lands. The team now proposes to work on 53,400 hectares covering 151 villages. The project team along with the communities of 12 villages has prepared work plans for the conservation, management, and development of natural resources. Since the commons in the area are mainly gomal lands under the revenue department, the project is planned to be worked with JFM agreements and the panchayats. The possibility of bringing all natural resource management whether on revenue wastelands, forest lands, or grazing lands under the panchayat institution is being explored.

In Gujarat, project activity began in the Dahod area in 1998. Thirty-one villages comprising 179 hamlets in the catchment of river Kali, with a total area of 20,149 hectares were surveyed for rejuvenation activity. A total of 5250 hectares of common land including 3603 hectares of forest land, 1507 hectares of grazing land, and 140 hectares of revenue wasteland were identified on which the work began. In 2000, 8 hamlets were organized and 172 hectares of common lands were treated with soil and water conservation measures on both forest and grazing lands. A total of 160 hectares has been re-vegetated with saplings and seed dibbling.

## Case Study of Mallenahally Village TGCS in Karnataka

Mallenahally in Kolar district is one of the villages adopted by NTGCF in 1989. A team of researchers from the Indira Gandhi Institute of Development Research (IGIDR) carried out a study of this TGCS to analyse the economic impact of land regeneration programmes with specific reference to TGCS summarily presented.[1]

The oldest TGCS in Karnataka state is located at Mallenahally. The forest department leased 20 hectares of land (classified as wasteland) to the TGCS for a period of 20 years. Of the 350 people in the village, almost the entire male labour force is engaged in agriculture either as cultivators or labourers or both. The other occupations in the village include trading and washing clothes. With about 500 acres of common property land, the village depends heavily upon its produce. Tables 8.2 and 8.3 present a profile of the village and the TGCS.

[1]For more details, see Parikh and Reddy (1997).

Table 8.2
Householdwise Membership Details of Mallenahally TGCS

| By Landholdings | | By Caste | | By Gender | |
|---|---|---|---|---|---|
| Landless | 7 | Forward | 48 | Male | 59 |
| Marginal Farmer | 43 | Backward | 8 | Female | 7 |
| Small Farmer | 14 | SC/ST | 9 | | |
| Big farmer | 2 | OBC | 1 | | |
| Total | 66 | | 66 | | 66 |

Source: Field data base.

Planning activities began in the early 1990s. The issues concerning the species to be planted, provision of saplings, funds for land development, and aftercare and technical inputs were jointly decided by the villagers and the TGCS staff. Of a total of 44,284 plants, a large percentage (44 per cent) belonged to the eucalyptus variety and the rest belonged to cassia (29 per cent) and acacia (13 per cent) varieties. The survival rate of plants has been found to vary between 60 and 70 per cent depending on the species.

It may be useful to review financial and economic aspects. The major cost items included are wage labour for land preparation, transplantation, and aftercare, establishment costs, costs of chemical fertilizers and pesticides, trenching and pond desilting, and other similar expenses. The cost per hectare per year worked out to be Rs 1621. The total amount spent on the Mallanahally TGCS for the period 1990–5 was Rs 194,543. On the benefits side, the important products reaped included fuelwood, pulpwood (mainly from eucalyptus), fodder, and grass. During the 1992–3, 11 tonnes of fodder were obtained, of which 9 tonnes were distributed to the TGCS members at Rs 8 per tonne and the remaining 2 tonnes were sold in the market at Rs 300 per tonne. The concept of reward for collectivization is thus built into the framework. Table 8.3 shows the summary of financial returns per hectare from the third year onwards.

It is observed that the financial return per hectare per year is Rs 1183 over a five-year period. When these results are projected over a 60-year period, the net present value per hectare of plantation comes to Rs 61,500 while the costs amount to Rs 23,500. From the point of view

Table 8.3
Financial Returns of Mallenahally TGCS, 1992–5

| CPR Produce | Year 3 | | Year 4 | | Year 5 | | Total |
| --- | --- | --- | --- | --- | --- | --- | --- |
| | Qty | Price | Qty | Price | Qty | Price | Recovered |
| Fodder in Tonnes | | | | | | | |
| Given to members | 9 | 8 | 6 | 8 | 3 | 10 | 150 |
| Sold in the market | 2 | 300 | 1 | 400 | 1 | 400 | 1400 |
| Fuelwood in Tonnes | | | | | | | |
| Given to members | | | | | 15 | 40 | 600 |
| Sold in the market | | | | | 6 | 600 | 3600 |
| Construction poles (No.) | | | | | | | |
| Given to members | | | | | 40 | 5 | 200 |
| Sold in the market | | | | | 40 | * | * |
| Pulp wood in Tonnes | | | | | | | |
| Sold in market | | | | | 252 | 540 | 136,080 |
| Total | 672 | | 448 | | 140,910 | | 141,990 |
| Financial Returns/ha/year: Rs 1183 | | | | | | | |

Notes: Price is in Rs per unit; No benefits accrued for the first three years; *not planned.
Source: Field data base.

of the TGCS, the benefits are derived from plantation products and the grants received from the NTGCF whereas the costs are the expenses incurred on planting and aftercare operations. For a 60-year period, the total benefits summed to Rs 9,459,300 and the costs to Rs 1,097,433. The internal rate of return (IRR) is found to be 23.73 per cent. If grants from NTGCF are considered as benefits, then the total benefits amount to Rs 9,710,058 and the internal rate of return to 48.3 per cent. Assuming the cost of land is Rs 5000 per hectare and the market-borrowing rate is 12 per cent, the study further re-estimated the IRR after accounting for the land cost etc. With these assumptions, the net benefits for TGCS during the 60-year period are Rs 9,459,300 and the costs are Rs 563,722 (considering only additional land cost) and Rs 978,012 (considering only additional interest costs). When both land cost and interest cost are considered together, the total costs go up to Rs 1197,433. The IRR corresponding to only the land cost is 18 per cent, and for only interest cost is 15.74 per cent. When both are considered, the IRR drops drastically to 11 per cent implying that the high profitability is eroded when market rates for land and capital are considered.

Besides the aspects mentioned above, a major thrust in the programmes of rural development is the distribution of benefits to local communities, particularly to the landless and poor. Due to the various plantation products like timber and other goods and services that accrue to different social strata, the income of the landless increased by 22 per cent with an additional total benefit of Rs 16,649. Each household in this group got Rs 1136. Referring to the question of equity, a significant factor is that the percentage increase for the high-income groups is only marginal (that is, 2 per cent).

From the analysis of the Mallenahally TGCS, an important policy conclusion emerges. The plantation is beneficial from both economic and social angles and that the activity needs to be sustained and bettered over the years. The evidence from this study suggests that these benefits can form a rationale for starting plantation programmes even in a market driven economy.

Further to the study by IGIDR, the same TGCS was studied in 1996 by NTGCF where an attempt was made to identify and ascertain issues that play a crucial role in managing CPRs through the institution of a TGCS. The study revealed that villagers were happy with the functioning of the TGCS, which they viewed as an economic source. Among the benefits accruing from the TGCS, fuelwood was ranked the highest, followed by employment generation and fodder/grass. Despite apprehensions about benefits not reaching the poor, the survey revealed that there was no caste, ethnic or income group that had a strong or adverse impact on the performance of the TGCS.

CASE STUDY OF SARNAL TREE GROWERS CO-OPERATIVE SOCIETY IN GUJARAT

The village Sarnal, located in Thasra taluka in Kheda district of Gujarat, lies on the left bank of river Mahi. The Sarnal TGCS was registered in 1987–8. It acquired 35 hectares of revenue wasteland, located in a large ravine area between the village and river Mahi, on lease from the Government of Gujarat. The land is highly eroded with gullies of depth as much as 30 metres. The Institute of Rural Management, Anand and the IGIDR Mumbai conducted a collaborative research for NTGCF to design an appropriate framework of natural resource accounting for TGCS for the year 1994–5.[2] Such

[2]For more details of the study, see Parikh and Reddy (1997).

accounts not only help in making appropriate internal decisions but also help in presenting a correct picture to outsiders, particularly policy makers. It would be useful to understand the approach used.

The following parameters were used to account for the physical, financial, and socio-economic-environmental parameters of the Sarnal TGCS. The amount of standing tree biomass was estimated by the weight and volume of timber, small wood, and bamboo. The total wood volume of standing trees of the Sarnal TGCS was around 3336 metric tonnes of which around 2909 metric tonnes was fuelwood and 427 metric tonnes of timber. In other words, only 13 per cent of the total green wood weight was in the form of timber. In addition, the bamboo biomass was about 47 metric tonnes. The total value of the standing green wood and bamboos was estimated at about Rs 12.4 lakh. Similarly, the sale quantities and values of fuelwood, grass, seeds, and other minor forest products in the Sarnal plantation were estimated.

The study then estimated the changes in the quality of soil due to the plantations by the Sarnal TGCS. The parameters used in estimating the soil quality were the major soil nutrients, pH, and electrical conductivity. For purposes of comparative analysis, the soil quality of the plantation was compared with that of the adjoining five-hectare plot of revenue wasteland used for open grazing and other needs of the villagers. It was found that the average levels of nitrogen and phosphorous were higher in the TGCS land but still much below the prescribed medium levels. Though the level of potash is also higher in the TGCS land, its levels in both the wasteland and the TGCS land are well above the prescribed level. The pH level of the TGCS land is higher than that of the wasteland but still below the prescribed level. Also, the levels of electrical conductivity in both the wasteland and TGCS land were found to be well within the prescribed low limit. It also appears that tree plantation in the TGCS had improved the quality of soil. The study estimated the total incremental value of nitrogen, phosphorous, and pH in the plantation soil to be Rs 26,398. These values were quantified using the market prices of the cheapest fertilizers required to provide the same amount of these nutrients.

The valuation accounting was pursued further to trace indirect effects such as the impact of the Sarnal TGCS on atmospheric carbon. The study assumed 45 percent carbon in the dry weight of the total tree biomass available in the estimation of the amount of carbon sequestered. Using this assumption and with the given standing wood biomass of the Sarnal TGCS, the total amount of carbon sequestered during the period 1987–8 to 1994–5 was estimated as 909.58 metric tonnes. The alternative cost of carbon reduction are in the range of Rs 168 per metric tonne of carbon, which amounts to a contribution of about Rs 59,000 by way of carbon sequestration during 1994–5. The value of the total carbon sequestration during 1987–8 to 1994–5 by this TGCS was estimated at Rs 152,809.

The study also estimated the financial and economic benefits of the Sarnal TGCS to members and non-members. It estimated the net internal financial benefit to be a low Rs. 760 during 1994–5 whereas the net financial benefits to the outsiders is of the order of Rs. 4.15 lakhs for the same year.[3] The high incremental benefits are due to standing tree biomass. The high study also estimated the net social and economic benefits from the project to be Rs. 58,909. It is important to note here that this net benefit was created mainly due to environmental gains because of CPR management, which might not figure in the calculations of outsiders.

In summary, the revenue land management strategy adopted by the NTGCF is an option which can be replicated in the country. Though the initial catalytic role is played by the Federation, sooner or later, village communities under various other collective action and participatory systems can follow the successful methods in different states under different agro-climatic conditions and reverse the cycle of land degradation.

---

[3]It should be noted, however, that the value of the growth in the standing tree biomass is completely ignored in the financial calculations and that the interest rate used on the grants received from NTGCF by the TGCS is 12 per cent.

# 9

# Watershed Development on Forest Lands: The Case of Sukhomajrians

Watershed development as a strategy in rural development was introduced in India in 1974, (reviewed in Chapter 6). Watershed development is an integrated way of managing commons by bringing water, land, soil, and forest managements strongly linked to the source of water and its *in-situ* management. People's participation in watershed development is a crucial catalyst for its successful and cost effective implementation. This is because the watershed approach requires that every patch of land located in a watershed be treated with appropriate soil and water conservation measures and used according to its physical capability. For this to happen, it is necessary that every farmer having land in the watershed accepts and implements the recommended watershed development plan. There are some components of a watershed development plan such as bunding, levelling, etc., which can be implemented individually by the farmers involved and there are many others such as check dams, waterways, etc., that can be implemented only through collective action. This means that for a successful implementation of any watershed development plan, participation of the people is necessary at the individual as well as collective levels on common property land resources in the watershed.

One can cite a large number of successful watershed programmes in India; some of the earliest ones with certain special characteristics are:[1]

1. The Mittemari Project: This project is in the Kolar district of Karnataka, and was launched in 1984.

2. Participatory and Integrated Development of Watersheds (PIDOW): This project was started in 1986 in Gulbarga district of Karnataka.

3. The Ralegan–Siddhi Project: This project was launched in 1980 in the Ahmednagar district of Maharashtra.

4. Sukhomajri Watershed Project: One of the first experimental projects in Haryana, launched by CSWCRTI around 1980.

The oldest of these projects is presented as a case study in this chapter. Incidentally, what was started as an experimental watershed programme ultimately led to replication in a large number of villages in Haryana; created the institution of HRMS; has been instrumental for the evolution of the concept of cyclic system of development. Therefore, it is appropriate to re-examine and understand this programme for its creative and innovative approaches. That is the story of Sukhomajri.

ABOUT SUKHOMAJRIANS

Sukhomajri is one of the many clusters of villages in Haryana situated in the lower Shivalik range of the Himalayas. The Shivalik mountains are a treasure house of a variety of CPRs that provide food, fodder, and water to the people of this region. They are also a part of the catchment area of rivers such as Jhajhar and Sukhna, and feed water to the man-made recreational Sukhna lake to beautify the city of Chandigarh. In the past, this village (and many other surrounding ones) had witnessed severe soil erosion, forest denudation, and declining land productivity. Since the 1970s, however, the government and the people of the region acted together by adopting an unconventional watershed management approach and fully incorporating a new institution of people's participation. Village societies under the common title of HRMS came into existence in the late 1970s in many villages (Singh

---

[1]It may not be easy to produce a complete list of all the major watershed projects in India. However, Farrington et al. (1999), Katar Singh (1994b), Sengupta (2001), and several recent books cite a number of examples and illustrations.

and Hegde, 2001). Followers of the original Sukhomajri model of participatory watershed development are often called as 'Sukhomajrians'. They follow the philosophy of CVP,[2] a mantra originally conceived and developed by late P. R. Mishra. Why are the village societies called 'schools'? Under CVP, every member of the society is a student. Hence the society itself is called a school.

What was the situation in and around Sukhomajri in the 1970s? There were many instances of continued ecological degradation, unabated by the state government or even the people themselves. For instance, the soil run-off from the catchment of Sukhna river over time used to accumulate silt to the tune of about 40 hectare metres per year in downstream Sukhna lake; severe loss of fertile soil in agricultural lands was reported; and the forest cover in the foothills of the Shivaliks had gradually declined. In the uplands, fodder grass and fuelwood shortages were becoming acute. The people of Sukhomajri, traditional cattle-rearers (Gujjars), used to leave their cattle, sheep, and goats to graze therein, increased their goat population, reduced the cattle stock (as a result of the fodder crisis) and accepted the declining milk and crop yields as their inevitable destiny.

As is typical of development processes in many parts of the world, early attempts to arrest this unabated environmental degradation were made by the central and state governments, using conventional methods of environmental protection through a Chandigarh based institution, CSWCRTI. These included wire fencing, contour bunding, planting of trees on contour trenches, constructing check dams, restricting the entry of cattle in the forests, etc. People of the village reacted indifferently to these governmental measures, and quite often broke them to take their cattle into the forests. Free grazing continued on a large scale. Repeated conventional actions were repelled by counteractions or inaction by the villagers, a typical instance of a repeated game of the non-cooperative type (discussed in Chapter 5). One can term this phase of development as a non-cooperative stage in watershed development. This may also be called the first phase of development in Sukhomajri.

This chain was broken in 1978, when an agreement was reached between CSWCRTI and the HRMS of the villagers that if the

[2]This concept has already been elaborately described in Chapter 5.

CSWCRTI built dams with storage tanks in the catchment areas to supply water to the community (irrigation and drinking water), the villagers would stop grazing their animals in the watershed areas and resort to stall feeding which they knew would reverse the degradation of forests. Simultaneously, the CSWCRTI—in collaboration with the forest department—undertook a large-scale operation of planting fodder grass and several species of trees, with labour being contributed by the entire village. Irrigation water from the tanks (initially distributed by the government agencies) supplied to the nearby fields led to a rise in crop productivity. This was the second phase of major governmental initiative with community participation and contribution.

The third stage in the process was the state of emerging conflicts about the distribution of irrigation water, and their eventual resolution with the founding of a Water User's Society (in 1981), to which the management of irrigation tanks including the distribution of water was transferred. Rules of water distribution such as 'equal water rights', rules on the number of discharges and water rates were worked out and implemented. In the final stage of development, the empowerment of the village society in the management of several other CPRs emerged. The forest department made a departure from normal practice and gave exclusive rights to manage and use fodder and bhabbar grass cutting, with local labour and distribution and sale to the village society on a contract basis (following a co-operative game theoretic model, already presented in Chapter 5). The villagers worked out rules of sharing the grasses and the payments to be made to the society. The acceptance and adherence to all such rules, norms, and procedures seemed almost universal by 1985 when the process of participatory development had reached a mature stage. Thus, there is an instance of active participation of the people in the management of all components of CPRs such as irrigation water, forests, common land, fishery, etc. All these developments in Sukhomajri and among the Sukhomajrians are to be attributed to late P. R. Mishra, crusader and leader of the participatory movement on CPR management in India.

Initial financial support by the government and persistent leadership by P. R. Mishra (as a catalytic institution) followed by sharing of forest produce between the society and government converted what would have been a prisoner's dilemma, with repeated non-cooperative actions and realizations, into a co-operative game with sustainable development.[3] A crucial component of the process was an agreement on the division of household labour between PPR based activities (livestock and land related activity) and CPR conservation (model presented in Chapter 4). This led to CPR conservation and also increased productivity of PPRs.

A case study on watershed development in five villages is presented in this chapter.[4] Of these, Sukhomajri, Dhamala, and Jattanmajri have the Sukhomajri model of watershed management with different degrees of effectiveness. The other two villages, Prempura and Tanda, did not follow them. Tables 9.1 and 9.2 show the demographic background and the process of participatory institution building in these villages. Tables 9.3 and 9.4 present the impact or performance of CPR management in the villages. Some of the major observations on the participatory watershed development in these villages can be highlighted.

1. The per cent of households owning land in Sukhomajri is much higher than that in other villages.

2. Sukhomajri is nearly a mono-caste village; the others are not so.

3. The degree of participatory CPR management (measured as an index) is very high in Sukhomajri, followed by Jattanmajri, Dhamala, and Prempura, and is nil in Tanda.

4. By 1986, the extent of soil run-off from the Sukhna river had come down to 1.6 hectare metres per year (from 40 hectare metres prior to 1960).

5. The crop and milk yield rates had gone up substantially in the CPR participatory villages.

6. The number of buffaloes among the Sukhomajrians increased and the number of goats declined to nil.

7. In Sukhomajri village, the average fuelwood availability increased by more than 30 per cent.

8. Effectiveness of participatory institutions and their impact on PPR and CPR productivity varied coherently. Income from PPRs as reflected in 'within village income generated' was higher among the

---

[3]It may be useful to recall a discussion between late Daulat Ram, an old resident of the village and late P. R. Mishra in 1978: When asked to whom the forest belongs, Daulat Ram replied, 'Forest belongs to us'. Ten years prior to this the same villagers responded that the forest belongs to the forest department!

[4]For more details of these watershed development projects, see Chopra et al. (1990), Chopra and Kadekodi (1991), and Singh and Hegde (2001).

Sukhomajrians as was the average farm income per acre of operational holding. The availability of fodder from CPR's was also higher in Sukhomajri as indicated by the fodder consumed per animal.

9. The investment in afforestation and desilting irrigation tanks along with the creation of participatory institutions resulted in benefits to the households, the village society, and the government. A summary of these benefits is presented in Table 9.5. The IRR in market prices varies from 19 to 36 per cent for different villages. Some details of the income, employment, and livelihood support benefits have been already presented in Chapter 4.

Table 9.1
Demographic Profile of the Villages, 1986

|  | Sukhomajri | Jattanmajri* | Dhamala* | Prempura* | Tanda* |
|---|---|---|---|---|---|
| Population | 538 | 321 | 401 | 227 | 336 |
| No. of households | 83 | 78 | 90 | 30 | 60 |
| Caste Composition (No. of households) | | | | | |
| Gujjars | 80 | – | – | | 24 |
| Jats | 2 | 22 | 25 | | – |
| Harijans | – | – | 20 | 2 | – |
| Pandits | – | 8 | 6 | | |
| Others | 1 | 8 | 17 | 26 ** | 34 ** |
| Average no. of residents | 6.49 | 8.02 | 5.89 | 8.12 | 5.79 |

Notes: * Data relate only to households covered in the study by *Chopra et al* (1990); ** These households are from the community of Bagadia Sikhs.
Source: Chopra *et al.*(1990).

## A COST–BENEFIT MODEL OF PARTICIPATORY DEVELOPMENT

How to measure participation? Participation itself can be assessed in terms of the degree of community involvement in CPR management (Lise, 1997).[5] As seen from Tables 9.2 and 9.3, these have been identified, with Sukhomajri having the highest index of participation (that is, unity), and village Tanda with the lowest with value zero. (for more details, see Chopra *et al.*, 1990, Chapter Four). How can the

[5]A conceptual framework and method of indexing has already been discussed in Chapter 5.

Table 9.2

Process of Emerging Institutions and Activities

| Village | Membership (No. of Households*) | Formation of Society | Years of Initiation of Institution Building | | | | | | |
|---|---|---|---|---|---|---|---|---|---|
| | | | Stall Feeding | Fodder Contracting and Distribution | Bhabbar Contracting and Distribution | Fishing | Water Distribution | Road | Drinking Water |
| Sukhomajri | 70 | 1981 | 1979 | 1982 | 1986 | 1983 | 1981 | 1985 | 1982 |
| Jattanmajri | N.A. | 1981 | 1982 | 1982 | 1986 | – | 1982 | – | – |
| Dhamala | 70 ** | 1982 | 1984 | 1982 | 1986 | 1985 | 1984 | – | – |
| Prempura | 15 | 1985 | 1986 | 1986 | NA | – | – | – | – |
| Tanda | 10 | 1984 | 1984 | 1986 | NA | – | – | – | – |

Notes: *Membership data are obtained from interview records only; ** The Dhamala society had an initial membership of 70 which dropped to 25 eventually; A dash indicates absence of management of the relevant activity by the village society; NA not available

Source: Chopra et al. (1990).

235

Table 9.3
Villagewise PPRs and CPRs; 1986–7

| Sl. No. | | Units | Sukho-majri | Jattan-majri | Dhamala | Prempura | Tanda |
|---|---|---|---|---|---|---|---|
| | | PPRs per household | | | | | |
| 1 | Cultivated land | Acre | 109.80 | 66.40 | 100.60 | 24.60 | 39.20 |
| 2 | Av. size of operational holding | Acre | 1.34 | 1.66 | 1.48 | 0.88 | 0.67 |
| 3 | Percentage households owning land | per cent | 90.36 | 62.25 | 41.18 | 75 | 77 |
| 4 | Cattle population | Number | | | | | |
| | Buffalos | 1977 | 136 | 82 | 111 | NA | NA |
| | | 1986 | 182 | 116 | 161 | 18 | 67 |
| | Cows | 1977 | 28 | 2 | 21 | NA | NA |
| | | 1986 | 6 | 2 | 12 | 26 | 23 |
| | Goats | 1977 | 89 | 2 | NA | NA | NA |
| | | 1986 | 10 | 2 | 5 | 0 | 0 |
| | Draught animals | 1986 | 89 | 37 | 44 | 29 | 62 |
| 5 | Av. no. of milch animals | Number | 2.32 | 2.95 | 2.16 | 1.54 | 206 |
| 6 | Percentage households owning milch cattle | Per cent | 94 | 90 | 74 | 93 | 90 |
| | | CPRs | | | | | |
| 7 | Forest land | Acre | 1219 | 597 | 517 | NA | NA |
| 8 | Storage capacity of irr.tanks | HAM | 9.16 | 3.96 | 6.67 | 0 | 0 |
| | | No. of tanks | 4 | 2 | 2 | 0 | 0 |
| 9 | Command area | Acre | 92.66 | 59.30 | 130.96 | 0 | 0 |
| 10 | Common land | Acre | 118 | 99 | NA | 115 | NA |
| | | CPR–PPR linkages | | | | | |
| 11 | Av. irr. land per operational holding | Per cent | 23.57 | 2.49 | 12.07 | 0 | 0 |
| 12 | Household getting irrigation | Per cent | 49 | 8 | 22 | 0 | 0 |
| 13 | Av. fodder per animal | kg/day | 29.69 | 20.02 | 13.39 | 19.83 | 20.97 |
| 14 | Degree of participation | Index | 1 | 0.62 | 0.33 | 0.26 | 0 |

*Notes:* NA = not available; HAM = Hectare metres
*Source:* Chopra *et al.* (1990).

Table 9.4

Villagewise Impact from Participation

| | Units | Years | Sukhomajri | Jattanmajri (for 32 hhs) | Dhamala (for 68 hhs) | Prempura | Tanda |
|---|---|---|---|---|---|---|---|
| **1 Productivity** | | | | | | | |
| Wheat yield rate | Quintal / acre | 1977 | 2.75 | 3.27 | 4.32 | NA | NA |
| | | 1986 | 5.80 | 6.50 | 5.40 | 3 | 4.10 |
| Maize yield rate | Quintal / acre | 1977 | 2.46 | 3.24 | 4 | NA | NA |
| | | 1986 | 4.95 | 5.1 | 4.50 | 3.45 | 4.40 |
| Milk yield Buffalo | Litre / animal / day | 1977 | 2.32 | 3.24 | NA | NA | NA |
| | | 1986 | 3.01 | 3.37 | 3.41 | 1.86 | 2.16 |
| Cow | | | NA | NA | 1.65 | 1.37 | 1.68 |
| **2 Income in 1986** | | | | | | | |
| Average farm income per acre of operational holding | Rs/acre | 1986 | 2603.85 | 2050.20 | 1205.20 | 962.80 | 1849.40 |
| Average income from dairying per animal | Rs | 1986 | 961.36 | 761.69 | 968.42 | 373.75 | 186.05 |
| Average income from rope making per female | Rs | 1986 | 0 | 0 | 0 | 653.71 | 667.24 |
| Average outside income per household | Rs | 1986 | 10,232 | 10,634 | 10,324 | 4795 | 3303 |
| Average household income | Rs | 1986 | 16,370 | 28,329 | 14,700 | 7454 | 5928 |
| Average income per capita | Rs | 1986 | 2523 | 3530 | 1882 | 919.44 | 952.72 |
| Average within village income per capita | Rs | 1986 | 1012.99 | 1005.54 | 821.49 | 399.27 | 505.16 |

(Contd.)

237

(*Table 9.4 Contd.*)

| | Units | Years | Sukhomajri | Jattanmajri (for 32 hhs) | Dhamala (for 68 hhs) | Prempura | Tanda |
|---|---|---|---|---|---|---|---|
| **3  Consumption in 1986** | | | | | | | |
| Average consumption per capita | Rs | 1986 | 2552.36 | 2541.96 | 2284.81 | 2001.43 | 2606.12 |
| Average fuelwood consumption per capita | Rs | 1986 | 203.66 | 202.66 | 135.9 | 98.57 | 133.26 |
| Average fuelwood consumption per household | Rs | 1986 | 1246.50 | 1450.50 | 1036.35 | 805.08 | 798.24 |

*Notes:* NA is not available;
*Source:* Chopra *et al.* (1990).

Table 9.5
Incremental Annual Income from and Economic
Evaluation of Investment with Participation

| Sl. No. | Beneficiary Group | Mode | Units | Sukho-majri | Jattan-majri | Dhamala |
|---|---|---|---|---|---|---|
| 1 | Households | Crop Production | Rs | 180,187 | 24,385 | 72,203 |
| | | Dairying | Rs | 40,080 | 69,117 | 38,198 |
| | | Stall feeding | Rs | 19,788 | 24,401 | 20,683 |
| | | (i) fodder production | Rs | 12,757 | 17,931 | 16,270 |
| | | (ii) organic manure | Rs | 7031 | 6470 | 4413 |
| 2 | Village Society | Fodder & bhabbar grass contract | Rs | 3667 | 3667 | 3667 |
| | | Wheat distribution | Rs | Neg | Neg | Neg |
| | | Fisheries | Rs | 1200 | 1800 | Neg |
| 3 | Government | Fodder & bhabbar grass contract | Rs | 22,581 | 15,912 | 16,172 |
| | | Desiltation of downstream lake | Rs | 31,712 | 34,371 | 13,329 |
| | IRR at market prices | | Percentage | 19.0– 19.5 | 36.5– 37.0 | 35.5– 36.0 |
| | B/C ratio at 12 per cent | | Number | 2.06 | 2.76 | 3.80 |

Note: Neg = Negligible.
Source: Chopra et al. (1990).

effectiveness of CPR management be evaluated? Here, treating 'with and without people's participation' as the possible alternative scenarios, a cost–benefit analysis may come in handy. In this methodology, the costs and benefits (both direct and indirect) are to be identified and measured. The direct investment through conventional programmes of the government plus the private investments on PPRs constitute the total investments. The direct public investments are in the construction of irrigation tanks and  maintenance of forest ranges. Private investments include those on cattle, purchase of agricultural equipment and rope making machines, etc. The indirect investments are  the costs of preservation, defined as those incurred in the creation of community and private assets that provide incentives for people's participation. In this manner, the community invests in a number of ways through indirect participation. With these investments, community assets are created in the form of irrigation dams, systems of water distribution, and so on. There are also direct costs incurred by the village community in the maintenance of the water tank etc.—recurring costs. How can the benefits be identified? The beneficiaries of preservation through people's participation may be divided into three categories: households in the village economy, the HRMS or the village society itself, and the government. Who are the beneficiaries representing the government? The forest department gains directly in terms of income from fodder and bhabbar grass contracting to HRMS and the Chandigarh administration in its reduced cost of desilting (which is an indirect benefit). The true benefit from participatory CPR management, as compared to a situation of 'no participation', is the incremental income or gain from participation, which is relevant for the cost–benefit model (Table 9.5). Prempura, a village where no investments were made in community assets till 1986, and no participatory institutions existed, represented the 'no participation' situation. It was, therefore, treated as the benchmark for the estimation of incremental income to the households. The net present value benefits at a social rate of discount of 12 per cent and the IRR are tabulated in Table 9.6 for alternative cases at three stages of the cost–benefit analysis. In the first stage, all inputs and outputs are valued at market prices; in the second stage, labour and capital are valued at shadow prices; in the third stage distributional weights (calculated from income distribution patterns in the project region as compared to that without project situation) are used.

The IRR for all villages is greater than 12 per cent, the cut-off social rate of discount usually adopted by the Planning Commission. The rates of return for Dhamala and Jattanmajri are higher than those for Sukhomajri, partly because of relatively lower initial investments. Whereas shadow pricing of labour and capital reduces the IRR for Sukhomajri by about 5 percentage points, the corresponding decreases for Dhamala and Jattanmajri are 12 and 8 percentage points, respectively. The results for the latter two villages are also more sensitive to the use of distribution weights. The IRRs increase from 24.5–25 to 48.5–49 for Dhamala and 27.5–28 to 41.5–42 per cent for Jattanmajri. After using distribution weights, the IRR for Sukhomajri is in the range of 18.0–18.5 per cent. Though the range in which the IRR lies is lower for Sukhomajri than for Dhamala and Jattanmajri it is important to note that 81.5 per cent of the annual benefits from the

Table 9.6
Economic Evaluation of Investment with Participation:
Alternative Decision Criteria

| Units | NPSB at 12 per cent (Rs '000) | BC ratio at 12 per cent | Range of IRR |
|---|---|---|---|
| Stage 1 (at market prices) | | | |
| Sukhomajri | 398 | 2.06 | 19.0-19.5 |
| Dhamala | 287 | 2.76 | 36.5-37.0 |
| Jattanmajri | 313 | 3.80 | 35.5-36.0 |
| Stage 2 (with shadow price of labour and capital) | | | |
| Sukhomajri | 194 | 1.33 | 14.5-15.0 |
| Dhamala | 190 | 1.74 | 21.5-25.0 |
| Jattanmajri | 248 | 2.41 | 27.5-28.0 |
| Stage 3 (with distribution weights) | | | |
| Sukhomajri | 518 | 1.89 | 18.0-18.5 |
| Dhamala | 802 | 4.09 | 48.5-49.0 |
| Jattanmajri | 758 | 5.30 | 41.5-42.0 |

Notes: Net present social benefits (NPSB) and BC ratios are computed at 12 per cent rate of discount. The shadow price of labour is taken as 90 per cent of market wages and the shadow price of investment ($P_l$) is computed as:

$$P_l = \frac{(1-s)R}{r-s\,R} = 1.75$$

where as s=0.23, R=0.18, and r=0.12.

Assuming governmental income as numeraire, distributional weights for incomes of Sukhomajri, Dhamala, and Jattanmajri societies are taken as 1.51, 2.91, and 2.46, respectively.

Source: Chopra et al., 1990.

project accrue to the village economy in Sukhomajri. This is perhaps on account of the higher level of development of participatory institutions in Sukhomajri.

Desilting of irrigation tanks is intended to be done co-operatively by the villagers. In the absence of such a community effort, investment in tanks would have to be undertaken at periodic intervals. On the assumption that in the absence of participation this additional re-investment would be undertaken once in every six years, it is found that, the IRR falls from the range of 14.5–15.0 to 11.5–12.0 per cent; the difference between the two is an indication of the contribution from participation. This numerical estimate does not, of course, purport to measure the full implication of a participatory approach.

One of the assumptions made in this analysis is that the income from the forest lease is a net benefit to the government. In the 'non-participatory situation', the forest department would have received an alternative income from private contracting. In reality, however, this income would be lower due to ineffective government policing, and the consequent appropriation could then vary from zero to the amount of the contract. Setting the government's net benefit on this account at zero, the IRR is found to decline by only 0.5 percentage points, thereby implying that the government's revenue benefit is not crucial in this participatory development model.

In summary, the Sukhomajri model shows the strength in sharing CPR management by the communities, thereby linking CPR management with PPR returns. The net result is livelihood and ecological sustainability (discussed in Chapter 4).

# 10

# An Institution of Creating CPRs out of PPRs
## The Case of Chakriya Vikas Pranali

WHAT IS CHAKRIYA VIKAS PRANALI?

A community based institution evolved to pool private lands to develop as a CPR is presented in this chapter as a case study. This new institution called Chakriya Vikas Pranali (CVP)—best translated into English as Cyclic System of Development—has been in operation since 1987 in several villages of Palamau district of Jharkhand. An NGO, Society for Hill Resources Management School (SHRMS) has been active since 1985–6 in initiating, supervising, monitoring, and spreading the concept of CVP in villages in Bihar and Jharkhand. In essence, the approach is pooling private lands with an objective of regenerating degraded lands to be managed by village societies. In the process, a CPR is created as well.

How does this CVP process get started? How does it function? How does it grow? What are the gains from CVP? Answers to some of these questions are presented in Box 10.1.

One-time investment grants are sought by SHRMS from some donor agency to revive land productivity and raise the ecological level of the villages. The SHRMS works very closely with the people to convince them about the need to pool land and water resources to reverse the cycle of degradation. Private lands and water bodies are pooled into a common property from among the poor marginal and small farmers, totally on a voluntary basis. Village households designated as 'students' are in the core of the community management and decision making system. Investment decisions on soil and water conservation, purchase of seedlings, nursery development, flood and drought pruning, etc. are made collectively. Indigenous knowledge is pooled and revived in bringing the degraded lands into productive and ecologically sustainable common assets.

Uniformly, a three-tier, agro-forestry programme is introduced on the pooled lands. It consists óf vegetable and crop agriculture in the lower terrains, citrus and other fruit crops and fodder growth in the middle terrains, and timber, bamboo, and long-term fruit plantations in the upper-most tier. Until the plantations and crops start yielding regular incomes, that is, during the interim period, students are paid stipends (generally below minimum wages). Once the plantations start yielding returns, the final agricultural and forest produce is shared according to agreed formulae. Four major stakeholders are identified in this situation. The students and landowners get one-third share each. One-third share is saved as village fund for further investments on land and water management. The last 10 per cent of the produce is kept aside as *kalyan kosh*, and is used for giving loans, for emergency assistance, welfare, and for research and  development purposes.

What is the net gain from CVP? Under CVP, a balance is reached between environmental preservation and livelihood sustenance (a concept elaborately stressed in Chapter 4). For instance, almost from the first year itself, the first tier crops start supporting basic livelihood. Vegetables, rice, several types of grams (grown 2–3 times a year) keep the people above the subsistence level of living. While the people gain from medium-term productive activities such as growing papaya, guava, mango, citrus fruits, sapota, etc. (either annually or once in two years), the process helps in  protecting land from soil erosion. The third tier plantations such as bamboo, teak, sal plantations, etc. provide growth to the village economy, enhance carbon sequestration, sustainable forestry, and environmental security.

---

**Box 10.1: Features of Chakriya Vikas Pranali**

• Village is a unit of natural resource management.
• Operationalizing the development process involves bringing people together, introducing appropriate technology, institution building, and imparting confidence to people about self-reliance. Some element of leadership is necessary at this stage.
• There shall be a need for only a one-time grant or financial support to start the CVP activities in a village.
• Enrolling members of the households as 'students' of the CVP School. This includes those who pool their lands, as well as people without lands but willing to participate under CVP. For all practical purposes, no government official is a member of the Management Committee, as the government has not provided any land, except for an initial 'seed money' grant (under IRDP, NREP, or some other schemes).
• Pooling degraded private lands belonging to marginal and small farmers, to create a common land. In the event, forest and panchayat lands are also available, they can also be pooled, on the same lines as private lands.
• Pooled land is initially used to create village nursery and three-tier agro-forestry programmes.
• All activities such as land development, water harvesting, plantation, protection, harvesting, and marketing of the produce etc., will be guided by community decisions.
• The first principle of water management is 'arresting water where it falls' or *in situ* as the basic water harvesting technology.
• Other water harvesting technologies are traditional and quite well known to the local tribals: tie-ridge, ring-ridge, strip trenches, check dams, small ponds, bunding, *nallas*, deep wells, etc., are various alternatives depending upon the terrain. These techniques also act as soil conservation measures.
• Technical support on farming and marketing will be made available through interaction between villages and the existing governmental and NGO institutions.
• The plantation programme is broadly divided into three tiers: In the lower beds, short duration crops, tubers, and vegetables are to be planted. In the middle terrains, medium duration fruit and medicinal plants are to be planted. In the upper ridges, long duration energy and timber plants are to be grown.
• The plantation and agro-forestry programme will ensure three types of returns: annual, once in 2–3 years, and once in 6–8 years. These returns can be suitably used by the households for short-run basic needs such as food and clothing, medium-term requirements such as schooling, house repair, and festivals, and long-term needs of marriages, house building, etc.
• The sharing system is unique in CVP. The income from the produce is shared between those who have participated, and some is retained for village development. All the participant students are paid a stipend on a daily basis during the period of land development, nursery development, etc. After the harvest is ready, one-third share of the net produce will again go to the students; the second slice of one-third share will be distributed among those who have contributed lands; and one-third share will be set aside as a village fund. The last slice of 10 per cent will be used for community welfare.

Chakriya Vikas Pranali, which was initiated in 1987 in just five villages in Palamau district of Jharkhand, has by now spread to a large number of villages in Jharkhand and Bihar. By 1994, a realistic and reliable picture had emerged in several villages about the potential of this process. By then about 1762 households were involved in the CVP programme covering about 2730 acres of land. Table 10.1 shows the summary for 30 villages, where land regeneration programmes have been going on for over 10 years. In order to study the CVP design and progress, the following definitions and indicators are used.

Investment: Net investment is defined as expenditure on nursery, plantation, and soil and moisture conservation, whereas gross investment includes overhead expenses.

CVP Fund: There are three components of income namely, student fund (student stipend plus income to land owners), village fund, and sale incomes that are set aside as *kalyan kosh*. The CVP fund is the total income from all these three.

Household savings rate is defined as the ratio of student fund to total CVP Fund.

Village savings rate is defined as the ratio of village fund to total CVP Fund.

CVP growth rate is the ratio of village savings rate to CVP investment /CVP fund ratio. The CVP investment/CVP fund ratio stands roughly as an approximation to the incremental capital–output ratio in CVP.

From the experience of CVP, it can be seen that employment, household income, and net village savings rate are much higher than those attainable under many other development programmes. Second, the corresponding investment to land ratio is also quite small, with an average investment of about Rs 3750 per acre as a one-time investment.[1] Both these indicators imply a very high rate of growth at the village level. Chakriya Vikas Pranali villages have a potential growth rate of 3.45 per cent. [2]

---

[1] Under the usual IRDP, watershed, and other such programmes, the estimates of investments are as high as Rs 3900 per acre (Chopra and kadekodi, 1993).

[2] A model of CVP growth has already been presented in Chapter 5.

Table 10.1
Experience of CVP in 30 Villages of Palamau

| Performance Indicators | Units | Total Over 1987-94 |
|---|---|---|
| Gross investments | Rs '000 | 10,848.927 |
| Net investment | Rs '000 | 10,248.232 |
| Sale income * | Rs '000 | 418.768 |
| Student fund ** | Rs '000 | 642.360 |
| Village fund ** | Rs '000 | 353.179 |
| Total CVP fund *** | Rs '000 | 1414.307 |
| Households | Number | 1900 |
| Students | Number | 265 |
| Area covered | Acres | 2730 |
| Seedlings raised | No.('000) | 6091 |
| Plantations undertaken | No. ('000) | 4753 |
| Graftings done | No. ('000) | 95 |
| Investment/CVP fund | Ratio | 7.246 |
| Investment/student ratio | Rs per capita | 38,672 |
| Investment/area ratio | Rs per acre | 3753.930 |
| Household income rate | Per cent | 45.420 |
| Village savings rate | Per cent | 24.970 |
| CVP growth rate | Per cent | 3.446 |

Notes: 1. All the figures shown in this table are with respect to CVP activities only. Other private and governmental investments, and incomes are not shown here; *refers to income from sale of produce so far and does not include accrued income from trees, bamboo, etc., which would mature only after another 3–4 years; **shows the actual savings and deposits made in these accounts; ***CVP fund here is interpreted as the savings out of CVP activities and actual sale income. Growth rates shown here, therefore, portray the potential of only CVP.
Source: Field data.

MICRO-LEVEL ANALYSIS OF CVP

The community-oriented plantation and land regeneration CVP programme is analysed in some detail for three selected villages namely, Tandwa, Sakanpiri, and Chapri. Following the logic of net productivity contributed by the community as an indicator of its contributions, the community treats the surplus value generated as village fund as the value of community contributions.

Using the data on seedling, sapling, and other plantation programmes, along with the data on soil-moisture control, participatory labour deployment etc., the cost and income profiles are estimated for the three

villages. Tables 10.2 (a to c) show some of the major performance
indicators of the three villages with community participation.

Table 10.2.a
Summary Performance Indicators, Tandwa Village

|  | 1987–8 | 1988–9 | 1989–90 | 1990–1 | 1991–2 | 1992–3 | 1993–4 |
|---|---|---|---|---|---|---|---|
| Cum. land pooled (acre) | 0 | 2 | 47 | 57 | 69 | 95 | 105.5 |
| No. of community students | 93 | 93 | 93 | 93 | 93 | 93 | 93 |
| Cum. seedlings /acre | 0 | 9000 | 2936 | 3561 | 3522 | 2958 | 2848 |
| Cum. plantation/acre: (Number) | 0 | 0 | 1900 | 2374 | 2482 | 2260 | 2178 |
| Inv./acre (Rs '000) | 0 | 39.85 | 5.99 | 6.31 | 6.12 | 5.42 | 5.18 |
| Unit inv. cost/seedling (Rs) | 0 | 1.14 | 0.63 | 0.59 | 0.62 | 0.60 | 0.60 |
| Unit inv. cost/sapling(Rs) | 0 | 0 | 1.46 | 1.26 | 1.13 | 1.12 | 1.11 |

*Source*: Field database.

Table 10.2.b
Summary Performance Indicators, Shakanpiri Village

|  | 1987–8 | 1988–9 | 1989–90 | 1990–1 | 1991–2 | 1992–3 | 1993–4 |
|---|---|---|---|---|---|---|---|
| Cum. land pooled (acre) | 0 | 1.5 | 28.5 | 43.5 | 52.5 | 83 | 103 |
| No. of community students | 58 | 58 | 58 | 58 | 58 | 58 | 58 |
| Cum. Seedlings /acre: | 0 | 12,000 | 1702 | 2218 | 2333 | 2693 | 2560 |
| Cum. Plantation/acre: | 0 | 0 | 765 | 1394 | 1508 | 1489 | 1506 |
| Inv./acre (Rs '000) | 0 | 34.24 | 3.66 | 3.64 | 3.71 | 3.94 | 3.98 |
| Unit inv. cost/seedling (Rs) | 0 | 1.13 | 0.77 | 0.64 | 0.67 | 0.57 | 0.58 |
| Unit inv. cost/sapling (Rs) | 0 | 0 | 1.46 | 0.99 | 0.92 | 1.00 | 1.13 |

*Source*: Field database.

Table 10.2.c
Summary Performance Indicators,  Chapri Village

|  | 1987–8 | 1988–9 | 1989–90 | 1990–1 | 1991–2 | 1992–3 | 1993–4 |
|---|---|---|---|---|---|---|---|
| Cum. land pooled(Acre) | 50 | 65 | 82 | 97 | 122 | 148 | 168.6 |
| No. of community students | 89 | 89 | 89 | 89 | 89 | 89 | 89 |
| Cum. Seedlings /acre | 1188 | 1145 | 1426 | 1771 | 1868 | 2025 | 1967 |
| Cum. Plantation/acre | 1009 | 931 | 1194 | 1385 | 1429 | 1426 | 1419 |
| Inv./acre (Rs '000) | 2.75 | 4.70 | 4.26 | 4.43 | 3.92 | 3.99 | 4.13 |
| Unit inv. cost/ seedling (Rs) | 0.73 | 1.34 | 0.93 | 0.78 | 0.70 | 0.64 | 0.64 |
| Unit inv. cost/sapling (Rs) | 1.63 | 2.83 | 1.93 | 1.60 | 1.33 | 1.30 | 1.32 |

*Source*: Field database.

In most of the villages, the programme started around 1987–8. The first cycle of investment ended around 1993–4. Since then, the villagers have been protecting and reaping either some or all the three tier produce, namely, food crops, vegetable crops, fuel and fodder, small timber, and in some instances even long timber and bamboo. However, much of the timber produce will mature only in the coming five years.

How can the performance of CVP as an institution of creating CPRs be assessed? For this purpose, a cost–benefit analysis may prouide some answer under the following major assumptions.

1. An average survival rate of 70 per cent is assumed for all the major plantations. This is partly based on the community's field information, and from experience elsewhere (Indian Institute of Public Opinion, 1991). Comparable figures from social and farm forestry are 67.0 per cent for Karnataka, 53.6 per cent for Tamil Nadu, 68.7 per cent for Utter Pradesh and 67.7 per cent for West Bengal.

2. Gestation lags from the end of plantation to the stage of yielding benefits are based on the field experience.

3. The life of the project is determined by the expected life of fruit plants such as lemon, orange, guava, chikoo, musambi, etc. Timber is said to be ready for harvesting after about 10 years of maturity.

4. The prices of the produce are based on the actual current rates. For instance, 58 timber trees were sold for Rs 11,000 in Chapri in 1995. In case of other produce, some averages were arrived at, based on the records of weekly and monthly sales or use patterns. The ultimate prices or values used are Rs 50 for a fuel and fodder plantation per year, income from fruit plants at Rs 50 per tree per year, timber at Rs 188 per tree, each bamboo at Rs 20 per pole, and other minor timber at Rs 100 per tree.

5. (For several reasons income from vegetables, and marginal crops is not accounted.) Firstly, only a minor part of the pooled land is put to these crops. Second, income data on these two products were incomplete since a substantial part of these are consumed as homegrown. Third, much of the sale incomes from these on a day-to-day basis are utilized for routine expenditures such as cartage, transport cost, and payments for hired labour. The impression one has from the field is that the income from vegetables is of the order of Rs 200 per acre and is spent on various routine expenses.

6. Out of the income, the households get a share of 60 per cent as

consumption benefits. The corresponding accounting components in the village records are the student share (30 per cent) and landowners share (30 per cent). The remaining 40 per cent of the income is the surplus value generated by the community, attributable to their community labour (and includes providing indigenous knowledge, and technology, etc.). In terms of accounting, they are recorded as village fund (30 per cent), and *kalyan kosh* (10 per cent).

7. The village fund (30 per cent) is assumed to be used for further developmental works. This share is treated as savings, which are in turn invested. A shadow price on this investment is applied as $Ps = 1.54$ (based on a best rate of return of 18.5 per cent and a social discount rate of 12 per cent (Murty et al., 1992). Likewise, the initial investment costs are adjusted directly by the shadow price of savings (at a premium of 1.54).

8. The students (that is, labour) working on the programme are paid a stipend (around Rs 10 to 15 per day), which is much lower than the minimum wage rate (around Rs 25 per day). As the stipend, by and large, reflects only the resource cost, the case for the usual adjustment for unskilled labour does not arise.

9. The opportunity cost of degraded lands, brought under CVP is very difficult to assess. No firm data on the income from such lands prior to pooling are available. Interviews with the villagers reveal that some minor pulses were grown as rain fed crops. However, as a measure of the opportunity cost of land—on the basis of a study on crop outputs in Palamau district by Chopra and Kadekodi (1999)—an average income per acre of Rs 1066 is used.

Table 10.3 shows the investment flows from 1987–8 onwards out of grants and donor aids. Generally, investments on this three-tier, agro-forestry programmes are spread over a period of five to seven years, with peak investments in the third and fourth years. Table 10.4 gives the estimated income streams up to 2004–05. These are projected using the price, survival and income estimates, and assumptions made earlier.

The summary of a social cost–benefit analysis is presented here. Let the benefit, investment, and opportunity cost (of land) be denoted by $B_t$, $K_t$, and $O_t$, respectively. The basic labour cost incurred as stipends is paid out of the investment costs only. On the basis of the assumptions and parameters already mentioned, the net present value benefit (NPVB) can be expressed as:

$$NPVB = \sum \left[ a.B_t + (1-a).P_k.B_t \right] - P_k.K_t - \left[ a.O_t + (1-a)P_k.O_t \right],$$

where $a =$ the share of benefits going as consumption, the rest as investments; and $P_k =$ the shadow price of capital.

The benefit–cost ratio is defined as the ratio of the present value benefit stream, corrected (with appropriate shadow prices) to the sum of corrected present value investment cost and opportunity cost of land. The present values are computed at 12 per cent social discount rate (Murty *et al.*, 1992).

Table 10.3
CVP Investment Flows in the Three Villages

(Rs '000)

| Years | Chapri | Tandwa | Sakanpiri |
|---|---|---|---|
| 1987–8 | 137 | 0 | 0 |
| 1988–9 | 168 | 80 | 51 |
| 1989–90 | 444 | 202 | 53 |
| 1990–1 | 802 | 78 | 54 |
| 1991–2 | 489 | 63 | 36 |
| 1992–3 | 112 | 92 | 132 |
| 1993–4 | 105 | 32 | 83 |
| 1994–5 onwards till 2004–05: each year * | 7 | 5 | 4 |

*Notes:* *This is mainly maintenance expenditure.
*Source:* Field database.

Table 10.5 shows the performance indicators as derived from the cost–benefit model of CVP. The NPVB minus the 60 per cent share of the income enjoyed as student and landowner funds (for consumption) is redefined as the contribution attributable to community participation. In the accounts of CVP, this is equivalent to the village fund and *kalyan kosh* (appropriately adjusted by shadow prices). Since the direct consumption benefits and the opportunity cost of land are already accounted for in arriving at the NPVB, this measure represents the value contributed by community labour, over and above the labour, which is compensated as in any other agricultural activity.

Table 10.4
Income Flows from CVP

(Rs '000)

| Year | Tandwa | Sakanpiri | Chapri |
|------|--------|-----------|--------|
| 1992–3 | – | – | 1766.10 |
| 1993–4 | 832.80 | 229.20 | 2774.20 |
| 1994–5 | 1837.80 | 464.70 | 4092.50 |
| 1995–6 | 195.80 | 481.20 | 4391.60 |
| 1996–7 | 2459.70 | 631.80 | 5644.00 |
| 1997–8 | 2564.20 | 831.20 | 4367.90 |
| 1998–9 | 2725.80 | 1251.20 | 4482.10 |
| 1999–2000 | 7529.40 | 2131.50 | 4190.30 |
| 2000–1 | 6309.50 | 5938.50 | 3660.80 |
| 2001–2 | 4793.90 | 3256.20 | 3234.80 |
| 2002–3 | 6103.60 | 5442.40 | 4611.80 |
| 2003–4 | 1631.80 | 2753.80 | 2281.70 |
| 2004–5 | 261.40 | 213.50 | 533.80 |

*Source*: Field database.

The overall gain from the land regeneration programme can be viewed by considering the NPVB per acre. It ranges from Rs 10,000–Rs 11,000 per acre in Tandwa and Chapri villages to Rs 6500 in Sakanpiri. Certainly, these returns are much higher than in most parts of Jharkhand with irrigated or unirrigated crop agriculture (Chopra and Kadekodi, 1999). The net contribution towards ecological sustenance and regeneration of wastelands by the communities amounts to Rs 3585 per community labour per year in Tandwa village, Rs 2884 in Sakanpiri, and Rs 6058 in Chapri.

Table 10.5
Benefit–Cost Analysis of CVP

| | Tandwa | Sakanpiri | Chapri |
|------|--------|-----------|--------|
| Benefit/cost ratio | 5.05 | 4.85 | 7.15 |
| NPVB: (Rs million) | 10.75 | 5.56 | 14.48 |
| Net present value community contribution: (Rs million) | 2.707 | 1.358 | 4.378 |
| NPVB/Acre: (Rs) | 11,710 | 6557 | 10,168 |
| Net community benefit/student per year: (Rs) | 3585 | 2884 | 6058 |
| Net community benefit/acre: (Rs) | 2949 | 1601 | 3074 |

*Source*: Field database.

The regenerated area has received about 25 per cent of contribution from community labour, a fact which cannot be ignored. In replicating such CVP programmes, this element of community benefit needs to be recognized and properly rewarded. Only under such a transparent and rewarding system there will be a greater scope for the replication of such CPR land development programmes.

## CONCEPTUALIZING CVP AS A REPLICABLE MODEL

Based on the case studies presented here, as well as based on the dynamic growth of CVP institutions discussed in Chapter Five, a number of questions arise. Among them, the most commonly raised is on replicability of such community based institutions. Replication of local level community institutions requires several preconditions. Some of them have been extensively analysed in Chapter Five. The notable ones are: economic incentives to pool resources, guarantee about stability of the institutions in the long run and the need for transparent sharing rules. Apart from these, the existence of leadership is most important to make the replication to reach other situations. A set of design principles were also referred to in Chapter Seven.

Replication of community based institutions should always begin with basic needs of the community as the starting point. While attending to those, the sharing rules should be strictly adhered to and well demonstrated. It is then possible to add other social and economic activities for community management, including social responsibilities. As discussed in the design of CVP, this is done by guaranteeing incomes to all from the very start of the community management of resources. Creation of village development fund is a sound idea from the point of view of long run development, but is not convincing to the community in the initial stage of the process. That is basically because of not having sufficient trust on the system. That is why a leadership is added as the most required social institution for replication. Limits to replication will come as and when, any of these conditions are either not fulfilled or violated.

# 11

# Water as CPR:
## Cases of Traditional Systems, Community Management, and Sharing Principles

INTRODUCTION

Water is a CPR in general, unless it is owned by individuals in the form of, say, private wells and used by them. The CPR management of lands and forests by communities is a well-known phenomenon, already discussed and demonstrated in this book. However, this is not universally the case with water resources. As reviewed in Chapters 1 and 3, community participation and co-operative management of irrigation systems have existed since ages in India. Water management in ancient India was linked to sacredness, minimal state management, collective panchayat system, and a transparent allocation system (Agarwal and Narain, 1997: Chapter 3). The traditional *ahar* system practiced in the Gangetic plains and the *johad* systems in Rajasthan are only some living examples of indigenous water management technologies that are relevant even today. Over time, however, many of these traditional arrangements and systems have been replaced by state management. Today, about 36.8 per cent of different irrigation systems are under state management, mainly as canal irrigation. The rest of the irrigation comes from private or community owned sources such as private canals (1.11 per cent), tanks (6.93 per cent), wells (48.89 per cent), and several other sources. Traditionally, water rights always existed with the village communities (Vani and Asthana 2000). It was only after the Land Acquisition Act of 1874 and the Water Act of 1975 that the management of this CPR was transferred to the governments. With the tragedy of this CPR, new and emerging institutions in water management need to be studied.

The case studies presented in this chapter throw light on the manner in which different participatory institutions and activities have facilitated the efficient management and utilization of tank irrigation systems, drinking water supply, and water for livestock in India.

## ON IRRIGATION SYSTEMS

Two different types of irrigation systems, one traditional and another modern are presented here to highlight the importance of developing indigenous irrigation systems. The studies focus on the irrigation systems of Tamil Nadu: the indigenous tank irrigation system in the *zamindari* area of Ramanathapuram and the modernized Tamraparni system with three reservoirs added to the traditional tank irrigation system—diverting water through anicuts and channels.[1]

## The Case of Village Kandadevi in Ramanathapuram District

At the outset, a brief look at the history of Ramanathapuram district would be useful. This region was ceded to the British in 1792 and was under a permanent land settlement from 1802 to 1948 (when the same was abolished). It stands as an example of the most famous irrigated *zamindari* tank tracts in southern India. The average rainfall in the district is around 890 millimetres. The northeast monsoon accounts for two-thirds of the rainfall, which occurs during the months of October to December. The district extends from the hills to the sea. The marked slope, therefore, causes quick loss of water. Except for the Vaigai, there are no perennial rivers here.

Consider the case of Kandadevi village. It has ten tanks, classified as

[1]These case studies are taken from Sengupta (1991), with his generous permission to abridge them for presentation here.

parts of a chain of tanks, which are fully rainfed (Table 11.1). Tenaru is a small natural drainage channel.

Table 11.1
Tanks and their Ayacuts in Village Kandadevi

| S. No. | Name of tank | Ayacut (ha.) | Sources of supply |
|---|---|---|---|
| 1 | – | 9.20 | Drainage of a tank in previous village |
| 2 | – | 4.70 | Drainage of another tank in previous village |
| 3 | Kandadevi big tank | 39.60 | Tenaru river through a feeder channel (2 km long) |
| 4 | Kandadevi and Kandankattan Tank | 51.60 | Kandadevi big tank |
| 5 | – | 20.20 | Kandadevi big tank |
| 6 | – | 20.20 | Kandadevi big tank |
| 7 | – | 7.90 | Kandadevi big tank |
| 8 | – | 13.00 | Kandadevi big tank |
| 9 | – | 16.00 | Kandadevi and Kandankattan tank |
| 10 | Siruvali | 45.70 | Tenaru river and Kandadevi big tank |

Source: Based on Sengupta, 1991.

When these tanks are full, there is sufficient water for three months. Together they irrigate 91.2 hectares of agricultural land. The whole ayacut is sown with paddy, the common variety used being IR 50. It is single cropped and all the holdings have direct access to water from the channel and branches. Landholdings are mostly owner cultivated and there are hardly any large landowners. A total of 15.5 hectares is given in tenancy and both owners and tenants reside in three hamlets (called *tolas*) around the ayacuts.

Systems where water is appropriated as common property require the users to (i) construct additional channels for appropriation, (ii) allocate water amongst themselves, and (iii) maintain the physical works within their jurisdiction. Efficient and effective utilization of such common property water resources is, therefore, highly dependent upon the nature of understanding between all the beneficiaries. Normally, a rational person will always try to maximize his individual benefit. It is often seen, however, that though an individual gains only marginally in the short run, the benefits that he reaps in the long run more than overshoot this. Thus, major co-operation is commonly observed among co-users of common property water resources in the area of operation and maintenance, in allocation, and in conflict resolution.

The process of water allocation and design of co-operation is as follows.

1. In 1978, the inhabitants of a village located upstream on the Tenaru river improved their diversion structure in such a way that there was no release beyond this dam. At that time, Kandadevi and two other villages came together and about 500 people opposed this. On being informed, the PWD and the police came to the spot to remove the new structure.

2. Water distributors locally called *neerpaichys*, (consisting of four persons), distribute water from the tank. The neerpaichys work for three to four months of the year. They have full power over the tank water. They open the sluices every morning and close them in the evening during the irrigation period. If any villager other than the neerpaichy tries to open the sluices, he is punished by the village panchayat.

While initially the neerpaichys were hereditary, farmers now appoint them after the tank has received water. The requirement for candidature is that the person must be either an owner or a tenant in the ayacut. The Kandadevi villagers usually assemble in the evening in an open ground near the temple. A meeting is conducted and presided over by important landowners in the ayacut. After appointing the neerpaichys, they are taken to the village temple to take an oath that they will remain impartial in their duty. The cultivators pay them in cash at the rate of Rs 25 per hectare per month and the neerpaichys themselves collect this money.

3. During water scarcity in the tank, people assemble in formal meetings and decide how much of hectarage can be saved through irrigation with the remaining supply. It is then converted into some measure of land per holding. Every cultivator thereafter encloses that much of an area irrespective of his total holding. The neerpaichys implement the distribution to these enclosed parts.

While distributing water in such a manner, it is technically impossible for the neerpaichys to identify fragments of holdings belonging to a particular individual. Thus, the decided size is not on the basis of individual ownership but marked off as parts of every plot. Holdings of occupants may be fragmented and such occupants get more than one enclosure of their holdings irrigated. In Kandadevi village, there were in all 502 fragments of individual holdings with no common boundary in the whole ayacut. Many farmers whose holdings were not fragmented occupied 282 of these fragments and 80 farmers occupied the remaining 220 fragments. In both cases, the average size of a fragment of land was about 0.18 hectares. Thus, the bigger landowners through their fragmented holdings receive several shares of water. At the same time, this principle of distribution favours the very small landholders who may get their entire holdings irrigated even during a situation of water scarcity.

This method of joint management of the irrigation resource has proved efficient over time. In enclosing parts of the plot, no real measurement is undertaken. Farmers merely determine the area by visual estimates. If one of the enclosures looks bigger, the neerpaichy uses his discretion.

Another important aspect of any joint management of irrigation systems is its maintenance. Repair works on the 2 km long Tenaru river channel is taken up once a year during the off-season. In addition to this, the need for repairs may arise if a breach occurs after a heavy rainfall. If such a need arises the villagers assemble at a convenient spot to discuss the issue and take necessary action. Information regarding the meeting is relayed through neerpaichys or drummers. In the meeting, they decide a date for the work. On that day, every family is required to send at least one worker, usually an able-bodied member. If this is not possible, a labourer is sent to represent the family or a day's wage is contributed. Group work is taken up when repair work of the distributaries or field channels is required.

The third element of the CPR design is transparency. Just as in the case of allocation and maintenance of the irrigation systems, information dissemination takes place in an informal manner. Information circulates among the people of Kandadevi tola. Since all shops are at Kandadevi tola, the people from neighbouring villages also assemble here and formal meetings are convened when necessary. The village panchayat has the responsibility of announcing and calling meetings and presiding over meetings to appoint neerpaichys. Decision making is guided mostly by technical considerations and customs, and decisions are reached by consensus. No voting or regulation of membership is necessary. The organization does not maintain any records, nor does it collect any financial subscription. Participation and absenteeism are only noted on the spot.

While the above-mentioned case is a traditional case of co-operative management of irrigation systems, it is not an example of a typical traditional organization. While the construction occurred way back in the past, maintenance and allocation works persist and are being done efficiently. Part of the commitment to work arises from kinship ties and close neighbourhood. At the same time, a major contribution to the sustenance of this management method is the manner in which water distribution satisfies all the participants. Local traditions also influence such co-operation. The oath-taking ceremony of the newly appointed neerpaichys (with breaking of coconuts in front of village temple deity) is one example.

In conclusion, it may be said that while such organized activity may not be commonly observed in many parts of India, and that wide differences exist in the levels of efficiency and functional effectiveness, it can be safely said that five to ten per cent of the tank-type irrigation systems still remain efficient organizations as in the case study described.

## The Case of Chatrampudukulam Village in Tamraparni River Catchment

The Tamraparni river is the southern-most perennial river in peninsular India. The irrigation system in this area is an old one, but still has the characteristics that have facilitated in bringing about its modernization. Originating in the Western Ghats, this river traverses a distance of about 120 km before emptying itself in the Gulf of Mannar. The catchment area of the river alone is 2500 sq. km and that of its seven tributaries is about 3300 sq. km. The average rainfall in the catchment area varies between 600 to 1100 mm. Rice is the main cultivated crop. The Tamraparni area has a long history of irrigation activity.

Chatrampudukulam is one of the many villages along this river. It has three reservoirs built over 40 years ago. The biggest tank, which has the same name as that of the village, gets water through the Kodagan channel originating at the fourth anicut on Tamraparni river. For the last 30 years, the PWD has not been involved in any recognizable cleaning work except minor ones on the Kodagan channel; one such work was carried out in 1987. The whole ayacut is always cultivated with rice. Farmers' activities of paddy sowing, plantation, etc., takes place simultaneously with the release of water in the feeder canal by the PWD.

The official ayacut as per the PWD is 284.9 hectares. There are three sluices in the tank and a drainage channel is used for irrigation. A number of repair works are required for example, for the movable shutters provided by the PWD. There are numerous sub-branches from the channel. Every plot has access through a field channel and because of the completely haphazard pattern of plot locations; there are several sub-laterals and branches.

The traditional irrigation system discussed earlier showed the ownership of land to be concentrated in one village. This is not the case here. The ayacut of the Chatrampudukulam village is owned by 24 hamlets of eighty villages and a nearby town. Farmers' associations are spread across these different hamlets. The members belong to several castes and religious groups, three major ones accounting to 80 per cent. Each of these castes is found on only one or the other side of the ayacut. This gives a clue about the caste dominance, residential locality, and ownership of a specific part of the ayacut.

When the Chatrampudukulam tank is in the process of being filled, some people guard the upper sluices and prevent others from diverting the flow. A tank at a lower level to this tank receives its supply from another sluice and, therefore, if its sluice is open, the entire water gets diverted to it. This necessitates guarding the sluice throughout the process of filling up of the Chatrampudukulam tank. While the tank is officially run by the PWD, in practice, the villagers operate it.[2] There is one neerpaichy for the tank. Requests for letting water are made to him by the cultivators. Generally, he complies with every request if there is water and if there is scarcity, no such requests arise because of the *Kandavettu* system. Every channel is supplied with water for a few consecutive days and when all the plots are irrigated, the farmers inform the neerpaichy.

It is around the neerpaichy and his operations that the irrigation organization in Chatrampudukulam revolves. A family of neerpaichys holds the present post since generations. There is a nominal farmers' association to look after all irrigation-related matters. However, the

[2]As noted in Chapter 1, this was the game the British played on the people, by constituting PWDs but making the people participate as labourers.

neerpaichy is the leader to be consulted in all matters. The neerpaichy has a respectable position in the village.

The Kandavettu operation is used during periods of scarcity, when the tank contains insufficient water. During the Kandavettu in 1984, the farmers' association had appointed 15 labourers for two days to work in two groups (day and night), for the distribution of the remaining water from the tank to all lands. The distribution started from the tail-end of the channels to the upper reaches. Persons from all major castes are represented in the group. The labourers are paid by collecting contributions from the cultivators at a rate that meets all expenses adequately. Whenever these association fees are not paid during the Kandavettu, the association threatens to stop water. This makes all the farmers pay their dues regularly. The Farmers' Association also undertakes other works related to allocation. It also makes petitions to ministers and political figures lobbying for the release of water into the channel at certain times.

The maintenance work of the channel is also undertaken by farmers due to lack of interest taken by the PWD. Wage labourers do all repair works. Even if a few farmers participate, they are paid at the rate of Rs 12 per day. Thirty years ago, farmers themselves used to engage in these works. In the Tamraparni system, however, a transition has occurred and labourers are employed. The farmers contribute only financially to meet the wages and other expenses. The persons who organize the channel maintenance works and collect money (usually through local leaders), either belong to the dominant caste or are influential persons, elected to village offices.

The Farmers' Association has been functioning for the last thirty years at least. The association has still not taken a formal shape, despite efforts to do so. Therefore, the *modus operandi* is somewhat flexible and changes from year to year to meet the contingencies at hand. Members, mostly landowners and in some cases tenants, are listed in the association and are required to make financial contributions as demanded by the association. Except for an annual general meeting, the association does not conduct any regular meetings of members. Participants number between 200 and 300. But, one does not see much of participation at large. Formal meetings of office-bearers take place for the resolution of conflicts between individual farmers. Every year, there are about twenty such meetings. The association does not collect any monthly subscription or donations. Indeed, the impetus is felt only when there is some work that requires considerable expense. For each channel, generally two or three persons are entrusted to make the collection. They are allowed to retain 10 per cent of the collection. Collection has always been the weak point of the Chatrampudukulam village. Evidently, the major problem arises in the central channel where there is no single predominant caste. One of the drawbacks of the association in effecting stringent measures in collections is that it does not have any legal standing to restrict others from accessing the water.

Election of office bearers is usually through consensus. They do not receive any remuneration. This leads to caste leaders and prominent people being elected. However, a conscious effort is made to elect members from all castes and from the major hamlets.

In summary, what has brought stability to the water management system in Chatrampudukulam village is the construction of three reservoirs during the long period from 1943 to the 1980s. This helped to bring institutions such as rational water use and sharing, economization of flows in the old channels and into the river. It also enabled the construction of a hydropower plant. All these have enhanced crop productivity and stabilized livelihood.

INSTITUTIONS SPECIFICALLY ADDRESSED AT SHARING OF WATER

Of all the CPRs, it is water for which it is the most difficult to set equitable distribution or sharing rules in respect of water. As argued by Vani and Asthana (2000) and Kadekodi (2000)et. al, should water be available to all the concerned citizen on equal basis or on a need basis? The question can be sorted out by treating water as a fundamental right. In the case study reviewed in Chapter 9, we have already seen that the Sukhomajrians share water on equal rights basis irrespective of ownership or non-ownership of land. Drinking water is any way very basic to human life. What about water rights for animals? What about water for sanitary use? These are other questions linked to sustainable development. Such issues can be resolved by analysing the carrying capacity of water as a CPR in specific situations. Considering all the major uses of water (leaving the recreational use of water for the moment), some case situations are presented here, which address these and other water sharing questions.

The Pani Panchayat Experiment

The meaning of *Pani Panchayat* is water co-operative. As an institution, it is based on the concept of managing water resources at the community level. The ultimate objective of this type of institution is to conserve water while sharing it equitably with the village community.

The origin of Pani Panchayat goes back to the frequent droughts that occurred in different parts of Maharashtra. After the 1972 drought, water conservation projects were initiated and executed on a large scale by the government, which were appreciated by the people.[3]

What was the experience of those projects? Planning and implementing the works in different villages over a period of one year (1972), enabled the people and the government alike to realize that only conservation work in the absence of further distribution measures would tend to sharpen the disparity in underdeveloped areas. As a result, in 1974, village Naigaon in Pune district of Maharashtra was selected for a watershed action project. Naigaon is a typical drought-prone village. The average annual rainfall is 500 mm, with about 32 rainy days. On a small micro-watershed of this village, an earthen check dam was constructed to capture run-off from an area of 80 hectares. By conserving a run-off of about 28,000 cubic metres every year, protective irrigation could be provided to about 8 hectares of land for two seasonal crops. This increased the total agricultural food grain production from 10 quintals to 100 quintals.

*Gram Gourav Pratisthan,* headed by late V. B. Salunkhe, is a trust which executes programmes for community irrigation based on the Pani Panchayat model. Unlike governmental watershed programmes, it first realized that sharing and distribution rules are a must for the success of any CPR water management. Its main aim is to facilitate efficient harvesting and equitable sharing of scarce water resources. In 1986, 51 schemes were functioning, providing irrigation to 1500 hectares of land and benefiting 1800 families. Before the schemes, people would migrate in search of employment after harvesting a seasonal rain fed crop. Today, with irrigation available, people are able to stay on their own land. Earlier, income from agriculture was hardly Rs 1500 per hectare; it has now increased to about Rs 30,000 per

---

[3]It was late V. B. Salunkhe, who conceived this idea, which was liked by both the government and the people.

hectare. This has brought many families above the poverty level. These families have been able to improve their economic status through increased productivity of their lands and greater food security. The highly successful community action has facilitated higher food production through appropriate cropping pattern, grasslands development, tree cover on barren lands, and zero water run-off.

Lessons from this NGO experiment in over 50 villages and several others have raised hopes of having a panchayat stylized water management system within village economies. The lessons and concepts from Pani Panchayats are summarized in Box 11.1

---

**Box 11.1: Concepts   and Lessons from Pani Panchayat**

- Only community oriented group schemes should be undertaken.
- Water is to be shared on the basis of number of family members and not on the basis of land holdings. Families with greater than 2.5 acres of land holding must remain under rainfed conditions.
- Water rights do not accompany land rights. If any land is sold or transferred, the water rights revert back to the community.
- Beneficiaries will have to share part of the capital and maintenance costs of water harvesting systems. Invariably a formula of 20 per cent is applied.
- Project beneficiaries administer, manage, and operate the system, making way for leadership within the village.
- Crops such as sugarcane, requiring heavy water, are not permitted under the shared water system.
- Landless families also get a share of water, which they can share with the landowners, thereby gaining some income.

*Source:* Agarwal and Narain (1997).

---

## Community Controlled Groundwater Exploitation

The unplanned and uncontrolled development of groundwater under current public policies, which subsidize tube wells often, leads to poor groundwater management. As groundwater is a CPR, its management requires collective action, operationalizing some of the design principles mentioned in Chapter 7. Otherwise, it would become an open access resource (referred to in Chapter 1). Most of the problems can be minimized or even overcome if suitable statutory institutions are initiated with people's participation.

Take the case of three farmer water users' associations (water users society) that have been formed in the tail-portion of the command of the upper Godavari project near Waghad dam in Nasik district of

Maharashtra. The total water supply delivered to the three societies is 5,034,000 cubic metres per annum; 2,080,000 cubic metres in the *kharif* season and 2,954,000 cubic metres in *rabi* season. The societies have entered into an agreement with the Irrigation Department and receive water on a volumetric basis. They distribute this among individual farmers; and in turn collect water fees and remit them to the government.

Before the societies were formed, hardly 25–30 ha of land was irrigated in the official command area of 1150 ha. Now about 400 to 500 ha are being irrigated in rabi season. This has resulted in a rise in groundwater table in existing wells. The societies have been successful in convincing the farmers that this additional groundwater should be tapped for irrigation through their combined efforts and the formation of societies. The new wells will not be owned by the farmers but by the societies. The societies are now charging for incremental irrigated area from the existing privately owned wells at Rs 100 per ha per watering. The farmers have also resolved that no individual will construct new wells in the command area of the present surface system and the entire additional water made available through groundwater recharge will be exploited by the societies on a community basis and supplied equitably to all farmers.

Traditional *Johar* System

Johads are the traditional check dams, quite prevalent in Rajasthan. Through embankments, rainwater is arrested and stored. They are based on local mud and local human capital. But certainly, their maintenance requires continual involvement of the people of the village. Tarun Bharat Sangh, a leading NGO, undertook revival of such locally relevant technologies under the leadership of Shri Rajendra Singh, immediately after continuous droughts of 1985 and 1986 in Rajasthan.

Consider another case of water resource management through community action. Madalvas is a small village in the Rajgarh tehsil of Rajasthan. It is in a rainshadow with erratic rainfall. There is an acute water shortage. In 1985, a team of five young graduates, forming Tarun Bharat Sangh, came to the village and discovered that the problem of water was not one of scarcity but of improper management. They found that due to the lack of maintenance, the johads had become non-functional.

As a result of active people's participation, many johads were built up. This resulted in improved productivity of land—the production of maize doubled to 16 quintals per hectare in spite of the fact that rains were not good. About 30 hectares of wastelands have been reclaimed after the johads were constructed.

There were 12 wells in the village and many of them used to dry up during drought years. Now most of them have high water levels because of the johads, which can be used for raising crops, for animal and domestic uses.

To regenerate the wastelands adjacent to johads, a large number of saplings have also been planted. In order to manage and protect their forest it was decided by the Gram Sabha that if anyone cuts branches of a tree or grazed animals in a protected area he would be fined and expelled from the society. Since then every year saplings are being planted on all types of common lands and protection of plantation is the responsibility of every villager.

The major lesson from all these case-studies is that *in-situ* management of water by communities themselves can resolve most of the typical CPR-open access problems of water management, be it in the foothills of Himalayas or the plateaus of Tamil Nadu.

# References

Agarwal, Anil and Sunita Narain (1997), *Dying Wisdom: Rise, Fall and Potential of India's Traditional Water Harvesting System*, Centre for Science and Environment, New Delhi.

Alchian, Armen and H. Demsetz (1973), 'The property Rights Paradigm', *Journal of Economic History*, Vol. 33, pp. 16–27.

Anderson, L. G. (1997), *The Economics of Fisheries Management*, John Hopkins Press, Baltimore.

Anderson, L.Q (1977), *Economic Impacts of Extended Fisheries Jurisdiction*, Science Publishers, Ann Arbor, Michigan.

Anonymous (1998), *Joint Forest Management: Update*, Society for Promotion of Wastelands Development, New Delhi.

Antia, N. H. and Gopal K. Kadekodi (2002), *Dynamics of Rural Development: Lessons from Ralegan Siddhi*, Monograph, The Foundation for Research in Community Health, Pune and Centre for Multi-Disciplinary Development Research, Dharwad.

Arrow, K. (1951), *Social Choice and Individual Values*, Wiley, New York.

Atkinson, A. B. and J. E. Stiglitz (1980), *Lectures on Public Economics*, McGraw Hill International, Singapore.

Axelrod, Robert (1990), *The Evolution of Co-operation*, Penguin Books, Harmondsworth.

Bagchi, K. S. and M. Phillip (1993), *Wastelands in India: An Untapped Potential*, UPALABDHI, Trust for Developmental Initiatives, New Delhi.

Bahuguna, V. K. (2000), 'Van Sahyog', *JFM Network News Letter*, Vol.2, Issue 2, August–October.

Bali, J. S. (1987), 'Agro-industrial Watersheds: A Model for Removal of Poverty', *Journal of Soil and Water Conservation*, Vol. 31, No.2, pp. 98–105.

Ballab, V. and Katar Singh (1988), 'Managing Forests Through Peoples Institutions: A Case Study of Van Panchayats in Uttar Pradesh Hills', *Indian Journal of Agricultural Economics*, Vol. 43, No. 3, p. 296.

Bardhan, Pranab (1999), 'Irrigation and Cooperation: An Empirical Analysis of 48 Irrigation Communities in South India', *Economic Development and Cultural*

*Change*, Vol. 43, No.1, pp. 1–41.

—— (1993), 'Symposium on Management of Local Commons', *The Journal of Economic Perspectives*, Vol. 7, No. 4, pp. 87–92.

Basu, K. and A. Mishra, (1993), 'Sustainable Development and the Common Problem: A Simple Approach', in P. K. Bardhan, M. Datta Chaudhuri, and M. Krishnan (eds), *Development and Change*, Oxford University Press, New Delhi.

Berkes, F. (ed.) (1989), *Common Property Resources: Ecology and Community Based Sustainable Development*, Belhaven Press, London.

Bhatta R. and Bhat, M. (2001), 'An Economic Analysis of the Sustainability of Marine Fish Production in Karnataka', Report submitted to Indira Gandhi Institute of Development Research, Mumbai.

Bombla, D. R. and Arvind Khare (1984), *Estimate of Wastelands in India*, Society for Promotion of Wastelands Development, New Delhi.

Bon, Emmanuel (2000), 'Common Property Resources: Two Case Studies', *Economic and Political Weekly*, 15 July, pp. 2569–73.

Bromley, D. W. (1992a), 'The Commons, Common Property and Environment Policy', *Environmental and Resource Economics*, Vol. 2, No. 1, pp. 1–17.

Bromley, D. W. (ed.) (1992b), *Making the Commons Work: Theory, Practice and Policy*, International Centre for Self-Governance Publication, San Francisco.

Bromley, D. W. (1991), *Environment and Economy: Property Rights and Public Policy*, Basil Blackwell, Oxford, UK.

Bromley, D. W. and M. M. Cernea (1989), *The Management of Common Property Natural Resources: Some Conceptual and Operational Fallacies*, The World Bank, Washington, D.C.

Bruns, Bryan Randolph and Ruth S. Meinzen-Dick (2000), *Negotiating Water Rights*, Vistaar Publications, New Delhi.

Buchanan, F. (1870), *Journey Through the Northern Parts of Kanara (1801–2)*, Higgin Bothams Madras.

Buchanan, J. M. (1968), *The Demand and Supply of Public Goods*, Rand–Mcnally, Chicago.

Buchanan, J. M. and G. Tullock (1965), *The Calculus of Consent*, University of Michigan Press, Ann Arbour.

Butle, Erwin, Henk Folmer, and Wim Heijman (undated), 'Open Access, Common Property, and Scarcity Rent in Fisheries', forthcoming in *Environmental and Resource Economics*.

Chai, Ch'u and Winberg Chai (1965), *The Humanist Way in Ancient China*, Bantam Books, New York.

Chakravarty–Kaul, Minoti (1996), *Common Lands and Customary Law*, Oxford University Press, New Delhi.

Chandrakant M. G. and M. G. Nagaraj (1997), 'Existence Value of Kodagu Sacred Groves: Implications for Policy the Challenge of the Balance: Environmental Economics in India', Centre for Science and Environment, New Delhi, pp. 217–24.

Chandran, M. D. S. and M. Gadgil (1993), 'Kans-Saftey Forests of Uttara Kannada',

Proceedings of IUFRO forest history group meeting on peasant forestry, Freiburg, Germany, No. 44, pp. 49–57.

Chopra, Kanchan and D. V. Subba Rao (1996), *Economic Evaluation of Soil and Water Conservation Programmes in Watersheds*, Monograph, Institute of Economic Growth, New Delhi.

Chopra, K. and G. K. Kadekodi (1999), *Operationalising Sustainable Development: Economic, Ecological Modelling for Developing Countries*, Sage Publications, New Delhi.

——— (1993), 'Watershed Development: A Contrast with NREP/JRY', *Economic and Political Weekly*, XXVIII, No. 26, 26 June, pp. A61–7.

——— (1991), 'Participatory Institutions: The Context of Common and Private Property Resources', *Environmental and Resource Economics*, Vol. 1, pp. 353–72.

Chopra, K. and C.H.H. Rao (1992), 'The Links Between Agricultural Growth and Poverty', *Quarterly Journal of International Agriculture*, Vol. 31, No. 4, pp. 365–77.

Chopra, K. and S. C. Gulati (1997), 'Institutions for Management of Common Property Land Resources and Migration: A Study in Rajasthan', in Jyoti Parikh and S. Reddy (1997) *op. cit.*, pp. 257–77.

Chopra, K. and S. C. Gulati (2001), *Migration, Common Property Resources and Environmental Degradation: Interlinkages in India's Arid and Semi-arid Regions*, Sage Publications, New Delhi.

Chopra, K., Gopal K. Kadekodi, and M. N. Murty (1990), *Participatory Development: People and Common Property Resources*, Sage Publications, New Delhi.

Ciriacy–Wantrup, S. V. and R. C. Bishop (1975), 'Common Property as a Concept in Natural Resource Policy', *Natural Resources Journal*, Vol. 15, pp. 713–27.

Clague, Cristopher (ed.) (1997), *Institutions and Economic Development: Growth and Governance in Less Developed and Post-socialist Countries*, Johns Hopkins University Press, Baltimore.

Clark, C.W. (1982), 'Models of Fishery Requlation', in L.J. Mir man and D.F. Spulber (Eds): *Essays in the Economics of Renewable Resources*, North Holland Publishing Co. Amstesdam.

Cohen, J. M. and N. Uphof (1977), *Rural Development Participation: Concepts and Measures for Project Design Implementation and Evaluation*, Cornell University Press, Ithaca.

Commons, J. R. (1950), *Economics of Collective Action*, MacMillan Press, London.

Conrad, J. M. (1999), *Resource Economics*, Cambridge University Press, Cambridge.

Conrad, J. M. and Colin W. Clark (1995), *Natural Resources Economics: Notes and Problems*, Cambridge University Press, Cambridge.

Dahlman, C. J. (1980), *The Open Field System and Beyond: A Property Rights Analysis of an Economic Institution*, Cambridge University Press, Cambridge.

Daly, H. E. (1990), 'Towards some Operational Principles of Sustainable Development', *Ecological Economics*, Vol. 2, No. 1, pp. 1–6.

Darling, M. L. (1984), *The Punjab Peasant in Prosperity and Debt*, Cosmo Publications, New Delhi (first published 1925).

Dasgupta, Partha (1982), *The Control of Resources*, Basil Blackwell Publications, Oxford.

Demsetz, Harold (1964), 'Towards a Theory of Property Rights', *American Economic Review*, Vol. 62, No. 2, pp. 47–59.

Devlin, Rose Anne and R. Q. Grafton (1998), *Economic Rights and Environmental Wrongs: Property Rights for the Common Good*, Edward Elgar Publications, Cheltenham.

Eggertsson, T. (1990), *Economic Behaviour and Institutions*, Cambridge University Press, New York.

Ellis, Christopher J. (2001), 'Common Pool Equities: An Arbitrage Based Non-cooperative Solution to the Common Pool Resource Problem', *Journal of Environmental Economics and Management*, Vol. 42, No. 2, pp. 140–155.

European Commission for Latin America (ECLA) (1973), 'Popular Participation in Development', *Community Development Journal*, Vol. 8, No. 2, pp. 77–93.

Farington, John, C. Turton, and A. J. James (eds), (1999), *Participatory Watershed Development: Challenges for the Twenty-first Century*, Oxford University Press, New Delhi.

Ferndandes, Walter and Vijay Paranjape (eds) (1997), *Rehabilitation Policy and Law in India: A Right to Livelihood*, Indian Social Institute, New Delhi.

Field, A. J. (1984), 'Microeconomics, Norms and Rationality', *Economic Development and Cultural Change*, Vol. 32, pp. 683–711.

Folmer, Carl (ed.), *Game Theory and the Environment*, Edward Elgar Publications, Cheltenham UK, pp. 219–36.

Freitag, Sandria B. (1990), *Collective Action and Communities: Public Arenas and the Emergence of Communalism in Northern India*, Oxford University Press, Delhi.

Friedman, J. W. (1986), *Game Theory with Application to Economics*, Oxford University Press, New York.

Furubotn, E. G. and R. Richter (1991), *The New Institutional Economics*, J. C. Mohr, Tubingen.

Gadgil, M. and R. Guha (1992), *The Fissured Land: An Ecological History of India*, Oxford University Press, New Delhi.

Gadgil, M. and V. D. Vartak (1981), 'Sacred Groves of Maharashtra: An Inventory', in S. K. Jain (ed.) *Glimpses of Indian Ethnobotany*, New Delhi, pp. 279–94.

Godbole, A., A. Watve, S. Prabhu, and J. Sarnaik (1998), 'Role of Sacred Groves in Biodiversity Conservation with Local People's Participation: A Case Study from Ratnagiri District, Maharashtra', in Ramakrishnan, K. G. Saxena, and U. M. Chandrashekara (eds) *Conserving the Sacred: For Biodiversity Management*, Oxford and IBH Publishing Co., New Delhi, pp. 232–50.

Gokhale, Y., R. Velankar, M. D. S. Chandran, and M. Gadgil (1998), 'Sacred Woods, Grasslands and Waterbodies as Self-organised Systems of Conservation', in Ramakrishnan, K. G. Saxena and U. M. Chandrashekara (eds) *Conserving the Sacred: For Biodiversity Management*, Oxford and IBH Publishing Co., New Delhi, pp. 365–96.

Gordon, H. S. (1954), 'The Economic Theory of a Common Property Resource: The

Fishery', *Journal of Political Economy*, Vol. 62, No. 2, pp. 124–42.

Government of India, Ministry of Rural Development (2000), *Wastelands Atlas of India*, National Remote Sensing Agency, Hyderabad.

Government of India (1996), *Forestry Statistics of India*, ICFRIE, Dehradun.

Government of India (1996), *National Accounts Statistics*, Central Statistical Organisation (CSO), Department of Statistics, and Ministry of Planning, New Delhi.

Government of India (1999), *The State of Forest Report 1995*, Forest Survey of India, Government of India, Ministry of Forest and Environment, Dehradun.

Government of India (1992), *National Watershed Development Project for Rainfed Areas*, Ministry of Agriculture and Co-operation, New Delhi.

Government of India (1989), *Developing India's Wastelands*, Ministry of Environment and Forests, New Delhi.

Greenberg, J. (1990), *The Theory of Social Situations: An Alternative Game-theoretic Approach*, Cambridge University Press, Cambridge.

Guha, R. (1989), *The Unquiet Woods: Ecological Change and Peasant Resistance in Himalayas*, Oxford University Press, New Delhi.

Hamilton, L. S. and P. N. King (1984), *Tropical Forested Watersheds: Hydrologic and Soils Response to Major Uses or Conversions*, Westview Replica Editions, ND, USA.

Hardin, G. (1968), 'The Tragedy of Commons', *Science*, Vol. 62, pp.1243–48.

Hardin, Russel (1982), *Collective Action*, Johns Hopkins University Press, Baltimore.

Harriss, J., J. Hunter, and C. M. Lewis (1995), *The New Institutional Economics and Third World Development*, Routledge, London.

Hartwick, J. M. (1977), 'Intergenerational Equity and the Investing of Rents from Exhaustible Resources', *American Economic Review*, Vol. 67, No. 5, pp. 972–4.

Hicks, J. R. (1939), *Value and Capital, London*, Oxford University Press.

Hirshleifer, J. (1987), *Economic Behaviour in Adversity*, University of Chicago Press, Chicago.

Hoskin, W. G. and Dudley Stamp (1967), *The Common Lands of England and Wales*, Collins Press, London.

Howarth, R. B. (1991), 'Intergenerational Equilibria and Exhaustible Resources: An Overlapping Generations Approach', *Ecological Economics*, Vol. 4, pp. 237–52.

Howarth, R. B. and R. B. Norgaard (1992), 'Environmental Valuation under Sustainable Development', *American Economic Review*, Vol. 82, No. 2, pp. 473–7.

Howe, C.W. (1979), *Natural Resource Economics: Issues, Analysis and Policy*, John Wiley Publications, New York.

Hurley, T. M. and J. F. Shogren (1998), 'Environmental Conflicts with Asymmetric Information: Theory and Behaviour', in Nick Hanley, J. Shogren, and B. White (1998), *Environmental Economics: Theory and Practice*, Oxford University Press, Oxford.

Indian Institute of Public opinion (1991), A Report on the Surninal Rate of Trees, New Delhi.

Iyengar, S. (1988), 'Common Property Land Resources in Gujarat: Some Findings about their Size, Status, and Use', Gujarat Institute of Development Research, Working paper No.18, Ahmedabad.

Jeffery, Roger and Nandini Sundar (1999), *New Moral Economy for India's Forests? Discourses of Community and Participation*, Sage Publications, New Delhi.

Jensen, J. (1996), 'Watershed Development: Concept and Issues', in J. Jensen, S. Seth, T. Sawney, and P. Kumar, (1996), *Watershed Development: Proceedings of Danida's Internal Workshop on Watershed Development*, Watershed Development Co-ordination Unit, Danida, New Delhi, India.

Jodha, N. S. (2000), 'Wastelands Management in India: Myths, Motives and Mechanisms', *Economic and Political Weekly*, 5 February, pp. 466–73.

—— (1997), 'Management of Common Property Resources in Selected Dry Areas of India', in Kerr *et al., op. cit.*

—— (1996), *Sustainable Development in Fragile Environment: An Operational Framework for Arid, Semi-arid and Mountain Areas*, Centre for Environment Education, Ahmedabad.

—— (1994), 'Management of Common Property Resources in Selected Dry Areas of India', in John Kerr *et al., op cit.*, pp. 339–61.

—— (1992), *Common Property Resources. A Missing Dimension of Development Strategies*, World Bank discussion paper, 169, World Bank, Washington, D.C.

—— (1990), 'Rural Common Property Resources: Contributions and Crisis', *Economic and Political Weekly*, Vol. XXV, No. 26, p. A-65.

—— (1986), 'Common Property Resources and Rural Poor in Dry Regions of India', *Economic and Political Weekly*, Vol. 21, No. 27, pp.169–81.

—— (1985), 'Population Growth and the Decline of Common Property Resources in Rajasthan', *Population and Development Review*, Vol. 11, No. 2, pp. 247–64.

—— (1983), 'Market Forces and Erosion of Common Property Resources', Proceedings of a Workshop, ICRISAT, P.O. Patancheru, Hyderabad, India.

Kadekodi, Gopal K. (ed.) (2002 a), *Economics and Valuation of Biodiversity, Report of the Thematic Working Group for NBSAP*, Monograph, Ministry of Environment and Forests, Government of India.

—— (2002 b), 'Environmental Economics in Practice: Selected Case Studies from India', Gopal K. Kadekodi (ed.), Monograph, Centre for Multi-disciplinary Development Research, Dharwad.

—— (1998), 'Common Pool Resources: An Institutional Movement from Open Access to Common Property Resources', *Energy Resources*, Vol. 20, pp. 317–32.

—— (1997a), 'Peoples' Participation in Rural Development: An Institutional Touch to Reforms Process', in G.K. Chadha, and A. N. Sharma (eds), *Growth, Employment and Poverty: Change and Continuity in Rural India*, Vikas Publishing House, New Delhi, pp. 406–19.

—— (1997b), *Regeneration of Degraded and Wastelands: A Status Report on Data Gaps, Valuation, Implementation and Monitoring*, Monograph, Institute of Economic Growth, New Delhi.

—— (1995), 'Resource and Livelihood Linkages: The Context of Operationalising

Sustainable Development', in M. M. Skutsch and Hans Opdam (eds), *Towards Sustainable Development* University of Twente, Enschede.

—— (1992), 'A Model of Sustainable Village Development: The Case of peoples' Participation', *Indian Economic Review*, special issue, pp. 439–50.

—— (1990), *Planning for Coal Sector*, B. R. Publishing Corporation, Delhi.

—— (1988), *Planning for Coal Sector in India*, B.R. Publications, New Delhi.

—— (1982), *Economic Planning for Iron Mining in India*, Hindustan Publications, New Delhi.

Kadekodi, G. K. and Kanchan Chopra (1990), 'Cyclical Re-investment Strategy: An Alternative Approach To Rural Development', *Social Action*, Vol. 40, pp. 382–98.

Kadekodi, Gopal and S. C. Gulati (1999), *Root Causes of Biodiversity Losses in Chilika Lake: Reflections on Socio-economic Magnitudes*, Monograph, Institute of Economic Growth, New Delhi.

Kadekodi, Gopal, K.S.R Murty, and Kireet Kumar (2000), *Water in Kumaon: Ecology, Value and Rights*, Gyanodaya Publications, Nainital.

Kerr, John M., Dinesh K. Marotia, Katar Singh, C. Ramasamy, and William R. Bentley (eds) (1997), *Natural Resource Economics*, Oxford and IBH Publishing Co., New Delhi.

Khare, Arvind, Madhu Sarin, N.C. Saxena, S. Palit, S. Bathla, F. Vania, and M. Satyanarayana (2000), *Joint Forest Management: Policy, Practice and Prospects*, International Institute for Environment and Development, London.

Kohlin, Gunnar (2001), 'Contingent Valuation in Project Planning and Evaluation: The Case of Social Forestry in Orissa, India', *Environment and Development Economics*, Vol. 6, Part 2, pp. 237–58.

Lal, J. B. (1989), *India's Forests, Myth a Reality*, Natraj Publishers, Dehradun.

Larson, Bruce A. and D. W. Bromley (1990), 'Property Rights, Externalities and Resource Degradation: Locating the Tragedy', *Journal of Development Economics*, Vol. 33, pp. 235–62.

Lise, Wietze (1997), 'An Econometric and Game Theoretic Approach to Common Pool Resource Management: Case Studies in Rural India', Unpublished Ph.D. Monograph, Institute of Economic Growth, New Delhi.

Lokur, Vasudha (2000), *Social and Institutional Issues in Watershed Management in India*, Oikos India and International Institute of Rural Reconstruction, Philippines.

Luce, D. and H. Raifa (1957), *Games and Decisions: Introduction and Critical Survey*, John Wiley Publications, New York.

Malhotra, K. C. and Mark Poffenberger (1989), *Forest Regeneration through Community Protection*, West Bengal Forest Department.

Malhotra, K. C., Y. Gokhale, S. Chatterjee, and S. Srivastava (undated), *Sacred Groves in India: An Overview*, Indira Gandhi Rashriya Manav Sangrahalaya, Bhopal.

Marshall, Alfred (1949), *Principles of Economics*, McMillan and co., London, Eighth edition.

Mc Carthy, Nancy, E. Sadoulet, and Alain de Janvry (2001), 'Common Pool Resource Appropriation under costly cooperation', *Journal of Environmental Economics and Management*, Vol. 42, No. 3, pp. 297–309.

Mc Closky, D. N. (1975), 'The Persistence of English Common Fields', in Parker and Jones, *op. cit.*

Mearns, R. (1996), 'Community, Collective Action and Common Grazing: The Case of Post-socialist Mongolia', *Journal of Development Studies*, Vol. 32, No. 3, pp. 297–339.

Metrick, Andrew and M. L. Weitzman (1998), 'Conflicts and Choices in Biodiversity Preservation', *Journal of Economic Perspectives*, Vol. 12, No. 3, pp. 21–34.

Meyer, C. A. (1966), 'NGOs and Environmental Public Goods: Institutional Alternatives to Property Rights', *Development and Change*, Vol. 27, pp. 453–74.

Mill, J. S. (1985), *Principal of Political Economy*, Penguin Press, London.

Mitra, A. K. (1996), 'Irrigation Sector Reform: Issues and Approaches', *Economic and Political Weekly*, 30 March, pp. A31–7.

Mukerji, A. K. (1994), 'India's Forests: A Status Report: Concepts, Definitions, Trends, Controversies', Paper Presented in the International Workshop on India's Forest Management and Ecological Revival, New Delhi, 10-12 February.

Mukerji, S. D. (1995), Strategy for Joint Forest Management, *Wasteland News*, August–October, Society for Promotion of Wasteland Development, New Delhi.

Munro, G. R. and A. D. Scott (1985), 'The Economics of Fisheries Management', in A. V. Kneese and J. L. Sweeney, (ed.) (1985), *Handbook of Natural Resource and Energy Economics*, Vol. 2, Elsevier Science Publications, Amsterdam.

Murty, M. N. (1994), 'Management of Common Property Resources: Limits to Voluntary Collective Action', *Environmental and Resource Economics*, Vol. 4, pp. 581–94.

Murthy, M. N., B. N. Golder, Gopal, K. Kadekodi, S. N. Mishra, (1992), 'National Parameters for Investment Project Apprisal in India', Mimeograph, IEG working paper E/158/93.

Nabli, M. K., and J. B. Nugent (1989), 'The New Institutional Economics and its Applicability to Development', *World Development*, Vol. 17, No. 9, pp. 1333–47.

Nadkarni, M. V., S. A. Pasha, and L. S. Prabhakar (1989), *Political Economy of Forest Use and Management*, Sage Publications, New Delhi.

Nash, J. (1951), 'The Bargaining Problem', *Econometrica*, Vol. 18, pp. 286–95.

Ninan, K. N. (1998), 'An Assessment of European-aided Watershed Development Projects in India from the Perspective of Poverty Reduction and the Poor', Centre for Udviklingsforskning and Centre for Development Research, CDR Working Paper.

Norgaard, R. B. and R. B. Howarth (1993), 'Intergenerational Transfers and the Social Discount Rate', *Environmental and Resource Economics*, Vol. 4, No. 3, pp. 337–58.

North, Douglass C. (1990), *Institutions, Institutional Change and Economic Performance*, Cambridge University Press, Cambridge, pp. 33–68.

Oakerson, Ronald J. (1992), 'Analysing the Commons: A Framework', in D. W. Bromley (ed.), *Making the Commons Work: Theory, Practice and Policy*, International Centre for Self-Governance, San Francisco.

Olson, M. (1965), *The Logic of Collective Action: Public Goods and the Theory of Groups*, Harvard University Press, Cambridge, Mass.

Ostrom, E. (1990), *Governing the Commons: The Evolution of Institutions for Collective Action*, New York, Cambridge University Press.

Ostrom, Elinor (1994), 'Constituting Social Capital and Collective Action', *Journal of Theoretical Politics*, Vol. 6, No. 4, pp. 527–62.

Ostrom, Elinor (1998), 'Reformulating the Commons', Paper presented at the Fifth Biennial Conference of the International Society for Ecological Economics, Santiago, Chile, 15–19 November 1998.

Ostrom, Elinor (2000), 'Collective Action and the Evolution of Social Norms', *Journal of Economic Perspectives*, Vol. 14, No. 3, pp.137–58.

Ostrom, E. and R. Gardner (1993), 'Coping with Asymmetrics in the Commons: Self-governing Irrigation Systems can Work', *Journal of Economic Perspectives*, Vol. 7, No. 4, pp. 93–112.

Ostrom, E., J. Walker, and R. Gardner (1992), 'Covenants with and without a Sword: Self Governance is Possible', *American Political Science Review*, Vol. 86, No. 2, pp. 404–17.

Ostrom, E., R. Gardner, and J. Walker (1994), *Rules, Games and Common-Pool Resources*, University of Michigan Press, Ann Arbor.

Pangare, Ganesh and V. Pangare (1992), *From Poverty to Plenty: The Story of Ralegan Sidhi*, International Trust for Art and Cultural Heritage, New Delhi.

Parikh, J. and S. Reddy (1997), *Sustainable Regeneration of Degraded Lands*, Tata McGraw Hill Publishing Co., New Delhi.

Parker, W. N. and E. L. Jones (eds) (1975), *European Peasants and Their Markets*, Princeton University Press, Princeton.

Pasha, A. S. (1992), 'Common Pool Resources and Rural Poor: A Micro Level Analysis' *Economic and Political Weekly*, Vol. XXVII, No. 46, 14 November, pp. 2499–503.

Paul, Samuel (1989), 'Poverty Alleviation and Participation: The Case of Government Grassroot Agency Collaboration', *Economic and Political Weekly*, Vol. XXX, No. 2, pp. 100–10.

Pearse, A. and M. Stiefel (1979), 'Inequality into Participation', UNRISD, Geneva.

Picciotto, Robert (1992), *Participatory Development: Myths and Dilemmas*, Working Paper, Series 930, The World Bank, Washington, D.C., p. 9.

Poffenberger, M. and B. McGean (eds) (1996), *Village Voices, Forest Choices, Joint Forest Management in India*, Oxford University Press, Delhi.

Poffenberger, Mark (1990), *Joint Management of Forest Lands, Experiences from South Asia*, Ford Foundation, New Delhi.

Putnam, Robert., Robert Leonardi and Raffaella Nanetti: (1993), *Making Democracy Work*, Princeton, Princeton University Press.

Ramachandran, Asha (2002), 'Foisting Failure', *Down to Earth*, Vol. 11, No. 7, 31 August, pp. 38–9.

Rangachari, C. S. and S. D. Mukherji (2000), *Old Roots, New Shoots*, Winrock International Foundation and Ford Foundation, New Delhi.

Rao, CHH. (2000), 'Watershed Development in India: Recent Experience and Emerging Issues', *Economic and Political Weekly*, Vol. 35, p. 3943.

Ravindranath, N. H., K. S. Murali, and K. C. Malhotra (2000), *Joint Forest Management and Community Forestry in India: An Ecological and Institutional Assessment*, Oxford and IBH Publishing Co., New Delhi.

Richardson, Ann (1983), *Participation*, Routledge and Kegan Paul Publications, London.

Roy Barman, J. J. (1992), 'The Institution of Sacred Groves', *Journal of Indian Anthropological Society*, Vol. 27, No. 2, pp. 219–38.

Roy, Sumit (1995), 'New Institutional Economics, State and Development', *Economic and Political Weekly*, 29 July, pp. PE 65–72.

Runge, C. F. (1986), 'Common Property and Collective Action in Economic Development', *World Development*, Vol. 14, No. 5, pp. 623–36.

Sahai, B. (1993), 'Application of Remote Sensing for Environmental Management in India', *Space and Environment Report of the International Astronomical Federation*, 44th Congress, Graz, Austria.

Saleth, R. M. (1996), *Water Institutions in India: Economics, Law and Policy*, Commonwealth Publishers, New Delhi.

Samra, J. S. and B. L. Dhyani (1998), 'Elements of Participatory Watershed management in India' in National workshop on watershed approach for managing degraded lands in India challenges for 21st century, sponsored by Government of India, Ministry of rural areas and employment department of wastelands development, New Delhi.

Schlager, Edella and Elinor Ostorm (1992), 'Property Rights Regimes and Natural Resources: A Conceptual Analysis', *Land Economics*, Vol. 68, No. 3, pp. 249–62.

Seabright, P. (1993), 'Managing Local Commons: Theoretical Issues in Incentive Design', *Journal of Economic Perspectives*, Vol. 7, No. 4, pp. 113–34.

Sen, A. K. (1977), 'Social Choice Theory: A Re-examination', *Econometrica*, Vol. 45, pp. 53–89.

Sen, A. K. (1970), *Collective Choice and Social Welfare*, Holden-Day, San Francisco.

Sengupta, Nirmal (2001), *New Institutional Theory of Production*, Sage Publications, New Delhi.

—— (1997), 'Structural Adjustment Programme: Relevant Common Property Issues', in G. K. Chadha and A. N. Sharma (eds) *Growth, Employment and Poverty: Change and Continuity in Rural India*, Vikas Publishing House, New Delhi, pp. 420–34.

—— (1995), 'Common Property Institutions and Markets', *Indian Economic Review*, Vol. 30, No. 2, pp. 187–201.

—— (1991), *Managing Common Property: Irrigation in India and the Philippines*, Sage Publications, New Delhi.

Sethi, Rajiv and E. Somanathan (1996), 'The Evolution of Social Norms in Common Property Resource Use', *American Economic Review*, Vol. 86, No. 4, pp. 768–88.

Shah, S. L. (1985), *Planning and Management of Natural and Human Resources in the Mountains—A Micro Level Approach with Special Reference to Central Himalayas*, Yatan Publication, New Delhi.

Shanmugaratnam, N. (1996), 'Nationalisation, Privatisation and the Dilemmas of Common Property Management in Rajasthan', *The Journal of Development Studies*, Vol. 33, No. 2.

Singh, Chatrapati (1986), *Common Property and Common Poverty: India's Forests, Forest Dwellers and the Law*, Oxford University Press, New Delhi.

Singh, J. S. (1992), 'Man and Forest Interactions in Central Himalyas' in G. B. Pant (Monograph), Institute of Himalayan Environment and Development, Almora.

Singh, Katar (1995), 'The watershed management approach to sustainability of renewable common pool natural resources: Lessons from India's experience', Research Paper No. 14, Institute of Rural Management, Anand.

—— (1994a), *Managing Common Pool Resources: Principles and Case Studies*, Oxford University Press, New Delhi.

—— (1994b), 'Property Rights and Tenures in Natural Resources', in Kerr John M., Dinesh K. Marotia, Katar Singh, C. Ramasamy and William R. Bentley (eds), *Natural Resource Economics*, Oxford and IBH Publishing Co., New Delhi, pp.131–59.

—— (1992), 'Managing Common Pool Irrigation Tanks: A Case Study in Andhra Pradesh and West Bengal', Institute of Rural Management, Case Study No. 9, Anand.

—— (1991), 'Determinants of People's Participation in Watershed Development and Management: An Exploratory Case Study', *Indian Journal of Agricultural Economics*, Vol. XLVI, No. 3, pp. 278–86.

Singh, Katar, N. Singh, and R. P. Singh (1996), 'Utilisation and Development of Common Property Resources: A Field Study in Punjab', *Indian Journal of Agricultural Economics*, Vol. 51, Nos 1 and 2, pp. 249–59.

Singh, Katar and Ballab Vishwa (1996), *Cooperative Management of Natural Resources*, Sage India, New Delhi.

—— (1989), 'Afforestation of Village Common Lands: A Case Study of Aslali Village Woodlot in Gujarat', Case Study No. 4, Institute of Rural Management, Anand.

Singh T. P. and Ravi Hegde (2001), "Stake holders" analysis in Joint Forest Management: A Case Study of Haryana Shivaliks', in Gopal K. Kadekodi (ed.), *Environmental Economics in Practice: Selected Case Studies from India*, (Forthcoming).

Society for Promotion of Wastelands Development (1998), *Joint Forest Management Update*, New Delhi.

Solow, R. M. (1974), 'Intergenerational Equity and Exhaustible Resources', *Review of Economic Studies* (Symposium), pp. 29–46.

Somanathan, E. (1991), 'Deforestation, Property Rights and Incentives in Central Himalaya', *Economic and Political Weekly*, Vol. 26, pp. PE37–46.

Srivastava, Alka and Janaki Chundi (eds) (1999), *Watershed Management: Key to Sustainable Development*, Indian Social Institute, New Delhi.

Srivastava, H. C. and M. K. Chaturvedi (1989), *Dependency and Common Property Resources of Tribal and Rural Poor*, New Delhi, Commonwealth Publications.

Steins, N. A. and V. M. Edwards (1999), 'Collective Action in Common Pool Management: The Contribution of a Social Constructivist Perspective to Existing Theory', *Society and Natural Resources*, Vol. 12, pp. 539–557.

Stevenson, Glenn G. (1991), *Common Property Economics: A General Theory and Land Use Applications*, Cambridge University Press, New York.

Sugden, Robert (1984), 'Reciprocity: The Supply of Public Goods through Voluntary Contributions', *Economic Journal*, Vol. 94, pp. 772–87.

Sundar, Nandini (2001), *Branching Out: Joint Forest Management in India*, Oxford University Press, New Delhi.

Taylor, M., (1992), 'The Economics and Politics of Property Rights and Common Pool Resources', *Natural Resource Journal*, Vol. 32, No. 3, pp. 633–64.

TERI (1998), *Looking Back to Think Ahead: Green India 2047*, TERI, New Delhi.

Turton, Cathryn, Ben Groom and Michael Warner (1998), 'Scaling-up Participatory Watershed Development in India', Paper presented at the National Workshop on Watershed Approaches for Wastelands Development: Challenges for the 21st Century, 28–30 April 1998, New Delhi.

Vaidyanathan, A. (1991), *Integrated Watershed Development: Some Major Issues*, Foundation day lecture, Society for Promotion of Wasteland Development, New Delhi.

Vani, M. S. and R. Asthana (2000), 'Water Rights, Law and Policy in Uttaranchal: Empowered State and Eroded Public Rights', in Gopal K. Kadekodi *et al.* (2000) *op cit.*, pp. 205–38.

Varian, H. (1984), *Microeconomic Analysis* (2nd edition), Norton, New York.

Wade, R. (1987), 'The Management of Common Property Resources: Finding a Cooperative Solution', *World Bank Research Observer*, Vol. 2, No. 2, pp. 219–34.

—— (1987), 'The Management of Common Property Resources: Collective Action as an Alternative to Privatization or State Regulation', *Cambridge Journal of Economics*, Vol. 11, No. 2, pp. 95–106.

Walker, Thomas S. and James G. Ryan (1990), *Village and Household Economies in India's Semi-arid Tropics*, Johns Hopkins University Press, Baltimore and London.

World Resources Institute (1990), The World Bank in the Forest Sector: A Global Policy Paper, Summarised in Wastelands news 8(2), 1993.

# Index